How to do Educational Ethnography

the Tufnell Press,
London,
United Kingdom

www.tufnellpress.co.uk

email contact@tufnellpress.co.uk

British Library Cataloguing-in-Publication Data
A catalogue record for this book is
available from the British Library

paperback ISBN		*1872767 923*
	ISBN-13	*978-1-872767-92-5*
hardback ISBN		*1872767 974*
	ISBN-13	*978-1-872767-97-0*

Copyright © 2008 Geoffrey Walford
The moral rights of the authors have been asserted.
Database right the Tufnell Press (maker).

All rights reserved. No part of this publication may be reproduced, stored in a retrieval system, or transmitted in any form or by any means, electronic, mechanical, photocopying, recording or otherwise, without the prior permission of the publisher, or expressly by law, or under terms agreed with the appropriate reprographic rights organisation.

Printed in England and U.S.A. by Lightning Source

How to do Educational Ethnography

Edited by Geoffrey Walford

ETHNOGRAPHY AND EDUCATION

The *Ethnography and Education* book series aims to publish a range of authored and edited collections including both substantive research projects and methodological texts and in particular we hope to include recent PhDs. Our priority is for ethnographies that prioritise the experiences and perspectives of those involved and that also reflect a sociological perspective with international significance. We are particularly interested in those ethnographies that explicate and challenge the effects of educational policies and practices and interrogate and develop theories about educational structures, policies and experiences. We value ethnographic methodology that involves long-term engagement with those studied in order to understand their cultures, that use multiple methods of generating data and that recognise the centrality of the researcher in the research process.

www.ethnographyandeducation.org

The editors welcome substantive proposals that seek to:
- explicate and challenge the effects of educational policies and practices and
- interrogate and develop theories about educational structures, policies and experiences,
- highlight the agency of educational actors,
- provide accounts of how the everyday practices of those engaged in education are instrumental in social reproduction.

The editors are
   Professor Dennis Beach, University College of Borås, Sweden,
   Bob Jeffrey, (Commissioning Editor), The Open University,
   Professor Geoff Troman, Roehampton University, London and
   Professor Geoffrey Walford, University of Oxford.

Titles in the series include,
   Creative learning: European experiences,
      edited by Bob Jeffrey;
   Researching education policy: Ethnographic experiences,
      Geoff Troman, Bob Jeffrey and Dennis Beach;
   The commodification of teaching and learning,
      Dennis Beach and Marianne Dovemark;
   Performing English with a postcolonial accent: Ethnographic narratives from Mexico
      Angeles Clemente and Michael J. Higgins.

Contents

Preface
    Geoffrey Walford   vii

Chapter 1.
    The nature of educational ethnography
    Geoffrey Walford   1

Chapter 2.
    Selecting sites, and gaining ethical and practical access
    Geoffrey Walford   16

Chapter 3.
    For lust of knowing—observation in educational ethnography
    Sara Delamont   39

Chapter 4.
    Ethnographic interviewing: from conversation to published text
    Martin Forsey   57

Chapter 5.
    Video-enabled ethnographic research: A microethnographic perspective
    W. Douglas Baker, Judith L. Green and Audra Skukauskaite   76

Chapter 6.
    Bypass surgery: Rerouting theory to ethnographic study
    Mats Trondman   115

Chapter 7.
    Characterising social settings as the basis for qualitative research in ethnography
    Bob Jeffrey   141

Chapter 8.
    Ethnography and representation: About representations for criticism and change through ethnography
    Dennis Beach   165

Notes on Contributors   183

Preface

Geoffrey Walford

Ethnography is simultaneously one of the most exciting and misunderstood research methodologies and research products within educational research. What initially appears to be a straightforward process of 'hanging around' and writing about what has been seen and heard, with deeper familiarity, becomes a far more complex process. There are continual debates about how high quality ethnographic work should be conducted and presented, but there is also broad agreement. That broad agreement is illustrated within this volume.

This volume draws together chapters from a group of ethnographers of education. The chapters present individual views about the main aspects of doing ethnographic research, and each is based upon and illustrated by the authors' recent ethnographic research. While the authors share broad agreement about the nature of ethnography and how it should be done, there are also differences in emphasis between them. This is inevitable in a jointly written book such as this, and should not be seen as a weakness. As the nature of ethnography is heavily contested, it is instructive to offer insights into some of that contested terrain.

The first chapter of this book gives a general introduction to the nature and history of ethnographic work in education. It argues that ethnography is particularly appropriate for the investigation of many aspects of learning and teaching as there are strong similarities between the way people learn and the activities of conducting ethnographic research.

The second chapter covers three interlinked areas. It discusses the importance of choosing an appropriate site and offers advice on how to gain access to these sites in an effective yet ethical manner. It then discusses ethical issues which have gained in importance over the years, such that researchers are now much more reflexive about what they are doing and their possible effects on others.

Sara Delamont's chapter considers one of the two main ways in which data are generated in ethnographic work. Her discussion of observation and of fieldnotes uses her own recent work on *Capoeira* teaching as the main example. Similarly, Martin Forsey uses his recent ethnographic study of an Australian comprehensive school in crisis as his main example illustrating how to do interviews within ethnographic settings.

This is followed by a chapter by W. Douglas Baker, Judith Green and Audra Skukauskaite on a growing area of educational ethnography that focuses on the use of video and other technologies. The chapter by Mats Trondman uses the unusual analogy of heart bypass surgery to explain the role of theory. For him, theory is seen as the blood that flows through the heart of ethnography. He then discusses ways in which 'diseases' within ethnography can be cured.

The chapter by Bob Jeffrey shows how a particular six-fold characterisation can be used as a structure for observation and recording within ethnographic fieldwork. He uses examples from his creative learning work to show how the framework can be used. Finally, Dennis Beach examines the problems of writing and representations. He shows that concern with representation is far from new, yet there are particular issues when one wishes to present the results of critical ethnographic research.

Together, the authors of this book hope that it will give new insights to those already familiar with ethnography, and provide stimulation and advice to those newer to the field.

Chapter 1.

The nature of educational ethnography

Geoffrey Walford

- A doctoral student spends seven months in a Delhi slum amongst a group of poverty-stricken heroin addicts. His aim is to understand how peer learning occurs between them so that HIV/AIDS awareness programmes involving peer learning might be developed more effectively.

- Another doctoral student travels to China for well over a year to examine the processes by which knowledge of Chinese medicine are transmitted in three different Chinese contexts—she becomes a disciple of a *qigong* healer who teaches by imitation and repetition only, attends seminars by a senior Chinese doctor who encourages study of arcane medical classics, and becomes a member of a course at a College where standardised knowledge of Chinese medicine is inculcated.

- An academic spends several days each week in a primary school well-known for its creative teaching. He is another adult in the classrooms, but rather than helping children with their work, his main activities are looking and listening and making notes about what he sees and hears. Occasionally he will take out a tape recorder and encourage small groups of children to talk about their experiences of school.

- Another academic can be found one or two evenings each week in a local hall watching a group of young men and women and their teacher engaged in *Capoeira*—a form of dance and martial art originating in Brazil which is played, danced and fought to the music of the stringed *berimbau*. She is not taking part in the session, but is standing or sitting to one side scribbling in her notebook and occasionally asking questions.

What these four people have in common is that they are doing educational ethnography. They are, in order, Amar Dhand (2006a and b), Elizabeth Hsu (1999), Bob Jeffrey (Wood and Jeffrey, 1996, 2003) and Sara Delamont (2006, Stephens and Delamont, 2006). All four are engaged in ethnographic fieldwork that will eventually lead to published ethnographies about learning and teaching and about the perspectives of those involved in these processes.

The variabilities and consistencies of ethnography.

It can be seen from just the four brief examples given above that educational ethnography is hugely varied in its empirical focus. While the majority of studies are probably of schools and classrooms, others examine learning and teaching in a wide variety of diverse contexts. Further, while some are conducted in the researcher's own country and locality, others depend on extended periods away from home and may involve mastery of another language. What identifies them as ethnography?

As in much of social science research, dictionary definitions and word etymologies are not particularly helpful. The word comes from the two Greek words *ethnos*, meaning race, people or cultural group, and *graphia*, which is writing or representing in a specific field. In practice, various authors use the word in somewhat different ways.

Hammersley and Atkinson (1995: 1) discuss it in the following way:

> We see the term as referring primarily to a particular method or set of methods. In its most characteristic form it involves the ethnographer participating, overtly or covertly, in people's daily lives for an extended period of time, watching what happens, listening to what is said, asking questions—in fact, collecting whatever data are available to throw light on the issues that are the focus of the research.

In his guide to ethnography Fetterman (1998: 1) states:

> Ethnography is the art and science of describing a group or culture. The description may be of a small tribal group in an exotic land or a classroom in middle-class suburbia. The task is much like the one taken on by an investigative reporter, who interviews relevant people, reviews records, weighs the credibility of one person's opinions against another's, looks for ties to special interests and organisations, and writes the story for a concerned public and for professional colleagues. A key difference between the investigative reporter and the ethnographer, however, is that whereas the journalist seeks the unusual—the murder, the plane crash, or the bank robbery—the ethnographer writes about the routine, daily lives of people. The more predictable patterns of human life and behaviour are the focus of inquiry.

Bryman (2001) suggests five key features, the last of which moves beyond the process to the product:

1. Ethnographers immerse themselves in a society
2. to collect descriptive data via fieldwork
3. concerning the culture of its members
4. from the perspective of the meanings members of that society attach to their social world
5. and render the collected data intelligible and significant to fellow academics and other readers.

The academic journal *Ethnography and Education* similarly listed what it saw as the seven key elements of ethnography.

> The key elements of ethnographic research applied to the study of education contexts are:
> - the focus on the study of cultural formation and maintenance;
> - the use of multiple methods and thus the generation of rich and diverse forms of data;
> - the direct involvement and long-term engagement of the researcher(s);
> - the recognition that the researcher is the main research instrument;
> - the high status given to the accounts of participants' perspectives and understandings;
> - the engagement in a spiral of data collection, hypothesis building and theory testing—leading to further data collection; and
> - the focus on a particular case in depth, but providing the basis for theoretical generalisation.
>
> (Troman, 2006)

There are several things of note about these descriptions and lists, but one interesting feature is that none mention 'qualitative' or 'quantitative' data or methods. While it is now widely recognised that this crude division is largely unhelpful, ethnography is still generally thought of as being a 'qualitative' method or set of methods—indeed, some writers incorrectly use the term to be synonymous with qualitative methods. In fact, while ethnographers are unlikely to use sophisticated statistical analysis, they often generate quantitative data as well as qualitative notes and descriptions. Quantitative claims, which are frequently made in ethnographies, require quantitative data, so the use of structured observation, time-sampling and even surveys is required in addition to more open-ended participant observation and interviewing. The methods used depend upon the research questions that the study eventually tries to answer.

A little history

Historically, ethnography has been mainly associated with anthropology, but present day usage also has roots in sociology and, in particular, the Chicago School of sociology. Put simply, anthropology, and British anthropology in particular, developed during the late nineteenth century in order to understand the cultures of particular people who were usually regarded as 'primitive'. It frequently had links to ideas about the evolution of cultures and biological theories of progress. But the armchair theorists who first called themselves anthropologists mainly relied on information gained from missionaries and travellers to various parts of the Empire and other African and Asian countries. While there were attempts to systematise the information that such travellers might provide, particularly in the form of *Notes and Queries on Anthropology* (Urry, 1972), few anthropologists recognised the benefits of observing these other cultures for themselves and of coming to understand the culture through fieldwork. It was Bronisaw Malinowski who is usually given the credit for inventing fieldwork when he visited the Trobriand Islands in 1915-16 and 1917-18 from which he wrote *Argonauts of the Western Pacific* (1922) and other books. While the much later publication of his diaries raised questions about just how close to the 'natives' Malinoski actually got (Stocking, 1983), it was he who at least stated that his aim was to 'grasp the native's point of view' and who encouraged a generation of anthropologists to follow his lead. In the USA Franz Boas occupies a similar position to that of Malinowski, but without the emphasis on evolution and more of an emphasis on theory development. However Boas was not particularly interested in fieldwork. It was left to one of his students, Margaret Mead (1969 [1930]), to develop what she called 'participant observation' in her fieldwork amongst the people of Samoa.

Participant observation is also often associated with the sociology of the Chicago School—in particular during the period 1915-35 when Robert Park was in his ascendancy. Park had been a newspaper reporter and argued that first-hand observation of all walks of life was necessary to gain a full understanding of the urban environment. Using Chicago as the urban centre to be investigated, Park and Ernest W. Burgess are usually given credit for sending a stream of students to observe. Platt (1983), however, has argued that the facts do not really support this interpretation in that few of the studies of this period were actually based on participant observation. It was the second generation of Chicago School sociologists such as Howard Becker and Everett Hughes in the 1950s who really spread ideas about the importance of participant observation.

An interest in educational and learning issues was late in arriving in both anthropology and sociology and, even now, ethnography of education tends to be found more in department of education than in departments of sociology or anthropology. While some early anthropologists had generated data and written about such issues as child socialisation and the family, a specific educational emphasis only grew in the 1960 in both USA and UK. In part, this was due to institutionalisation of teacher education within the universities with its associated demands for academics to conduct research and publish. But it was also a reaction to the heavy emphasis on psychology in education and to quantitative survey-based educational studies in sociology. In short, many educationists wished to look inside the 'black box' of schools and investigate the micro cultures to be found inside.

Delamont and Atkinson (1995) have written about the division of labour in educational ethnography and argue that the majority of studies in the USA have been conducted by anthropologists while those in the UK have been done by sociologists or educationists. This has led to an interesting bias in the ethnic groups studied by Americans within the USA and in countries outside the USA. Up to the end of the 1970s, within the USA, Native Americans had been extensively studied followed by African Americans, while Africa provided the country base of the greatest number of overseas studies. In these figures there lurk remnants of a form of colonialism from which anthropology itself has gradually tried to free itself. In contrast, in the UK Delamont and Atkinson (1995) found far less work on ethnic minorities. At that time, most studies were urban-based and focused on social class and Anglo-Saxon Britons in secondary schools.

Anthropologists started entering the classroom in the USA somewhat earlier than in Britain. George Spindler started fieldwork in elementary schools in the early 1950s and, with his wife Louise, encouraged the development of a whole range of ethnographic studies (Spindler, 1982). In England, a series of studies were conducted by what is commonly called the Manchester School during the 1960s and 1970s. There, within a joint department of sociology and anthropology, doctoral students selected a range of sites which included schools. Three pathbreaking studies were conducted David Hargreaves (1967) who looked at a secondary modern school, Colin Lacey (1970) who did an ethnography of a boys' grammar school, and Audrey Lambart (1976) who focused on a girls' grammar school. The books by Hargreaves and Lacey started the shift away from the 'political arithmetic' tradition of British sociology of education (which examined social class issues in terms of inputs, outputs and class mobility) to the study of what was occurring within the 'black box' of schooling. Stephen Ball (1981), who was a doctoral student of Lacey, extended this series with his own ethnography of a comprehensive school.

The other main development that drove the development of ethnography in educational research was the so-called New Sociology of Education, with the edited collection by Michael F. D. Young (1971) being seen as central. This book brought together various chapters that derived from papers given at an annual conference of the British Sociology Association. Several chapters challenged the focus of sociology of education at that time and advocated a shift towards researching the curriculum, school knowledge, and power—again a move into the 'black box' of schooling, but this time at the even more micro level of the school classroom and the conduct of the teaching and learning activities. The Open University, which started in the early 1970s, took these viewpoints to heart and developed a range of courses (including *School and Society*, Hammersley and Woods, 1976) that were widely influential and taken by many teachers wishing to upgrade their qualifications. Peter Woods, Martyn Hammersley, Geoff Esland and Audrey Lambart were all at the Open University in the 1970, and Peter Woods went on to build a centre for school ethnography (e.g.,Woods, 1979, 1996) during the 1980s and 1990s.

Many people see the heyday of educational ethnography as being these last two decades of the twentieth century. There were many reasons for this, but two stand out. First, qualitative research was at its most valued, and research funding was available for studies that were exploratory. Research was not directed by a simplistic desire to establish 'what works'. Second, particularly in Britain, the pressure on doctoral students to finish within three or at most four years had yet to be applied. Many of the classic ethnographic studies within education are the results of a period of doctoral study which was far longer than is now required by funding agencies. These recent changes have meant that it is now more difficult for academics to obtain funding for ethnographic work and doctoral students no longer have the time required for extended periods of fieldwork or for thorough contemplation and analysis of the data generated.

Why is ethnography appropriate for educational issues?

Ethnography is a research strategy especially well-suited to the study of many learning, teaching and educational issues. It cannot, of course, answer all educational questions—there will always be a place for statistical surveys and randomised control trials—but ethnography can answer a range of questions where we are concerned to document and understanding learning and teaching processes. To indicate why this is true I shall a list of features of educational ethnography based upon an earlier version set out in Massey and Walford (1999). Rather than attempt to provide an exhaustive definition, this list identifies what might be seen as the minimum requirements for a research project to be called ethnographic, as opposed to, say, just qualitative or naturalistic. I will also show how these features make ethnography particularly relevant to studying education and learning. Fundamentally, there is a correspondence between the way in which children and others learn and the way that ethnographers go about their task. The parallels between the two processes are such that ethnography is well suited to the investigation of a range of research questions about the experience of learning.

1. A study of a culture

Ethnographers stress that we move within social worlds, and that to understand the behaviour, values and meanings of any given individual (or group), we must take account of their cultural context. In this respect, ethnography balances attention on the sometimes minute everyday detail of individual lives with wider social structures.

The word 'culture' is notoriously difficult to define, but it is hard to avoid in a discussion of ethnography. A culture is made up of certain values, practices, relationships and identifications. An ethnographer will try to define a particular culture by asking questions such as 'What does it mean to be a member of this group?' and 'What makes someone an insider or an outsider here?' The ethnographer tries to make sense of what people are doing by asking 'What's going on here? How does this work?' and hopes gradually to come to an understanding of 'the way we do things around here' (Deal 1985).

Answering those questions requires that the ethnographer be open to learn from those who inhabit that culture, and willing to see everything and suspend premature judgment on what should be selected as data. This quality of openness lies at the heart of ethnography, in its processes, purposes and ethics.

Schools are not total institutions but they still have a particular micro-culture which all children and teachers have to understand. Of particular interest in school ethnography is the potential clash of cultures between the culture that a child inhabits outside school in family or peer groups and the culture within school to which the child is expected to conform. The gradual enculturation process that ethnography entails enables elements of the school culture to be identified in a way unlikely to be evident by other research methods. By living through that process of getting to know the culture, an alert ethnographer can understand that which has become tacit knowledge to those who inhabit the culture.

2. Multiple methods, diverse forms of data

Cultures are complex and multi-faceted. To reach even a rudimentary understanding of them requires an openness to looking in many different ways. Different situations must be sampled many times—including the now widely accepted parameters of people, place and time—to establish what and who counts as being part of a culture.

Educational institutions are usually governed by time-specific activities. The timetable rules much of interaction within the organisation. Ethnography enables and demands that different places, times and people are sampled and that these contexts are taken into consideration in the interpretation of any data generated.

Data may consist of written documents, the researchers' own fieldnotes (including records of discussions, chance conversations, interviews, overheard remarks, observational notes), audiotapes and videotapes; quantitative data may also be included, such as the findings from surveys or structured observation. Gold (1997: 393) suggests that the fieldwork phase of an ethnography is complete only when 'both the ethnographer and his or her informants have exhausted their ability to identify other kinds of informants and other sorts of questions of relevance to the research objectives'.

Just as learning and teaching often demand multiple forms of input to be successful, so ethnography exploits a variety of research tools. In order to 'develop the story as it is experienced by participants' (Woods 1994: 311), and gain a multi-dimensional appreciation of the setting, the ethnographer must be prepared to consider many different types of data. These can be generated only through the use of multiple methods, which may include interviewing, observing, quantitative work, and assembling cultural artefacts. It makes sense then, that a study which uses only one field technique (however exhaustively) does not constitute an ethnography, since it can generate only one kind of data. A study that relies on interviewing only cannot reasonably be thought of as ethnographic.

These processes are again very similar to the way children learn both in and outside of educational institutions. They often adopt a 'magpie' attitude to information, picking up anything that looks interesting. They will generate enough data until they feel that they have enough to make sense of what is going on. In order to satisfy their curiosity they usually need many different forms of data and employ a variety of different methods to generate it—looking, listening, asking, watching, experimenting and so on.

3. Engagement

For learning to occur there needs to be engagement with the material to be learned. In particular, there often needs to be a relationship of trust between the learner and the teacher. Similarly, a basic tenet of ethnography is that 'observation of culture in situ' (Denscombe 1995: 184) is the best way of getting to know a culture intimately. Woods (1994: 310) agrees that the most prominent features of an ethnographic approach is 'long-term engagement in the situation as things actually happen and observing things first-hand'. Ethnographers work on the premise that there is important knowledge which can be gained in no other way than just 'hanging around' and 'picking things up'. Just as learning is a process that takes time, so ethnography is in a good position to be able to follow that process simply because it demands time taken in the field.

The principle of engagement by the researcher contains two elements: human connection with participants, and an investment of time. There is an assumption that, as the researcher becomes a more familiar presence; participants are less likely to behave uncharacteristically. Gold (1997: 394) explains: 'The fieldworker uses face-to-face relationships with informants as the fundamental way of demonstrating to them that he or she is there to learn about their lives without passing judgment on them …' The idea is that participants 'perform' less, and, as trust builds, reveal more details of their lives. So the success of an ethnography depends on the researcher developing and maintaining a positive personal involvement with participants (Denscombe 1995: 178), staying as close as possible to what and who is being studied, and returning perhaps many times to the field.

Part of how an ethnographer learns about a culture is through a process of enculturation, which takes time. Participants and settings need time to show what's going on. As the researcher enters the culture more deeply, new questions and avenues open up, requiring further investigation. 'Blitzkrieg ethnography' (Rist 1980), where the researcher spends only two or three days in the field, is therefore a contradiction in terms: prolonged period of investigation is essential for an ethnographer to get to know the ways of a culture.

Learners, too, need to spend time with others before they can begin to trust what they have to say. Learning is rarely a once-and-for-all process, but depends upon repeated engagement over time.

4. Researcher as instrument

Learning is a very personal activity. While a teacher may teach a class of 30, the individual child may take an idiosyncratic and highly personal path towards learning. Much detailed and useful background information on a setting is often subjectively informed, and an ethnographer is his or her own primary source of data. Whether the researcher's subjectivity is a weakness or strength is not the issue. It is seen simply as an inevitable feature of the research act.

The ethnographer must aim to keep an open mind about 'what is going on here' and what might be the best ways to talk or write about whatever is being studied. But recognising the presence of subjectivity is not the same as saying that anything goes. Somehow a balance must be struck between suspending preconceptions and using one's present understandings and beliefs to enquire intelligently. Dey (1993: 63-4) puts it this way:

> ... there is a difference between an open mind and empty head. To analyse data, we need to use accumulated knowledge, not dispense with it. The issue is not whether to use existing knowledge, but how [...] The danger lies not in having assumptions but in not being aware of them ...

Just as a learner needs continually to test what is being learnt against prior knowledge and to be aware of where there are gaps in knowledge, so the ethnographer has similarly to be aware of prior assumptions and lack of knowledge. To achieve such awareness, the ethnographer must constantly review the evolution of his or her ideas, reflecting on why particular decisions were made, why certain questions were asked or not asked, why data were generated a particular way and so on. Above all the ethnographer must try to articulate the assumptions and values implicit in the research, and what it means to acknowledge the researcher as part of, rather than outside, the research act.

5. Participant accounts have high status

Each person's account of the world is unique. What the researcher offers is an account which can be examined critically and systematically because the means by which it was generated is clearly articulated. It is often in the nature of ethnography that participants' accounts and actions appear to be in the foreground, and that the researcher has managed to 'get out of the way', acting only as 'information broker' (Goodson and Mangan 1996: 48). However, whether easily visible or not, it is the researcher who remains the highest authority, who selects from what has been seen and heard, and constructs the final account.

The researcher's power in this respect needs to be tempered for this account to be credible, such that we as readers feel that something of the culture has been illuminated rather than further obscured by the idiosyncrasies of a single observer/commentator. This can—and should be—achieved in at least three ways. First, as suggested earlier, the ethnographer must be culturally open-minded from the start, prepared to challenge his or her own theories and understanding, constantly testing them. This also implies that what people other than the researcher have to say has value as well.

Second, all claims about the culture must be based on some kind of empirical experience of that culture. Such evidence should be presented to or be available to the reader so that he or she can evaluate the claims made by the writer. It is in the nature of ethnography that a wealth of data is generated, recorded and stored; the writer's job is to share with the readers precisely which data have led to a particular claim.

A researcher may well be able to discover and articulate things about individuals and groups which they cannot see themselves, as well as things which neither the participants nor researcher can see at the outset of the study. However, participants hold knowledge about themselves which nobody else has. Thomas (1928: 572) argued that 'if men define situations as real, they are real in their consequences'. If this is true, then what people believe to be the reality of their world must be important information in understanding their activities, values, meanings and relationships and in working out what is going on. The most direct means of getting this information is to ask those people and to observe them in their everyday activities.

The third way to temper the researcher's power, is to give high status to participants' own accounts of their experiences and allow them to influence the researcher. This has methodological implications. Rather than relying on a preconceived framework for gathering and analysing data, ethnographers use their interactions with informants to discover and create analytical frameworks for understanding and portraying that which is under study. The procedures used in this direct and intimate acquaintance with the empirical world provide assurance that the data collected are grounded in informants' actual experiences (Gold 1997: 399).

An ethnographic approach is no automatic protection against an overly researcher-centric view of a culture, but it does at least allow the possibility of including multiple perspectives.

If we want to know more about children learning, it makes sense methodologically to investigate directly those who know best what it is like to be a child learning. Might an account of learning as seen through the eyes of learners challenge existing images of them and what they do? Almost certainly. As Fine and Sandstrom (1988: 12) write:

> Perhaps the most obvious goal of qualitative research with children is to get to know them better and to see the world through their eyes. On a deeper level, this style of research additionally assumes that minors are knowledgeable about their worlds, that these worlds are special and noteworthy, and that we as adults can benefit by viewing the world through their hearts and minds.

In recent years there has been a considerable growth in studies that try to gain the voices of children. Many of those involved with school improvement now believe that such views are vital (e.g., Rudduck at al., 1996). Yet teachers or inspectors are hardly the most appropriate people to be able to gain this information. Quick, one-off interviews with inspectors or teachers, all of whom have considerable power over learners, may give some new insights, but the sort of data generated by ethnographers who have built relationships of trust with children is likely to be of considerably more use and validity.

Enabling a relatively unheard voice to come to the attention of a wider audience is always a political act. This becomes even more significant when those individuals are speaking about matters in which they hold unique knowledge and which directly concern them. One could argue that people have a right to have a say in matters directly affecting them. There are both methodological and ethical implications of highlighting child learners' perspectives.

6. Cycle of hypothesis and theory building

The openness which has underpinned many of the elements so far is particularly evident in the ethnographer's constant commitment to modify hypotheses and theories in the light of further data. Gold (1997: 395) describes it as the 'running interaction between formulating and testing (and reformulating and retesting).'

In this type of enquiry, developing a theory is not so much an event as a process. As new data emerge, existing hypotheses may prove inadequate, the ethnographer's sense of what needs to be looked at and reported on may change, and explanations of what is going on may be supplanted by ones which seem to fit better. Such an approach is consonant with emergent design, another distinguishing feature of ethnography.

While it may not be clearly articulated, all learning occurs in a similar way to that described above. New information is tested against old understandings and these may be modified if there seem to be contradictions. Although not usually acknowledged, learning involves a process of theory development and testing which is closely aligned to the processes made explicit in ethnography. Ethnography should thus be a good tool for understanding elements of learning.

References

Ball, S. J. (1981) *Beachside Comprehensive*, Cambridge: Cambridge University Press.
Bryman, A. (2001) Introduction, in A. Bryman (ed.) *Ethnography*, London: Sage.
Deal T.E. (1985) The symbolism of effective schools, *Elementary School Journal*, 85(5): 601-620, reprinted in Westoby, A. (ed.) (1985) *Culture and Power in Educational Organisations*, Buckingham: Open University Press.
Delamont, S. (2006) The smell of sweat and rum: teacher authority in capoeira classes, *Ethnography and Education*, 1(2): 161-175.
Delamont, S. and Atkinson, P. (1995) *Fighting Familiarity: Essays on Education and Ethnography*, Cresskill, NJ: Hampton Press.
Denscombe, M. (1995) Teachers as an audience for research: the acceptability of ethnographic approaches to classroom research, *Teachers and Teaching: theory and practice*, 1(1): 173-191
Dey, I. (1993) *Qualitative data analysis: a user-friendly guide for social scientists*, London: Routledge
Dhand, A. (2006a) The practice of poetry among a group of heroin addicts in India: naturalistic peer learning, *Ethnography and Education*, 1(1): 125-141.

Dhand, A. (2006b) The roles performed by peer educators during outreach among heroin addicts in India: Ethnographic insights, *Social Science and Medicine*, 63: 2674-2685.
Fetterman, D.M. (1998) *Ethnography. Step by Step*, 2nd edition, London: Sage.
Fine, G. and Sandstrom, K. (1988) *Knowing children. Participant observation with minors*, London: Sage.
Hargreaves, A. (1991) Restructuring restructuring: postmodernity and the prospects for educational change, unpublished paper, Ontario Institute for Studies in Education
Gold, R. (1997) The ethnographic method in sociology. *Qualitative Enquiry*, 3(4):. 387-402.
Goodson, I. and Mangan, J.M. (1996) Exploring alternative perspectives in educational research, *Interchange*, 27(1): 41-59
Hammersley, M. and Atkinson, P. (1995) *Ethnography: Principles in practice, second edition*, London: Routledge.
Hammersley, M. and Woods. P. (1976) (eds.) *The Process of Schooling*, London: Routledge and Kegan Paul.
Hargreaves, D. H. (1967) *Social Relations in the Secondary School*, London: Routledge and Kegan Paul.
Hsu, E. (1999) *The Transmission of Chinese Medicine*, Cambridge: Cambridge University Press.
Lacey, C. (1970) *Hightown Grammar*, Manchester: Manchester University Press.
Lambart, A. (1976) The sisterhood, in Hammersley, M. and Woods P. (eds.) *The Process of Schooling*, London: Routledge and Kegan Paul.
Malinowski, B. C. (1922) *Argonauts of the Western Pacific*: London: Routledge.
Massey, A. and Walford, G. (1998) Children earning: ethnographers learning, in Walford, G. and Massey, A. (eds.) *Children Learning in Context*. Stamford CT: JAI Press.
Mead, M. (1969) *The Social Organisation of Manu'a*, [original 1930], Honolulu: Bishop Museum Press.
Platt, J. (1983) The development of the 'participant observation' method in sociology: origin myth and history' *Journal of History of the Behavioral Sciences*, 10(19): 379-393.
Rist, R.C. (1980) Blitzkrieg ethnography: on the transformation of a method into a movement.' *Educational Researcher*, 9(2): 8-10
Rudduck, J., Chaplain, R. and Wallace, G. (1996) *School Improvement: What can pupils tell us?* London: David Fulton.
Spindler, G. (1982) *Doing the Ethnography of Education: Educational Anthropology in Action*, New York: Holt Rinehart and Winston.
Stephens, N. and Delamont, S. (2006) Balancing the Berimbau: Embodied ethnographic understanding, *Qualitative Enquiry*, 12(2): 316-339.
Stocking, G.W. (1983) The ethnographer's magic: fieldwork in British Anthropology from Taylor to Malinowski, in Stocking, Jr, George W. (ed.) *Observers observed: Essays in ethnographic fieldwork*, Madison: University of Wisconsin Press.
Thomas, W.I. (1928) *The Child in America*, New York: Knopf.
Troman, G. (2006) Editorial, *Ethnography and Education*, 1,(1): 1-2.
Urry, J. (1972) Notes and Queries on Anthropology and the development of filed methods in British anthropology, 1870-1920, *Proceedings of the Royal Anthropological Institute of Great Britain and Ireland*, pp 45-57.
Wolcott, H. (2007) The question of intimacy in ethnography, in Walford, G. (ed.) *Methodological Developments in Ethnography*, Oxford: Elsevier.

Woods, P. (1979) *The Divided School*, London: Routledge and Kegan Paul.

Woods, P. (1994) Collaborating in historical ethnography: researching critical events in education, *International Journal of Qualitative Studies in Education*, 7(4): 309-321

Woods, P. (1996) *Researching the Art of Teaching: Ethnography for Educational Use*, London: Routledge.

Wood, P. and Jeffrey, B. (1996) *Teachable Moments: The art of teaching in primary schools*, Buckingham: Open University Press.

Woods, P. and Jeffrey, B. (2003) *The Creative School: A framework for creativity, quality and effectiveness*, (London, RoutledgeFalmer)

Young, M. F. D. (1971) (ed.) *Knowledge and Control: New directions for the sociology of education*, London: Collier-Macmillan.

Chapter 2.

Selecting sites, and gaining ethical and practical access[1]

Geoffrey Walford

Very many authors have written about the process of access to ethnographic research sites. Hammersley and Atkinson (1995), for example, devote a whole chapter to 'Access', Burgess (1984a) has 'Starting research and gaining access' for the title of his second chapter, while Johnson (1975) has a chapter that discusses 'Gaining and managing entree in field research'. Access is also a popular topic within the reflexive accounts written by educational ethnographers. The several collections of such accounts edited by Robert Burgess (1984b; 1985a and b) and Walford (1987a, 1991a, 1994, 1998a, 2002) have numerous examples of the genre. These accounts usually offer descriptions of successful and unsuccessful attempts to enter research sites such as schools and classrooms, and may then offer suggestions as to which tactics may meet with success. It is often suggested that access is fraught with difficulties and is one of the most problematic aspects of conduction ethnography (Troman, 1996). Some of these accounts go further and emphasise that, within ethnography, access is a continuous process and that, even after those with power within a school or educational organisation have been persuaded to give access, the researcher has continually to negotiate further access to observe classrooms and to interview teachers and students. It can be seen as a process of building relationships with people, such that teachers and students learn to trust the researcher to the point where they are prepared to allow the ethnographer to observe them with few restrictions and be open about their perceptions and beliefs. Access is thus never total, but might be seen as an incremental continuum, where the researcher is gradually able to move from the initial permission to enter the buildings to a series of developed and trusting relationships with some teachers and students. Access is a moment-by-moment process of negotiation and trust that can be rescinded at any time by headteacher, teachers, parents or students.

As access is recognised as a difficult process, there is a temptation to try to conduct any educational ethnography in an organisation with which the researcher already has links. For example, if the researcher already knows

---

1 This chapter draws upon several previously published articles including Walford 1999, 2001, 2005.

the headteacher of a school, the chances of gaining initial access are probably enhanced. If the researcher already works in an educational organisation, at one level, access to that organisation is already assured. But this selection of research sites according to perceived convenience of access is often a mistake. It is widely practiced, yet frequently leads to limitations in the research that might have been overcome if more thought had been devoted to the selection of an appropriate site for the research rather than 'making do' with a site that may be considerably less than ideal. Indeed, for many researchers the problems of gaining access seem to have been the defining factors in the choice of site rather than any thorough consideration of what the ideal site might be.

Thus, it is crucial that a distinction be made between site selection and access to that site. Site selection should be based upon the particular theoretical or practical issue that the researcher seeks to investigate, while the complexities of access may require some compromise with the ideal. Ethnography demands a focus on one or a very small number of sites, yet there is often a desire to draw conclusions which have a wider applicability than just that small number of cases. Within the ethnographic literature about education there is a plethora of examples where schools, or particular groups of children or teachers within schools, are researched because they are seen as typical (or, maybe, not untypical), or because they can offer insights into what may be occurring in other schools. It is not that such studies are without interest. They may well inform readers about contexts with which they are unfamiliar, but the temptation to make claims that cannot be warranted should not be given in to.

The debate about generalisability in ethnography is longstanding. Classic contributions include those by Becker (1990), Schofield (1990) and Stake (1995). There are several standard attempts to deal with this dilemma. The first is to recognise that, while strict generalisability is not possible in the statistical sense (for one or a small number of cases cannot possibly be an adequate sample drawn from a wider population of schools or classrooms) case studies or ethnographies can achieve transferability through thick description. It is argued that, if the authors give full and detailed descriptions of the particular context studied, readers can make informed decisions about the applicability of the findings to their own or other situations. Lincoln and Guba (1985: 316) describe the process as:

> Whether [working hypotheses] hold in some other context, or even in the same context at some other time, is an empirical issue, the

resolution of which depends upon the degree of similarity between sending and receiving (or earlier and later) contexts. Thus the naturalist [ethnographer] cannot specify the external validity of an enquiry; he or she can provide only the thick description necessary to enable someone interested in making a transfer to reach a conclusion about whether the transfer can be contemplated as a possibility.

As Seale (1999: 108) points out in a later discussion of this issue, it must be noted that it is not just the sending context but also the receiving context about which details are needed and, logically, this would require study of at least two cases. In fact this 'solution' to the problem is no solution at all for, in order to be able to judge whether a particular finding from an ethnographic study in one school is applicable in another, it is necessary to know as much about that second school as about the first. Lincoln and Guba (1985: 316) follow their logic through and argue that this means that one cannot generalise from a case study to a wider population unless one makes unwarranted assumptions about the wider population.

The second, and more successful, way in which commentators have tried to deal with the problem of generalisability is to argue for theoretical generalisation. Numerous authors (e.g., Bryman, 1988; Silverman, 1993; Yin, 1994) have sought to move away from statistical or empirical generalisation from case studies, and have proposed that the wider significance of findings from a particular ethnographic study can be derived through the strength of logical argument for each case. A case is significant only in the context of a particular theory, and logical inference replaces statistical inference. An extrapolation can be made between a particular case and a wider population only if there is a strong theoretical or logic connection between them. The strength of the theoretical reasoning is seen to be crucial. This means that the selection of the case to be studied is crucial. Rather than attempt to find a school or classroom that is typical or for which there is no reason to believe it is untypical, theoretical generalisation requires a clear theoretical basis for the choice. This may be seen as a version of Glaser and Strauss (1967) theoretic sampling, applied here to the initial choice of research site rather than the individuals and situations to be sampled once the site has been chosen. One possibility is seen as being that of choosing a leading-edge site for ethnographic research. For example, if a school is selected that is recognised for its pioneering work in information technology, then findings from that school might be of use to other schools not so far advanced. In contrast, Michell (1983) argues that the unusual case can be the most appropriate choice of research site, as the idiosyncratic can throw general principles into sharp focus.

This answer to the problem of choice of site and generalisation still has difficulties. For example, while a school may be perceived to be at the forefront of developments, it may not actually be so. It may be that the school has a particularly good marketing strategy, rather than any solid achievements. We need to know more about *all* schools before we can select the case study site. Similarly, it is only possible to judge a school to be idiosyncratic if a great deal is already known about the entire population of schools. The attempt to by-pass empirical generalisation through the idea of theoretic generalisation is, in the end, only of limited success. For there to be a convincing theoretical argument for extrapolation, there needs to be empirical evidence about the wider population. The same argument holds, of course, for claims that a school is typical or average. We simply cannot know how a case relates to the other possible cases in terms of particular relevant variables without empirical evidence about that wider population. We thus have to conduct a great deal of prior research before we can make any selection of a research site.

In practice, in most ethnographic case studies these problems of site selection appear to have been given less thought than necessary. While most ethnographic studies of schools and classrooms do not name the educational institution in which the research has been conducted, it is frequently evident (either from internal evidence or from personal communications) that a study was undertaken in particular locations simply because they provided convenient sites for the researchers. Often, a particular local school is known to the researcher, or contacts can be made through colleagues or friends. Researchers settle for research sites to which they can easily gain convenient and ready access rather than thinking through the implications of particular choices. The result is that there are too many ethnographic case studies where the choice of sites does not appear to be closely related to any theoretical objectives of the study. Further, while adequate justifications for the choice of sites are often not given, many authors explicitly or implicitly make claims not only about those particular sites, but also about broader, usually non-defined, populations of schools, classrooms, teachers or students within countries.

Of course, it is understandable that academics and research students should include convenience in their considerations of which sites to approach to try to gain access. There are time, financial and personal costs to be considered, and a distant location may involve accommodation away from home. Additionally, and obviously, case study and ethnographic research can only proceed where access has been achieved, and this is not always straightforward. There are obvious temptations to accept sites that appear to be readily available rather than work harder to try to achieve access to the most appropriate sites for the research. I do not believe access is as difficult as some would have us believe (see Walford, 1999a) but, however difficult it is, it is crucial that obtaining access is seen as a separate consideration from that of locating appropriate sites.

Some critics would claim that these limitations in terms of generalisability of findings make ethnography of little use in educational research. It will not come as a surprise that the authors of this book do not agree! There are several important ways that ethnography can contribute to educational knowledge. The most straightforward way is by selecting sites that are intrinsically significant and interesting in themselves, for themselves. Research questions that require some form of generalisation often cannot be answered through case studies, but generalisation need not be the goal at all. There are two main types of research question where case studies might be utilised. First, case studies can be used where the focus of interest is so important that it is sufficient to be able to show that particular events occurred in *any* school. Thus, if we are able to show that incidents that can be interpreted as racist have occurred in one school, many people would see this as an important finding in itself. The extent to which similar activities might be present in other schools is secondary—it is enough that they can be found in one school.

A second form of research question where case studies can be profitably employed relate to situations where particular cases are vital to understand because of their particular significance within policy formulation and implementation. I would argue, for example, that it was important to investigate the culture and activities of the first City Technology College, because its creation marked such a significant change in government policy (Walford and Miller, 1991; Walford, 1991b).

Of course, to say that particular cases or activities are important demands an answer to the question, Important to whom? It may be that case study or ethnographic methods are used where an evaluation of a particular policy is required. If, for example, a new way of teaching environmental studies is introduced in a school, several of the teachers and the senior management team might be expected to be particularly interested in the evaluation. The initial audience for such an evaluation thus might be rather small. However, an ethnographic study that contextualised the particular school and described the nature of the teachers and students involved would have a wider appeal. While readers could still not legitimately generalise the results of the study to any wider population, there is benefit in understanding what was successful and unsuccessful in that particular situation.

Selling your way to access

Once an ideal site has been selected, researchers need to develop a way of obtaining access to that site. In this section I argue that researchers have much to learn from sales people and that obtaining access to research sites has similarities to selling a product or service. The many popular sales and marketing books that abound in bookshops offer numerous insights about how to gain and maintain access. I am not suggesting that any of these books should be followed slavishly, or that their 'tried and tested' 'secrets of success' or 'vital ingredients' that lead to 'the perfect sale' should be taken too seriously. But what these books do is to encourage sales people to think about the access process and how they are presenting themselves and their products or services to potential clients and purchasers. We have to be clear how our research can be 'sold' to those who can grant us access and clarify what the potential benefits are to them. In selling, it may have become a platitude to say that 'people don't buy products, they buy benefits', but it is nonetheless true. Researchers need to be clear what benefits they, the process of research, and the research findings themselves can offer. In arguing for researchers to be able to make clear the benefits of their research I am not suggesting that all teachers and others concerned with education will only allow access if they see direct advantages for themselves. By and large, most teachers are prepared to act altruistically and accept the need for educational research that may only have long-term benefits. But it is important that they are able to see some benefits beyond those that accrue to the individual researcher's career.

One general structure often used when thinking about selling has the somewhat unfortunate acronym AIDS, where the four-fold formulation is: Approach, Interest, Desire, and Sale. In most of the following I will use entry to a school as the main example, but the discussion and suggestions are equally applicable to the many other institutions and organisations where learning occurs. Equally, although much of the discussion is framed around the initial entry to a school that might be granted by a headteacher, it also needs to be applied to individual teachers and students within the school.

Approach

The first step in selling is to seek the right people who are likely to want to buy your product or service. A great deal of work is done before any direct contact is made, for it is necessary to approach the correct people, and not waste time and energy on those who are unlikely customers. Similarly, in making an approach to a school or any other organisation to conduct research, the ethnographer needs to make sure that contact is made with the person most likely to be receptive to the research. Prospecting is the term used for looking for someone who might be sympathetic to whatever it is that you are selling. This requires research before making any approach. So, to obtain entry to a school to conduct an ethnography, it is worthwhile doing some preliminary research on people within a number of potentially suitable schools. One obvious possibility is to look for any university connections. Someone who has spent time doing their own research might be expected to be more likely to agree to outside research than someone who has not. It is relatively easy to find the academic qualifications of those in the senior management team of a school and the title of a dissertation for a Masters or doctoral degree can often be found from the university on the internet. If someone has a doctorate, it is worth seeing if they have published anything—again, this is easily done electronically. If a headteacher has researched and published on management structures or special educational needs, for example, this is certainly worth knowing before making any approach. The approach can then be framed to include elements that might be likely to appeal and potential points of conflict can be avoided.

It is important that the person approached is actually able to deal with the issue—in other words, able to grant access. In schools this is usually straightforward as the headteacher will be the obvious person. But this is not so in all schools—in some the Chair of Governors has a major say, while in others the Senior Management Team may expect to be consulted. So it is wise to investigate these people as well as the Headteacher and to try to discover where the power lies. Troman (1996) gives an example where the headteacher appeared to be enthusiastic about his proposed research, but where the Senior Management Team (who he did not talk with) rejected it. It is possible to see this as erroneously making his sales presentation to an individual when he should have insisted on making the presentation to the group.

Several books on selling emphasis that they are only systematising what they regard as 'common sense'. A 'referred lead' is a possible new client who has been suggested by an existing client. In attempting to gain access to a research site this might be seen as the use of a mutual friend or colleague. If there is someone else in the school who the researcher already knows, this person might be able to act as a 'link' and as a recommendation. Obviously, it is important here to contact the mutual friend or colleague first to ask for help and to try to ascertain the relationship between this person and the person able to grant entry. A further development of this idea is that it might be possible to exploit a shared experience or interest. Headteachers are more likely to give access if they can perceive the researcher as being 'one of us'. A researcher who is able to show some shared experience has a real advantage.

In my own early ethnographic work on boys' private boarding schools (Walford, 1986, 1987b), I approached access in a rather haphazard way. I wrote letters to Headmasters and had five refusals before one gave me an interview. I will discuss that interview in more detail later, but one of the important aspects was that the Headmaster spent time checking the question 'Are you one of us?' As I had briefly taught in three of these schools, he was able to answer that question in the affirmative, but only after he had extracted the name of someone whom we both knew from one of the schools who could act as a 'referee' for me. In this case, I had not contacted this person beforehand and I was not even sure that he would remember me with any clarity. But evidently the reference he gave (alongside the academic reference that was also demanded) was convincing, for an invitation to conduct the research soon followed. I had been lucky, for I had not thought through these possibilities beforehand.

One of the reasons I probably had so much difficulty in gaining access to the boys' public boarding schools was that I misunderstood the purpose of my letter to the schools. Had I read any of the 'selling' books beforehand, it might have been clearer that the purpose of any letter is to gain an initial interview, and not to gain access. Instead of a short letter that raised interest in the proposal without giving too many details, I wrote fairly long letters that included far too much information. Every additional piece of information gives a chance for an objection or problem to be raised in the mind of the reader. Detailed letters make it far too easy to find a 'good reason' to object. Thus, if a letter is to be used, it should be brief. If it is possible to include a referred lead or some aspects of common experience, then this is useful. If a letter is to be used, it should indicate that a telephone call will follow to try to fix an appointment. Having sent such a letter, it may be possible to use this as a way past any secretary who screens calls.

Denny (1997) puts the purpose of letters and telephone calls succinctly: 'Remember that the purpose of writing a letter is to sell your telephone call which should, in turn, sell the appointment. Another great principle of salesmanship: *you can only sell one thing at a time*' (Denny, 1997: 72, emphasis and sexism in the original). In a similar way, Kimball (1994: 87) uses large lettering to stress 'The purpose of the telephone call is to get the appointment.'

Interest

Once an appointment has been obtained, the preparation for and conduct of the interview must also be taken very seriously. In my experience, educational researchers tend to be apologetic about their research; they balk at the idea of selling themselves or their research to others. Yet, this may be what they must do if they are to gain access.

My early attempts to gain access to the boys' independent boarding schools are indicative:

> My interview with the headmaster of the first school to express interest lasted for only twenty minutes, but I experienced it as being far longer and more nerve-racking than any of the interviews I had for academic appointments. He was extremely sharp and shrewd and demanded precise answers to a range of questions about my purposes and methodology. I had envisaged presenting myself as an open ethnographer and had thus prepared only a fairly flimsy outline of the sort of areas in which I was interested—I intended, in true ethnographic style, to develop my research strategy once actually in the school. The headmaster, however, had a rather different views of how research should be conducted, where questions are tightly framed, questionnaires or interview schedules developed, and representative samples drawn from populations. It quickly became obvious that the role of 'open ethnographic researcher' was one which he would not entertain. (Walford, 1987b: 50)

I had done insufficient groundwork and I had allowed the prospect to control the situation. In this case I was able to retrieve the situation by showing considerable flexibility in my proposed research methodology, but I was very lucky. More thought about how to interest the Headteacher in the research would have greatly improved my chances.

Although there is now much greater concern about preparation for interviews, in particular where those interviews are with powerful people (for example, McHugh, 1994; Fitz and Halpin, 1994), I believe that many researchers would benefit by giving more thought to the process. However, most educational researchers do give consideration to some of the obvious aspects of self-presentation at interviews. Thought is given to how smart to look, what clothes to wear, and what degree of formality to try to adopt. Of course, we do not always get it right.

In my research on sponsored grant-maintained schools (Walford, 2000 a and b), for example, I went to interview the Headteacher of a Transcendental Meditation Primary school that wished to obtain state funding, but whose application was eventually rejected. I dressed reasonably smartly, but not in a suit. With a tie in my pocket, I checked whether I should wear it with the local taxi driver who was driving me to the school. 'No, they're all very laid-back. It's all very informal' he informed me. In fact, the staff were all very smartly dressed—all the male teachers had ties, and all the children were in stylish uniforms! I looked and felt out of place with my open collar.

But such aspects are trivial compared with the care that good sales people take with their interviews. The various sales books have pages of ideas about how to make sure your position in the room is a good one, how to control and interpret body language, how to deal with presentation aids and how to sell yourself as much as the product or service. But two points of emphasis in many of these books are the use of questions and the need to listen to the customer. In Denny's (1997: 85) words: 'If you were to ask me what I consider to be the single most important skill in mastering the art of professional selling, I would say it is the ability to ask questions.' Kimball agrees and states:

> [W]hen a professional salesperson makes a presentation, he or she will listen more than speak. In a presentation, you should listen—with the prospect talking—at least 55 percent of the time. If you are doing more than 45 percent of the talking, it's time to pull back on the reins, talk less, and listen more. You aren't going to persuade the prospect with your brilliant oratory. On the contrary, you persuade the prospect by getting him or her to talk.
> (Kimball, 1994: 106)

Whilst we should not take too seriously the exact percentages (they are hardly likely to be the results of systematic research), it is worth stopping and thinking about the general statement. My feeling is that it is unlikely that most educational researchers would try to interest anyone in their research in this way. For most of us, preparation for an initial interview means working out what we want to say; we hardly ever think of what our prospects might want to say. Yet, according to these sales books, questions can enable us to tune into the person and their thinking, and to identify their needs and motives. Questions can help to establish a greater rapport and, at the same time, give greater control to the person asking questions. They can help us to shape our presentation more carefully such that it is more likely to be accepted.

In a similar way, when trying to gain ethnographic access, listening to the headteacher's needs and desires can mean that the research proposal can be framed more closely to be more attuned to those requirements. Listening gives the salesperson 'buying signals' and indicates potential hesitations and objections. For the researcher, listening can give similar information about potential concerns which, as discussed in the next section, can then be dealt with before they are even voiced.

Within sales, presentational aids such as leaflets and power-point are seen as very important. Visual inputs can be particularly effective in selling, so some simple aids might be worth considering in trying to gain access. In particular, it may be worth trying to build and present an image of success, so taking along an example of the results of previous research might be helpful. A book based on previous research also has the advantage of slightly deflecting the discussion away from the details of the particular research that is being planned in this situation. A book about a related topic written by someone else might also have a similar effect. However, the aim would not be to deceive, simply to indicate the type of academic 'end-product' that the research might lead to.

Desire

There are two main aspects to raising the desire to purchase an item or service: overcoming objections and stressing benefits.

Within a selling interview numerous doubts may arise in the prospect's mind. It is usually thought better to deal with the most obvious possible doubts before they have been voiced. This shows that the salesperson is considerate and recognises that the prospect may have some misgivings. In research, the doubts that will probably most often come to mind are those that concern the smooth running of the organisation and the investment of time that staff and pupils might be asked to make. After all, the main purpose of schooling is not to act as a site for researchers. In contrast to many other educational researchers, the ethnographer is in a very good position to quell some of these doubts, as the objective is always to disrupt the everyday life of the organisation as little as possible. Any interviews are conducted at times convenient to those interviewed, and any observations are designed, as far as possible, to have little effect on those observed.

In an increasingly market-driven system, headteachers are often concerned about any potential bad effects on the school's reputation. Offering confidentiality and anonymity before these problems are raised is usually seen as a good tactic here but, in practice (as will be discussed in the next section), such offers are difficult to maintain.

Academic researchers often think of potential benefits only in terms of those that might eventually flow from the results of the study. Although this is of prime importance to the researcher, such benefits alone may be unlikely to convince headteachers. Such long-term research results offer no immediate benefits to the school and, if they do eventually materialise, all schools will benefit whether or not they agree to take part in the research. Again, this is not to say that it is impossible to gain access for projects that have only long-term benefits, but it is unwise to rely on other people's altruism as your only entry strategy.

An alternative is to offer more direct benefits. Thus many ethnographers have been prepared to become supply teachers when necessary or to take a class or two on a regular basis (e.g., Lacey, 1970; Burgess, 1983). This trade-off has obvious benefits for the school as it saves money, and it can have benefits for the researcher as well in that it can help in getting to know the school's culture and in providing a ready group of students. But the role conflicts can be great and the time involved in lesson preparation and marking can overwhelm the research. If this sort of benefit is to be offered, it is probably better to suggest help with sports or other extra-curricular activities.

What researchers often forget is the direct benefits to the school, its teachers and students that the process of research can bring. Just as headteachers can benefit from talking in confidence to someone else about the school, so teachers can benefit from discussions about their work and careers. Students, too, can benefit from the process of being asked to think about their learning activities, their examination preparation or their plans for the future. A good salesperson will ask past customers about what they liked and disliked about their purchases. If, at the end of any research, educational researchers were systematically to ask headteachers, teachers and students about what benefits they thought they had gained from the research process, future access procedures could be enhanced.

Of course, there is a need to be careful about the agendas of those with power. It is wise to resist any suggestion that the researcher's topic be shifted to one that focused on a particular problem for the school. It might be highly tempting, but such a focus may not only compromise the research, but may also lead to severe ethical problems. However, appropriate feedback to the school is an obvious benefit that most researchers can offer. If the focus is on bullying, for example, the researcher may eventually be in a good position to offer an in-service training session. The researcher's breadth of reading about the issue will be usually far greater than teachers have time for, so much of any feedback session can deal with general findings as well as the findings from the school itself.

Sale

The final stage is the 'sale'. The prospect agrees to pay for 10,000 wigits or, in our case, the headteacher agrees to grant access in return for the benefits that he or she believes will follow. Many of the suggestions in sales books may involve far more 'pressure' than most researchers would be willing to use, and are unlikely to be appropriate within the education system. But the idea of seeing 'objections as your friends' and the reminder that 'your objective is to close the sale, not to complete the presentation' (Kimball, 1994: 175) are well worth consideration.

There comes a time in all sales presentations when it is best to start closing the sale. This time might be before the salesperson has completed all that could be said, and before some features of the product have been covered. Thus, in an access interview, it may better to move to a decision at an unexpected time. When there are strong 'buying signals', it may be best to ask for a decision at that point. In the research context, such signals can vary considerably. They might include questions on the details of procedures to be followed, indications of who it might be thought desirable for the researcher to meet, or even comments on a more collegial basis. Such signals need to be interpreted with care, and equal care needs to be taken with the method chosen for closing the agreement.

If the researcher has really generated a desire to take part in the research, it may be possible to use the 'scarcity' tactic. As Kimball (1994: 176) states, 'People are motivated to buy when they feel the opportunity to buy may be lost.' Only a very limited number of schools will be involved in any ethnographic study, and the researcher selects particular schools to offer the opportunity to take part. The chance to be part of the research is limited, for the researcher does not have unlimited time or other resources. Is it too far fetched that researchers could generate a feeling that schools would be privileged to take part?

Another possibility, which may have only limited applicability, is the idea of the 'assumed close'. When the prospect has offered no objections, it may be possible to simply ask 'When shall I start? Would next Tuesday be okay, or next Wednesday? Even said light-heartedly, it might well work in some cases. Another possibility, when there are signs of uncertainty, is to 'pass down the hierarchy'. If entry to a particular school is very important, and the headteacher is showing indecisiveness, pressure to make a decision may just go the wrong way. In many ways it is easier to say 'no' than 'yes', and our objective should be to avoid giving the chance of a 'no'. A suggestion that it might be a good idea to talk with the Deputy Head or other appropriate members of the Senior Management Team, might be one way of avoiding the 'no'. The advantage is that once the research has been discussed with that person, it may be possible to again 'pass down the hierarchy' such that several members of staff become involved with the research before any decision is made. The school may drift into a positive decision without knowing it.

There is also the possibility of some negotiation on the 'price' to be paid by the school in return for the benefits expected. The decision to grant access is not a simple yes or no. Just as sales people are prepared to reduce their price and offer 'special discounts' to particular customers, so the researcher can negotiate the extent of access desired. In my rather chaotic negotiations for access to the boys' private boarding school, I originally asked for six weeks unstructured access which I actually thought was too short. I was granted four weeks, under more tightly specified conditions. If the cost to the school of granting access can be reduced, yet the same potential benefits are perceived to be forthcoming, then a deal might be easier to strike.

But is it ethical?

I have suggested that appropriate site selection is central to ethnographic research and that this means that more attention needs to be given to the process of gaining access to ideal sites. The enthusiasm and care with which good sales people approach selling should be a challenge for ethnographers who often give too little thought to tactics. Ideas from selling can offer many insights not only about how to gain initial access to the buildings of an organisation, but also in helping researchers with the continual process of gaining and maintaining access to the various people who work there.

But such methods of access, and indeed all of the research process, have to be ethical. I would argue that giving more thought to the benefits that might accrue to the school or other educational organisation is likely to make the research more ethical rather than less. Being positive about the research that you wish to conduct, and being able to show the benefits that could be obtained from being involved in the research, does not involve lying or even being 'economical with the truth'. If we can't find convincing benefits, then we should not be doing the research. Of course, there are some occasions when the major benefits of doing research do not accrue to the school, teachers or students who are the subjects of the research. There are times when potential benefits are gained by the wider society or wider social group, rather than those directly involved in the research. In many cases researchers can still obtain access by selling the benefits of feeling altruistic and of acting in such a way as to develop teaching as a research-based profession.

Ethical behaviour in research is not only desirable, but is now an essential part of obtaining permission from university and research institutions to be able to conduct research. Universities have a variety of ethical committees that demand that researchers show how they are going to conduct any research in an ethical manner before permission is given to start. This may involve following Codes of Practice from the British Educational Research Association (2004) or the American Educational Research Association. Such codes have been developed gradually over any years and cover many important issues concerning the relationships between researchers and participants and what is to be done with any data generated in the research.

There are some elements of ethnographic research, however, that can cause particular problems with gaining ethical approval and, more importantly, ensuring the researchers actually behave ethically when undertaking the research. Take, for example, the central tenet that all participants should give informed consent before they become part of the research. Informed consent means that potential participants should be told exactly what the research seeks to investigate and what will be done with any of the information that they give to the researcher. This is non-unproblematic even with highly statistical quantitative research as data are often archived and may be used by other researchers doing secondary analysis in ways that were never predicted by the original research. But in ethnographic work this problem is raised continually. Quite simply, being within an educational institution for a length of time means that discoveries are made about that institution that are unexpected. The initial focus for research often broadens to include features that were never part of the original plan. While ethnographers must attempt to give as full and accurate description as possible, this can only be a provisional description and participants have to accept that other aspects may eventually be written about. This demands a high degree of trust on the part of participants.

Sometimes participants will ask that they be allowed to see anything that is written and make any changes they feel are necessary before publication. This arrangement should be strongly resisted. First, there is the question of exactly who should have any veto. To agree to a headteacher's wish to be able to control publication means that the voices of teachers and students who might have other views are not heard. Such arrangements automatically give more power to those who already hold most power. Second, such an arrangement might lead to a vetoing of all publications and the results of years of work remaining unpublished. A good example of this is the work of Maurice Punch (1977) who conducted a study of the progressive Dartington Hall School. When some of the findings were perceived as critical of the school, the Chair of Governors, with whom the agreement had been made, forbade publication. It was only many years later that the study and an account of the whole disagreement were published (Punch, 1986). Third, such an agreement weakens the validity of any reports that are produced. If those with power have the right to censor publications, readers will always be concerned that only part of the story has been told. While ethnographers will often self-censor where it is felt inappropriate to include particular details, censorship by others makes the whole research project suspect.

A further problem in ethnography is that the list of those who might become participants is often not easily defined before the research starts. Many people other than teachers and students are to be found in schools for brief periods. Thus prospective parents, for example, become participants when they are shown round a school, but it would be inappropriate to force a description of the research onto them and try to obtain informed consent—unless, of course, the focus of the research includes relationships between prospective parents and the school. In most studies in schools it is usual for everyone who is most likely to be involved to be given written information about the research before it starts. In the case of children (defined as under 18) this also means that information is given to the parents or guardians. However, it would be giving too much power to a single person if research could not be conducted simply because one of the children, parents or teachers objected. In a case such as this a particular child or teacher would not be interviewed or take part in any special activities involving the research, but it would be unreasonable for one objection to curtail the whole research.

One common way that is used to try to reduce people's fears and encourage them to take part in research is to offer confidentiality and anonymity to both the research site and the individual people involved. For most researchers anonymity for individuals and research sites is seen as the standard ethical practice for educational research. Such a belief is embodied in the various ethical guidelines and codes of practice produces by such professional associations as the American Educational Research Association, the American Sociological Association, the British Sociological Association and the British Psychological Society. In a wide range of work the practice of giving a false name to a research site and to the people within it has become the norm. Anonymity has become the default option for most ethnographic work in education. Researchers do it, simply because it is seen as the ethical thing to do, and to protect those involved in the research from any potential possible harm or embarrassment deriving from publication of books or articles about them.

However, in ethnography there is a growing recognition that it is often actually impossible to offer confidentiality and anonymity. Further, it may be inappropriate and undesirable to try to do so (den Hoonard, 2002; Grinyer, 2002; Wiles et al., 2006). It often does not work, and it is hard to see how it can ever really work if what is being said in the reports is significant and worthwhile. The fundamental difficulty is that there are very many people involved with any organisation that is the site of an ethnographic study who know the identity of the researcher. In a school, for example, the headteacher, teachers, administrative staff and students all know (or should know) what is going on. In many cases the list may also include members of the governing body, parents and others connected with the school. The very essence of ethnography is that the researcher is present in the organisation over an extended period, and such exposure means that a great number of people come to know the researchers identity. With so many people knowing about the research, it is very difficult to hide the identity of the school or individuals involved if any of the reports have local or national exposure.

Nespor (2000: 549) summarises the overall problem:

> Anonymisation protects participants from identification and consequent harm or embarrassment only insofar as local people have no objection to what is written (or cannot be bothered to read it) and what is written is of too little import to attract the scrutiny of outsiders.

Not only is the true identity of the site known to those directly involved, in many cases it is relatively easy for an outsider to identify the school. Where convenience has been used as a main factor in the choice of sites, schools linked to the author's university education department are prime suspects. A few telephone calls from someone who appears to already know the identity of a research school can identify the particular site. Additionally, many researchers use a pseudonym for a school but give so much additional data that the school can be easily recognised. Alan Peshkin, who was one of Americas most well-known educational ethnographers, provides an interesting example. What turned out to be his last book before his death was of a private elite college preparatory High School to which he gave the name Edgewood Academy (Peshkin, 2001).

In one of the early chapters of this book Peshkin gave some basic facts about the elite school in which he conducted the research. He stated that the school was in New Mexico and gave the size of the campus and the foundation income. I checked the private schools in New Mexico in the Handbook of Private Schools (1991) that I had to hand—only Albuquerque Academy looked likely. I quickly found the schools website which verified the information given and then went into the schools library catalogue and looked under Peshkin. I found that the school had three copies of the book and the catalogue entry on it helpfully told me that Alan Peshkin spent approximately one year visiting and studying Albuquerque Academy as preparation for this book. It was absolutely clear which school was researched, and little attempt had been made to disguise its identity.

Similar difficulties with the anonymity of sites are evident in many published reports. Which British reader has not been able to unearth, for example, the real identities of Gewirtz, Ball and Bowes (1995) Local Education Authorities or Gerald Graces (2002) Catholic Diocese? Vulliamy (2004: 277) gives an example of a PhD thesis he was examining where he was able to identify an anonymised site simply by typing five consecutive words from a quoted Ofsted report into an internet search engine. Within seconds he was looking at the photographs and names of the teachers about whose working lives and views he was reading in the thesis.

But even if the identity of the community or organisation could be concealed, it is very unlikely that individual anonymity can be maintained through pseudonyms in relation to the other people involved. Robert Burgess (1985c) gives a good example of the negative impact of presenting some of his research on Bishop MacGregor School to the staff. While he had used pseudonyms for the four staff involved in the main department he studied, it was not difficult for the headteacher and others to identify individuals. Within a school, the headteacher and other teachers will know which teachers were involved in the research and a few details may be sufficient for them to identify each person quoted or whose activities are described in a report. Moreover, the people who are in a position to identify individuals are exactly those to whom exposure has the greatest potential risks of harm or embarrassment. For a teacher to be identified in a book or article as behaving in an incompetent or racist or sexist way, for example, could bring great harm on that person. While a few researchers might think such exposure to be acceptable, I do not believe it is ethically appropriate for the researcher to act as prosecution, judge and jury with no chance for the teacher involved to even present any defence.

Put simply, giving anonymity through pseudonyms to sites and people often does not work in ethnography. It does not protect organisations from exposure if the reports have sufficiently significant or damaging findings. And, even where the location of the site can be concealed, it does not protect individuals involved from harm that might result from exposure to those with the most direct power over them. Ironically, pseudonyms only act to protect people and organisations where there is little to protect them from.

Why, then, is the promise of anonymity so much an accepted part of most ethnographic and qualitative work? My guess is that anonymity is most frequently initially offered by researchers as part of an access strategy. It might be argued that, at a time when teachers and schools are the subject of so much external scrutiny and evaluation, offering anonymity takes some immediate pressure off them, and it is widely believed that they are more likely agree to research if the school is not to be mentioned by name in any report. If the research turns out to present the school in a good light, the school itself can break its anonymity. In a similar way, it is reasonable to believe that teachers will be more willing to agree to research if they know that their names will not be used in any report. Again, if the research shows them in a favourable light, they can identify themselves with it.

While promising anonymity is probably most often initially used as a means of fostering access, there may be further reasons for its almost unanimous acceptance in ethnographic work. One less altruistic reason for the use of anonymity is that it may benefit the researcher rather than the researched. It can be argued that the idea of anonymity allows researchers to write their books and articles with less concern for absolute accuracy and to base their arguments on evidence which may not be as strong as desirable. If named schools and people are being discussed the need for very strong evidence before claims are made becomes obvious. At the extreme, writers could be sued for libel in a way that is difficult to do where names are not used. Researchers are able to hide poor evidence behind the pseudonyms without those researched being able to make a challenge. Using pseudonyms means that readers are unable to verify any of the material presented in a research report. Even where a reader believes that he or she knows where the research was conducted and has contradictory information, it is impossible to challenge the findings as it is never entirely certain which site was the subject of the research (Wolfe, 2003). Indeed, naming a site in any criticism would break the guarantees of confidentiality offered by the original author.

But there are further equally worrying possibilities. Jan Nespor (2000) sees anonymisation as a representational strategy with interesting ontological and political implications, the most striking of which, he believes, have to do with the way anonymisation naturalises the decoupling of events from historically and geographically specific locations. In other words, the fact that we do not name a site gives the findings of the research a spurious generalisability. If we attempt to conceal details about a school, it becomes a more general place—a school that could be any school, a school which is just one example of many. Ethnographers thus implicitly invite readers to see their findings as being applicable to other situations. Yet, to be able to understand any school, readers really need to know the schools history and geographical location, its physical facilities and appearance, and the nature of the students it serves and the staff who teach there. Each school is unique in structure and organisation. The way it responds to change can only be understood in the context of its history and socio-political location.

While, as readers, we intellectually accept the lack of generalisability of ethnographic work, we may be seduced by the lack of specific details about the site and situation such that the significance of particular pieces of research expands to fill our general understanding of the issues. Thus, *Learning to Labour* (Willis, 1977) has been widely taken to explain why working class kids get working class jobs, yet it is based mainly upon a study of only 12 young men in a single school in a particular social, political and economic context (Walford, 2007). Similarly, *Beachside Comprehensive* (Ball, 1981) is seen as giving information on the effects of banding and streaming in secondary schools and *Rebels without a Cause* (Aggleton, 1987) is taken to explain some of the middle-class experiences of the transition from school to work. Jo Boalers (1987) work in two somewhat contrasting schools has been widely accepted as indicating the relationship between teaching styles, setting and gender and success in mathematics teaching, and Gillborn and Youdells (2000) ethnographic study of two schools has shown the nature of the A-C economy that has resulted in secondary schools as a result of recent policy changes.

The fact that none of the research schools is identified, implicitly gives the writer and reader the chance to broaden the findings of each study beyond the situation investigated. I am not implying that this is necessarily the authors' intention, but the use of pseudonyms gives a spurious generalisability of time and space to the results of specific studies. I recognise, of course, that giving the names of places and people does not automatically stop readers from making unwarranted generalisations—but it would certainly make writers more circumspect.

Conclusion

This chapter has argued for more attention to be given to the selection of research sites for ethnography and for sites to be chosen for specific theoretical reasons. Currently, many studies are conducted in sites which have been selected for convenience with the result that the contribution to knowledge that the studies make is open to question. Taking more care with site selection necessitates greater concern for the access process and it has been suggested that ethnographers have much to learn from sales people in presenting the benefits that their research can offer to potential participants.

Ethical behaviour is central to high quality research both in the access negotiations and in the conduct of the research, but it has been suggested that the use of anonymity may not always be the most ethical decision. Whilst anonymity is still the most common option (and is used by most of the contributors to this volume) it can have negative influences on the conduct and reporting of research and can lead both researchers and readers to make false generalisations from case studies.

References

Aggleton, P. (1987) *Rebels without a Cause*. London: Falmer.
Ball, S. J. (1981) *Beachside Comprehensive*, Cambridge: Cambridge University. Press.
Becker, H. S. (1968) Whose side are we on?' *Social Problems*, 14: 239-247.
Boaler, J. (1997) *Experiencing School Mathematics*, London: Falmer.

British Educational Research Association (2004) *Revised Ethical Guidelines for Educational Research,* Southwell: BERA.
Bryman, A. (1988) *Quantity and Quality in Social Researce,* London, Unwin Hyman.
Burgess, R. G. (1983) *Experiencing Comprehensive Education: A study of Bishop McGregor School,* London: Methuen.
Burgess, R. G. (1984a)(ed.) *The Research Process in Educational Settings: Ten Case Studies,* London: Falmer Press.
Burgess, R. G. (1984b) *In the Field.* London: George Allen and Unwin.
Burgess, R. G. (1985a) (ed.) *Field Methods in the Study of Education,* London: Falmer.
Burgess, R. G. (1985b) (ed.) *Strategies of Educational Research: Qualitative methods.* London: Falmer.
Burgess, R. G. (1985c) The whole truth? Some ethical problems of research in a comprehensive school, in Burgess, R. G. (ed.) *Strategies of Educational research: Qualitative Methods,* Lewes: Falmer.
Denny, R. (1997) *Selling to Win. Second edition,* London: Kogan Page.
Fitz, J. and Halpin, D. (1994) Ministers and mandarins: educational research in elite settings, in Walford, G. (ed.) *Researching the Powerful in Education,* London: UCL Press.
Gillborn, D. and Youdell, D. (2000) *Rationing Education,* Buckingham: Open University Press.
Gewirtz, S., Ball, S. J. and Bowe, R. (1995) *Markets, Choice and Equity in Education,* Buckingham: Open University Press.
Glaser, B. G. and Strauss, A. L. (1967) *The Discovery of Grounded Theory,* Chicago: Aldine.
Grace, G. (2002) *Catholic Schools: Mission, markets and morality.* London: RoutledgeFalmer.
Grinyer, A. (2002) The anonymity of research participants: assumptions, ethics and Practicalities, *Social Research Update,* Issue 36, Guildford, Department of Sociology, University of Surrey.
Hammersley, M. and Atkinson, P. (1995) *Ethnography: Principles in practice* 2nd edition, London: Routledge.
Handbook of Private Schools (1991) *The Handbook of Private Schools,* Boston, MA: Porter Sargent Publishers.
Johnson, J. J. (1975) *Doing Field Research,* New York: Free Press.
Kimball, B. (1994) *AMA Handbook for Successful Selling,* Lincolnwood, IL: NTC Business Books.
Lacey, C. (1970) *Hightown Grammar,* Manchester: Manchester University Press.
Lincoln, Y. S. and Guba, E. (1985) *Naturalistic Enquiry,* Beverley Hills: Sage.
McHugh, J. D. (1994) The Lords' will be done, in Walford, G. (ed.) *Researching the Powerful in Education,* London: UCL Press.
Michell, J. C. (1983) Case and situational analysis *Sociological Review,* 31(2): 187-211.
Nespor, J. (2000) Anonymity and place, *Qualitative Inquiry,* 6(4): 564-569.
Peshkin, A. (2001). *Permissible Advantage? The Moral Consequences of Elite Schooling.* Mahwah, NJ: Lawrence Erlbaum Associates.
Punch, M. (1977) *Permissive Retreat,* Cambridge: Cambridge University Press
Punch, M. (1986) *The Politics and Ethics of Fieldwork,* London: Sage.
Schofield, J. (1990) Increasing the generalisability of case study research, in Eisner, E. and Peshkin, A. (eds.) *Qualitative Inquiry in Education,* New York: Teachers College Press.

Seale, C. (1999) *The Quality of Qualitative Research*, London: Sage.
Silverman, D. (1993) *Interpreting Qualitative Data*, London: Sage.
Stake, R. (1995) *The Art of Case Study,* London: Sage.
Troman, G. (1996) No entry signs: educational change and some problems encountered in negotiating entry to educational settings.' *British Educational Research Journal,* 22(1): 71-8.
Van den Hoonard, W. (2002) (ed.) *Walking the Tightrope: Ethical issues for qualitative researchers*, Toronto: University of Toronto Press.
Vulliamy, G. (2004) The impact of globalisation on qualitative research on comparative and international education, *Compare*, 34(3): 261-284.
Walford, G. (1986) *Life in Public Schools*, London: Methuen.
Walford, G. (1987a) (ed.) *Doing Sociology of Education*, Lewes: Falmer Press.
Walford, G. (1987b) Research role conflicts and compromises in public schools, in Walford, G. (ed.) *Doing Sociology of Education*, London: Falmer.
Walford, G. (1991a)(ed.) *Doing Educational Research*, London: Routledge.
Walford, G. (1991b) Researching the City Technology College, Kingshurst.', in Walford, G. (ed.) *Doing Educational Research*, London: Routledge.
Walford, G. (1994) (ed.) *Researching the Powerful in Education*, London, UCL Press.
Walford, G. (1998a) *Doing Research About Education*, London: Falmer.
Walford, G. (1999). Selling your way in, in Massey, A. and Walford, G. (eds.) *Explorations in Methodology, Studies in Educational Ethnography, Volume 2*. Stamford, CT: JAI Press.
Walford, G. (2000) A policy adventure: sponsored grant-maintained schools, *Educational Studies*, 26(2): 247-262.
Walford, G. (2000) From City Technology Colleges to sponsored grant-maintained schools, *Oxford Review of Education*, 26(2): 145-158.
Walford, G. (2001). Site selection within comparative case-study and ethnographic research. *Compare*, 31(2): 151-164.
Walford, G. (2002) (ed.) *Doing a Doctorate in Educational Ethnography*, Amsterdam, Oxford, Elsevier.
Walford, G. (2005) Research ethical guidelines and anonymity, *International Journal of Research and Method in Education*, 28(1): 3-93.
Walford, G. (2007) Everyone generalises, but ethnographers should resist doing so, in Walford, G. (ed.) *Methodological Developments in Ethnography*, Amsterdam, Oxford: Elsevier.
Walford, G. and Miller, H. (1991) *City Technology College*, Buckingham: Open University Press.
Wiles, R., Charles, V., Crow, G. and Heath, S. (2006) Researching researchers: lessons for research ethics, *Qualitative Research*, 6(2): 283-299.
Willis, P. (1977). *Learning to Labour*. Farnborough: Saxon House.
Woolfe, A. (2003) Invented names, hidden distortions in social science, *The Chronicle of Higher Education*, 30 May.
Yin, R. K. (1994) *Case Study Research, second edition*, London: Sage.

Chapter 3.

For lust of knowing—observation in educational ethnography

Sara Delamont

The title comes from J. E. Flecker's (1947) poem, *The Golden Journey to Samarkand* an old fashioned verse in which various groups of people take it in turns to speak. A group of merchants and pilgrims are about to leave Baghdad for Samarkand, and explain their motives for the journey. The pilgrims seek a prophet, the merchants primarily intend to trade, but they are also motivated by the 'lust of knowing'. All good research is so motivated: and educational ethnography is no exception.

This chapter stands alone, but can be usefully read in the context of a book-length version of the same advice (Delamont, 2002), an essay-length account of how ethnographic research, in all disciplines, is conducted (Delamont, 2004), and a journal article which sets out my manifesto for high quality educational research (Delamont, 2005a). The book and the journal article have Flecker's poetry as metaphorical skeletons: the book uses the golden journey, the articles uses another poem, about the four gates of Damascus, as its framing device. One reason for these poetic excursions is given in the last section of this chapter.

The chapter deals with five things that inexperienced ethnographers find puzzling and problematic: how to observe, what to observe, what to write down, where to record observations, and what to do with the fieldnotes and other writings afterwards. The style is direct, with relatively few citations, illustrated with examples of the practicalities from ethnographic projects conducted since 1969. These include the doctoral study of St. Luke's, an elite girls' school, done in 1969. There are two confessional accounts of that research in Delamont (1984a, 1984b). There is also the first ORACLE (Observational Research and Classroom Learning Environment) Project done in 1977 and 1978, described in Galton and Delamont (1985) and Delamont and Galton (1986). However the majority of the concrete examples arise from my own current fieldwork because it is fresh, unfamiliar, and 'at the front of my head' (see Delamont, 2005b, 2005c; Delamont, 2006; Stephens and Delamont, 2006a, 2006b), and a project on operatic master classes that is about to begin. There have been technical advances since Delamont (2002), and the citations here are mainly to material published since 2002. My current fieldwork is a study of how the Brazilian martial art, *Capoeira*, is taught and learnt in the UK. It is an educational ethnography, but not a study of conventional schooling or higher education. *Capoeira* is done to music, and if you have never heard of it, think of a mixture of break dancing and karate done by agile Brazilians.[1]

The rest of the paper uses current research to illustrate the main points, so a partial account of the *Capoeira* fieldwork is interwoven with advice on how decent fieldwork is done. The model in my mind for the chapter is Blanche Geer's (1964) classic paper about the initial fieldwork encounters, in 1959, for the study of undergraduates at Kansas which was eventually published as Becker, Geer and Hughes (1968). Styles of fieldwork, or perhaps more accurately, styles of writing about fieldwork, have changed since 1964, but Geer's paper is still an insightful read, as Amanda Coffey, Paul Atkinson and I have written elsewhere (Atkinson, Coffey and Delamont, 2003). The subheadings for the following five sections are: Before the fieldwork; How to observe and record; What to observe and record; Types of record; What to do with the data; and then there is a brief afterword on The best bit of fieldwork.

Before the fieldwork

Good fieldwork comes from being interested in some aspects of the setting and its actors, *and* on having some foreshadowed problems grounded in social science. The more thinking and writing and reading that has gone into developing foreshadowed problems the better: but no one should think, write and read *rather* than go into the field and start observing. A pilot site is useful to practice a bit of observation too. It is sensible for students to explore their foreshadowed problems with their supervisors, and for employees on projects to discuss with the grant holders what the foreshadowed problems in the latter's mind were. It is vital to 'abandon' the foreshadowed problems if they are impeding the collection of good data: or, if not to abandon them, to put them to one side to focus on the core issues that are staring the researcher in the face.

My *Capoeira* project began, by accident, in November 2002, but the preliminaries do illustrate the importance of interest and foreshadowed problems. I teach a final year undergraduate module on Brazil, and had read an ethnography about *Capoeira* as it is practised, taught and learnt in Salvador de Bahia, a city in the north of Brazil, by Lewis (1992), which made it sound fascinating, both

1. When BBC One had station idents between the programmes showing dances and exercises performed by people in red, one of these was two men doing slow *Capoeira* on a roof above London, so most British people have seen *Capoeira* without knowing what it was.

in its own right and as an educational setting. *Capoeira* also appeared to be a lens through which to focus on Brazil itself. Paul Atkinson and I used Lewis's book as one example of how studying unusual settings helps fight familiarity in educational research (Delamont and Atkinson, 1995). I discovered there were classes in London, and thought I would try to organise studying them when I next had some sabbatical leave. It did not seem feasible to conduct any research from Cardiff, so I mentally put the idea 'on hold'. Then at the end of a lecture in November 2002 some of the students on the Brazil course told me that there was a *Capoeira* class advertised at a youth centre near Tolnbridge University which was a site I could get to. I went along to see what *Capoeira* was, partly out of curiosity and partly because I wanted to find something interesting to do fieldwork on.

The class turned out to be fascinating, and my diary records my excitement at discovering a great fieldsite for my purposes. Of course I did not understand most of what I saw and heard, but I wrote that I could see why Lewis (1992) had been captivated by *Capoeira*, and how it was fascinating. In that class there were several young men and women, including Neil Stephens with whom I have since published on the research, who I have watched change from absolute beginners to experienced *Capoeira* students. In the autumn of 2002 I was only able to watch two classes taught by Cadmus[2], and two where more experienced students helped beginners in the absence of a teacher. Then these classes folded, and both my research, and my colleague Neil Stephens's apprenticeship in *Capoeira*, ended. I was disappointed, and started to look for other possible things to study instead. However in 2003 another teacher Achilles who lived and worked based in Cloisterham, began to teach in a kickboxing gym in Tolnbridge and I went to meet him to see if I could watch his lessons. Neil Stephens was there, and Achilles was happy to be observed. So, twelve months after my two observations of Cadmus I wrote my first excited out of the field reflections, when I began to observe Achilles: 'So I have a fieldwork site again, hooray! Neil says the new teacher is nice, and there is a space to watch from'.

The general point here is that it does not matter whether the initial decision to try a field site for 'fit' comes from a book (whether an academic book or a work of fiction), or teaching, or a theoretical interest, or merely a desire to find

2 In the *Capoeira* fieldwork all the teachers and students are protected by pseudonyms. In *Capoeria* students are given a *Capoeira* nickname by their teacher when they receive their first belt, and I use pseudonymous *Capoeira* nicknames in all publications. All the teachers have pseudonyms from classical history and mythology (e.g., Cadmus, Achilles, Diomedes), and male students from *The Jungle Book*. The exception is Neil Stephens, my co-author, who has Portuguese *Capoeira* nickname, *Trovao* (Thunder), and I appear in the publications as *Bruxa* (Witch) an alternative to the real *Capoeira* nickname Achilles gave me.

an 'interesting' field site. However it is important to be reflexive about personal, biographical, financial and academic reasons for the choice, and to record these reflections systematically. As soon as a possible fieldsite opens up it is probably necessary to negotiate access, and submit the proposed research to an ethics committee. It is certainly vital to think about the access and the ethics, and to begin to write the reflexive 'diary' or its equivalent. Access negotiations and ethics are not discussed further here, but should be fully documented.

How to observe and record

Novice researchers are often very unclear about what they should be looking at, what sort of looking or watching becomes 'observation', and how to judge whether or not they are doing it 'right'. Precisely what to watch is often unclear not only to novice researchers, but also to experienced ethnographers. The textbooks are rarely specific enough and the 'confessional' or autobiographical accounts over-emphasise disasters and *faux pas* or danger and risk. (See Nordstrom and Robben 1995 or de Marrais, 1998 for example). It is valuable to read about doing ethnography on oil rigs or container vessels (Sampson, 2004), in opium dens or war zones, but they do not provide much practical help about what to look for in a mathematics lesson in a school on a wet Wednesday or a chemistry lecture in a university on a cold Friday morning.

Observation in educational settings *can* be dangerous, but in general the problems are over-familiarity and boredom. Because educational researchers have been pupils and students, and very often teachers and lecturers, it is hard to concentrate and 'see' things in our own culture. Going into schools in a different country provides instant 'strangeness', but in our own it is hard to force oneself to focus on what is happening rather than what one 'expects', 'knows' and is familiar with (See Delamont, 2002: 46-55). It is also hard not to judge. The researcher's job is to find out what the participants think is going on, what they do, why they do it, how they do it, and what is 'normal' and 'odd' for them. In much educational research it is easy to rush to judgement. One of the biggest problems in the first ORACLE project was that most of the observers sat in a 40 minute lesson and produced only a few lines of fieldnotes, often judging the events not describing them. So for example one ORACLE observer wrote:

> I find Mr. Mairs a very pleasant man who gets on with his job easily and confidently. However his lessons are tedious to observe. The children get on with their work with the minimum of fuss; they go up to him

individually for help; and consequently very little happens which is striking or noteworthy. (Galton and Delamont, 1985: 170)

and

At 3.30 p.m. those in St. Francis House went home—they had been given leave to do so by the head at assembly as it was St. Francis's Day. (I question the legality of this as children 9-11 were involved.) (Delamont and Galton, 1986: 152)

In both these examples the observed has judged events, but not recorded them. In the first a good observer would focus on how Mr. Mairs achieved the order left unanalysed; in the second on what actually happened when the sub set of children left the class early. In both cases the observer should have recorded far more detail what all the children were doing, what the room looked like, what textbook was in use, what the children wrote with and wrote on and many other details. Additionally, they should have been much more reflexive about their own potential impact on the classes, and they should also have examined why they were bored (in the first case) or disturbed (in the second). Good educational ethnography is not about hoping to see things that are 'striking' or 'noteworthy': it is about making the best description and analysis of what happens that one can.

My advice is to be very systematic about observing, and recording, some basic 'facts' in every setting: so for example in a school study I would sketch every 'room' or space entered for the first time. Classrooms, labs, staffrooms, library, changing room, hockey pitch, sick room, stock cupboard, gym, swimming pool, space for the bicycle racks and so on, and thereafter note where in that space the key actions take place. Then I would note what is displayed on the walls and door and noticeboards, officially and unofficially (for example, 'No Food or Drink to be Consumed in this Room' and the graffiti that states 'Robbie is fit' or whatever). The nature, location and condition of the furniture and fittings needs attention, as do the smell of any space (does the boys' changing room smell of hash, socks or chlorine?), and whether it is noisy or quiet (can you hear traffic, or bird song, or the dinner ladies clearing away lunch?). So observation is about using all the senses: not just sight.

Try to observe from different places or angles in the spaces you visit regularly: in the lecture hall sit in different places; in the staffroom spread yourself around among various cliques. Many ethnographers 'fall in with' one subset of pupils or students or staff and only observe and interact with them, as Cusick (1973) did. Where institutions have clerical staff, technicians, manual workers, their daily lives may provide real insights into the whole place: even if they are not the main focus, time with them can be rewarding. A day spent in one place, followed by a day following someone around will give good contrasts. Time matters—observe, and record, when things happen and how long they take: how long does it take to get coffee in the staffroom at morning break? How long to return a DVD to the library? How much time in a gym lesson do a keen boy and a reluctant one actually spend *moving* and how much queuing up or sitting? What percentage of the talk in the Spanish conversation class is in Spanish?

The most important things are to be reflexive, and not to slide into familiarity. Force yourself to think hard about what effect you are having, on what you need to know, on how to find out what you need to know, on changing your focus so the angles you get shift. Think about, and record, your strategies for staying alert, for making the familiar strange. Record whether you are too hot or too cold, whether it is quiet or noisy, what you could and could not do. Then think about how that affected what you could see, and what you understood of what you saw.

All these observations and reflections are only useful if they are recorded: everything needs to be written down, in one large record, or several smaller differentiated ones. In the next section there are concrete examples of what to record.

What to observe and record

Geer (1964: 382) stressed that if a process is a mystery, then sustained observation will clear it up. Note that this is a process: the longer you observe for the more your understanding should grow and develop. In what follows I have suggested some ways to observe and record: my emphasis is always on the concrete, because that is what fades. We all remember the emotions and outbursts—the delight, the anger, the embarrassment—but are likely to forget the details that are needed to write good ethnographic texts. So count things: how many pupils in the class? Males? Females? British Asian? African-Caribbean? Turkish? Somali? Are there enough Bibles in RE for every pupil to have one? How many of the Bunsen burners are working? Bodies matter: how are staff and students dressed? Who is clean, who smells? What is the state of people's teeth? What youth fashions are in vogue and do they mark out cliques?

How many people have all the necessary 'kit'? In the Oracle project, in the Coalthorpe Schools, the *only* boys who had perfect, complete kit for everything from rugby to art, from woodwork to swimming, were those from the local authority children's home. They had everything, it was all new, all fitted, and was all name marked with woven name tapes. Everyone else had some missing items, hand-me-downs, homemade items, things that were too big, or already too small, or were adapted—their art apron for example was an old shirt of their father's. What bodily skills are expected of students and pupils? Are nine-year-olds required to sit still for forty-minutes, to manage without lavatory visits for whole lessons, to use pens with liquid ink in? How many people have pierced ears, navels, lips, tongues, noses?

In some settings the researcher does not just observe, but talks to people in the setting, or even undertakes the activities themselves. Appropriate behaviour in a mathematics lesson would be inappropriate at the School Fete, and vice versa; a chemistry lecture is different from the bus trip to an away rugby game. To illustrate all these precepts I have described a typical piece of *Capoeira* fieldwork, in a new setting.

> It is a dark winter's night in Fordhampton, a British town. I have been externalling a PhD thesis at the university, and decided I would stay overnight at my own expense and go to a *Capoeira* class taught by Master Sicinnus. I met him when he visited Achilles's class a few months ago, he said I should visit when I was in Fordhampton, and my research collaborator, a *Capoeira* student I call *Trovao* has checked his website for me so I know where to go (the St. Costas and St. Damian Church Hall) and when (Beginners 7.00 to 8.30, Advanced 8.45 to 10.15). Skipping over finding the hall and re-introducing myself to *Mestre* Sicinnus, what will I look at and record?
>
> I draw the hall, noting the floor (wooden, stone, matting?), any equipment (a ballet bar, exercise mats, hula hoops), whether there are changing rooms, showers so people can wash after class and go out, a kitchen, lavatories, wall mirrors, weight training equipment etc. Do people change in the changing rooms, or have they come with their *Capoeira* kit on under their street clothes, or do they just change in public view? If the latter, is it men only, or both sexes? Is there a clock? Is it right? What temperature is it in here? What notices are posted? Do they say 'no drugs, no guns, no knives' or 'Can you help with the Bingo on

Wednesdays?' or 'The mother and baby club need raffle prizes—donations to Mrs. Williams *please*' or all three? Do they stress keeping everything locked up, and are the windows covered with wire netting or bars? On my diagram I will mark where I stood or sat, and if I had several observation points I will record these on the diagram or in the notes. If I sit on an exercise machine, or a bench, or on the floor, that needs to be written down, and if I move to see something, hear something or even join in, it could be important.

I count the students, by sex and race, and if there are children I note that too. I record how many were prompt, and add any latecomers. *Capoeira* in Britain is done in uniform, and I count how many people are in full kit, of which types, in partial uniform, and in ordinary clothes. Beginners' classes usually have lots of people in ordinary clothing, advanced students generally own uniforms, so a clothing census in a beginners class will be an indication of how new they are to *Capoeira*, or how energetically Mestre Sicinnus sells clothing to novices.

Capoeira groups mostly have a grading system with belts of different colours. If I know the colour hierarchy of Sicinnus's group, a count of the belts will tell me how many of those present are beginners and how many more advanced. If I do not know the hierarchy, I record the colours anyway and ask later, or look on the website. A typical class opens with a warm up, of running, stretching and bending. Most teachers train with a CD of *Capoeira* music on. I will find out what the CD is and record that, and describe the warm up—how many press-ups? Squat thrusts? Lunges? Does Sicinnus do all the warm up, or mostly yell instructions, or get an advanced student to lead it for him?

Once the *Capoeira* teaching begins I now record what each move taught is, by its Portuguese name, and in as much technical detail as I can. I note what Mestre Sicinnus says, verbatim if I can: so my notes will include things like 'S yells 'Look ahead, look ahead!'', or 'S stresses the angle of the kicking leg'. If the students are strangers to me, so I do not yet know their names, I'll give them brief descriptions (large man in red kit—'LMRK') or mnemonics (girl looks like Kelly Holmes—KH). If I later get introduced, or watch the class again I'll add their real and *Capoeira* names into the notes retrospectively.

As the class proceeds I might record a variety of other things. Some are factual such as how sweaty people are, how the money is collected, whether there is live music. Others are more judgemental, such as how hard the lesson is and how fiercely the people play. However I am careful to record the signs I use to make these judgements. I have watched over 200 lessons, so I can tell a simple one from a hard one, as it would be rated by students who have been learning for 3 years or so, but I will note both my judgement and the way the students in that class are responding to it. So I might write 'All but two of the men are struggling to do this sequence, and it seems hard to me'. That is very different from the ORACLE observer's 'I question this decision', or 'his lessons are tedious'.

What to write down

In the two previous sections I have stressed recording everything possible—in this section the focus is on how to record. Fieldwork is only as good as the fieldnotes, and the fieldnotes are only as good as the way(s) they are written, written up and analysed.

If I did the *Capoeira* myself, I would not be able to write any notes in the classes, because I would be upside down, dripping with sweat, and struggling to walk on my hands for much of the lesson. The two outstanding monographs on learning *Capoeira* by Lewis (1992) and Downey (2005) were written by men who became skilled players themselves. Neil Stephens and I have written about the differences between learning a physical activity and merely watching it learnt (Stephens and Delamont, 2006a). Because I watch lessons and do not do *Capoeira* myself, I can write notes at the time, as I usually could in all the school ethnographies I have done.

In situ I write scribbled notes in spiral bound reporters' notebooks—I use abbreviations and mnemonics which I can decipher, and aim to record as much as I can. I do not try to write legibly for anyone else to read these notes, they are only an *aide-memoire* for me. Generally I advise researchers to cultivate an illegible handwriting style and personal shorthand, because it affords the researcher some privacy, in case someone looks at the notebooks. I date each entry, record the time down the left hand side every four to six minutes, and scribble furiously. A ninety minute class might cover twelve to twenty sides of such a pad.

As soon as I get home, or back to wherever I am staying or into a quiet space, I write up those notes into an A4 spiral bound lined book. This is a much more detailed account, based on the fieldnotes, but amplified, and with some reflections, commentary and cross-referencing added. Twelve sides of the reporters' notebook will take 20 to 30 A4 sheets when expanded. These notes will not be in beautifully grammatical English, but there will be sentences.

To illustrate and amplify my notetaking and their subsequent writing up, I have introduced an extra step into the process. That is I have provided a 'translation' of the original notes taken in the gym. So in the Fordhampton class I might scribble '8.32 S yells 'Stop'. Circles them, S dem GBACM, S rdea IL GBACM neg, rol, au cw Dems routine 6 times. Says 'Train with yr frnd. Play with begs'. Pairs.' Of course that is incomprehensible to anyone but me, especially the technical description of the *Capoeira*. What it means to me is set out below:

> 8.32 Sicinnus yells 'Stop'. Circles them.
> Sicinnus demonstrates with the Green Belt African Caribbean Man.
> Sicinnus does a *rabo de arraia*, left leg.
> Green Belt African Caribbean Man does a *negative*, a *role*, an *au* clockwise.
> Sicinnus and man demonstrate routine 6 times.
> Sicinnus says 'Train with your friend. Play with the beginners.'
> They pair up and practice.

While that is still very cryptic, and very technical, but my 28 'words' mean the 56 'words' in the expanded version to me. The things in single quotes are Sicinnus's actual words. After demonstrating how those 28 'words' would be written up in the out of the field book the events are, very briefly, explained. In the A4 book I would write that up to: '*Mestre* Sicinnus yells 'Stop'. He circles the class and calls up the Green Belt African-Caribbean man to demonstrate with him. Sicinnus does a *rabo de arraia*, kicking with his left leg. The Green Belt man drops to a *negativa*, does a *role*, and then an *au*, clockwise.[3] Sicinnus and the African-Caribbean Green Belt Man demonstrate this routine six times. Then Sicinnus tells them to get into pairs 'Train with your friend' and practice that routine, and adds 'Play with the beginners', that is, he wants his regular students to pick novices to practice with to help them, improve, not just practice among themselves.' This level of description should be making what I observed a little clearer. It should be apparent that I saw something that was pretty normal or familiar to me. Teachers routinely call the students into a circle round them, pick one student to help them demonstrate a paired sequence that, subsequently, everyone in the circle will practice with a partner after the demonstration.

---

3   *Rabo de arraia, negativa, rol* and *au* are the Portuguese names of a kick, an escape, a 360 degree turn and a cartwheel.

For lust of knowing—observation in educational ethnography 49

There is an example of an equivalent set of notes written in real time, and then written up out of the field in Delamont (2002: 60-64) about a cookery class for a group of slow learners.

This strategy only works if the abbreviated, scribbled notes are written up very soon after they are made. While everything is fresh in my mind. I try to write up within two hours of the end of a class, and always write up within twenty four hours. In the next example, from the beginning of a routine Tolnbridge class of Achilles's, I have set out the material as it would look in the reporters' notebook.

> Friday May 26th Tolnbridge 2006
> TUSC
> 7.10 A. arrives with X and Y, drum. High 5's Jagai, hugs me—'Hey Bx'—changes—14 present ( )
> 7.14 A. starts warm-up [.........]
> 7.23 Pairs. A. sits on bench—I say 'OK?' 'Tired' expl. Sauna. Leaps up—whistles—circ. Dem Trovao—cap.

This would mean, to me, the following:

> Friday May 26th Tolnbridge 2006, Tolnbridge University Sports Centre
> 7.10 Achilles arrives with Xerxes and Yarrow, and the drum. Achilles high fives Jagai, hugs me, saying 'Hey Bruxa'. Changes. There are 14 students present.
> 7.14 Achilles starts the warm-up [.....]
> 7.23 They train in pairs. Achilles sits on the bench. I say 'Ok?' Achilles says he is tired, needs a sauna. He leaps up, whistles. He circles them round him, demonstrates with Trovao a capecada.

These notes from a class I watch every week, are equally opaque to an outsider, but I can write them up as follows.

> Friday May 26th 2006 Tolnbridge, Tolnbridge University Sports Centre
> 7.10 Achilles arrives with Xerxes and Yarrow from his Cloisterham group, carrying the drum. As he comes across the hall he exchanges

High Fives with Jagai, and as he reaches me, hugs me saying 'Hey Bruxa'. He puts down the drum and his bags, takes off his jeans, pulls on his *Capoeira* abbadas (trousers), takes off his shoes and sweatshirt to reveal a *Capoeira* singlet.

There are fourteen students present (List of their names).

7.14 Achilles calls them to form lines facing him and begins his usual warm up routine.

[......]

7.23 They go into pairs to practice. Achilles sits down on the bench. He looks depressed or exhausted, so I sit next to him and say 'Are you ok?' Achilles says he is tired—he got home at three a.m. (because the Cloisterham were doing a performance at a night club) has taught two ninety minute lessons there already today, and he needs a sauna. I put my arm round his shoulder, sympathise, and ask if he can rest over the weekend.

He leaps up, whistles to stop the paired practice, circles them, calls Trovao to demonstrate with him, and demonstrates the *capecada* (a head butt) to the chest, on Trovao.

A comparison of the original notes from the Sicinnus lesson, and its out of the field version, with the original version of the Achilles lesson and its written-up account reveals several differences. In the latter there are the names of individual students, and much more personal interaction between me and Achilles, which is not in the original fieldnotes at all. It should be obvious which is the class I observe regularly, and could even be said to 'belong' to. I know all the students by name, and I had a conversation with Achilles which I did not note at the time but wrote in after the class, just as I describe Achilles's arrival and his clothing change at more length. As long as the longer version is written while the evening is fresh in my mind that is fine—but if I were to leave the task for a few days it would be hard, if not impossible to fill in all the mundane events, and even, arguably, slightly dishonest.

If I want to quote from my fieldnotes, it is the amplified fieldnotes in the A4 book that I use—and they are the record I can read a year later and still make sense of. As the books fill up I separate them, storing the reporters' notebooks in work and the A4 ones at home, in case of fire, flood or theft. I number the books, and keep a record of which book covers a specific date range—so I know that Book 30 starts on March 14th 2006 and ends on April 12th 2006. I can usually remember roughly when things happened so I can use that record to locate the fieldnotes I want. For example one group of students gave Achilles a bicycle as a birthday present, and when Neil Stephens and I decided to write about that incident it was easy to find it because we knew it had occurred in May 2005.

I try to keep these books pretty 'factual'—and record my reflections elsewhere, as I explain in the next section. Other researchers, who want their bodily sensations, thoughts and feelings to be rolled up into their fieldwork might only keep one multifaceted record.

I keep both my original scribbled abbreviated notes and my written up 'out of the field' notes in handwriting, because that is how I work best. If I were more technologically innovative, or richer, I could work differently. There are other ways to keep the records. Many ethnographers dictate their fieldnotes: traditionally on to tape to be transcribed by a secretary, but today people also use voice recognition software to put their notes 'into' the computer. Once such software is trained to the voice it works well. It is sometimes possible to take a laptop into the field and type the notes straight in; and that works indoors, in dry places, and safe spaces. A project on chemistry lectures could be recorded on a laptop, while one on swimming teachers, or outreach work in high crime neighbourhoods could not be. In some settings the fieldnotes could be spoken into a digital recorder which would enable them to be turned to written text rapidly.

Today most researchers will dictate their out-of-the-field notes, or use voice recognition software, or word-process them. Having them in machine readable form means that it is easy to index and code them, and to prepare them for an analytic software package (CAQDAS) (Fielding, 2001). If you want to mix 'facts' and reflection, then using a software package that allows you to tag and mark passages helps keep different types of text clearly labelled for your own clarity, is sensible. Geer (1964: 372) used the *comments* she had recorded during her early fieldwork to explore how foreshadowed problems are refocused and reframed in the beginning of a project. She spent six hours a day in the field, then dictated her notes, adding some comments or 'an interpretive summary' (p. 373). Her classic paper is based on thirty-four comments from the first eight days.

Types of record

In this section the focus shifts to different types of record. I try to keep my commentary separated from the 'factual' record in the A4 books, by ruling lines across the text and putting comments in, marked off. These, though are usually not auto ethnography or reflections or confessions, but rather low level comments. So I might, when writing up my Fordhampton notes put in:

> Sicinnus *never* demonstrated with a woman tonight, and I found the whole class on the aggressive side—more like the ones in New Zealand than Achilles's usual sessions.

Or

> I was surprised by the large number of students in the advanced class who could sing verses, even though they weren't, as far as I can see, Brazilian or Portuguese. I wonder if Sicinnus has singing classes, or requires singing verses for belts?

These comments form the topics I try to explore in future observations, in informal and formal interviews, and in discussions with Neil Stephens especially when we write papers. My more reflexive, critical self and confessional comments are kept physically separate from the on-going field notes, in other types of notebook which I will describe next.

I have an A5 spiral bound book on-going that I use for keeping my reflections in tranquillity: ideas I am having, things to follow up, possible papers to write, items to read, theory and so on. So it is there I would write: 'I must sort out the belt order in Sicinnus's group—why do I *always* leave it till after fieldwork, instead of sorting it out *before* I observe?', or 'I nearly skipped fieldwork tonight as I was *so* tired' or 'I wonder why I always feel sick and scared before I walk into a new class—even when I know rationally that Sicinnus would be cheerful when I arrived, and his students would be cool about my presence. I've *never* had a hostile reception—typically the teacher sees me, and a big smile appears—so why do I dread the entrance?' or 'I wonder if I can use Loic Wacquant's idea of the pugilistic *habitus* to make sense of Sicinnus's classes—Perseus's don't feel pugilistic but his *do*. If I had Bourdieu's advice on that …..'

I keep a fourth type of notebook—again the reporter style but with different cover designs (currently Winnie the Pooh, while the fieldnotes are in books with blue and silver foil covers)—in which I put notes from books and theses, a list of pseudonyms used in the publications from the project and quotes from fieldnotes or publications that could make good titles for papers. It is here I have a list of quotes from Landes (1947), Browning (1995) and other useful things I have read, that have been, and will be, titles. So the papers called *Balancing the berimbau* which was a quote from Trovao, and *No place for women among them* which is from Landes (1947) had titles that were already in a list of *potential* titles. When I write up my fieldnotes I keep an eye open for things I need to follow up which go into the A5 book, and for potential titles, which go into 'the list'.

What to do with the data

Novices often separate data analysis from data collection. Coffey and Atkinson (1996) aimed their book on analysis at such unfortunate people, who have mistakenly allowed their data to pile up unanalysed because they separated the two activities. It is absolutely fatal to separate analysis and writing up from the fieldwork. My A5 notebook is, essentially, the beginning of the analysis and the Winnie the Pooh books have the genesis of the publications. The analytic themes and categories, arising from the data, from literature, from one's own head, are constantly interacting with the data as they are collected: the ongoing research is led by, and leads, the theorising and vice versa. When I watched Sicinnus's class and wrote in my original notes.

> 10.20 Roda continues: 2m. fierce—Ok? ACGMB buys game, fiercer. Hands Up.

in the out of the field book I expanded that to:

> 10.20 The roda goes on. Two men are playing, or rather competing. It is fierce. Sicinnus does not signal to them to tone it down, or stop them, or warn them of danger or anything. Unlike Achilles or Perseus, this is tough. The African-Caribbean Green Belt Man buys the game, and it gets even fiercer. I stop clapping and put my arms and hands up in the classic defensive position both so I won't get kicked, *and* so I signal to Sicinnus and anyone else who notices that I understand that standing in the roda can be dangerous and I am (a) experienced and (b) alert.

After the lesson I wrote the question about Loic Wacquant's (2004) notion of the pugilistic *habitus* quoted earlier, followed by a note to myself to discuss the concept with Neil Stephens and see if it could be developed further. The phrase 'pugilistic *habitus*' goes into the Winnie the Pooh book as a possible title.

I then go back through the twenty A4 books and search for all the examples of aggression in rodas, and 'code' them, looking to see if my impression in Sicinnus's class is supported by the data. My coding is very old fashioned—I use colours, and stick removable coloured labels on the pages where themes occur—so where I have something coded as 'authenticity claim' or 'Brazilian-ness' or 'Inversions', for example, there are red, green and lilac coloured markers. I do not like using highlighters or coloured ink to mark the actual text, because I want to be able to remove codes and re-code the same, handwritten text. It would be much better to get the A4 books wordprocessed and use a software package, but I feel too comfortable with my old methods to change now. So if I want to look back over the fieldnotes from two-hundred lessons and explore the concept of 'pugilistic *habitus*' or, more sensibly, because it is a broader category, 'aggression: used and prevented' I will choose a colour, say pink, and code incidents of it, or comments on it, from October 2002 to the present. I would always start at October 2002, and come forward, through the fieldwork period.

The notes from St. Luke's, and from the ORACLE project, are in the attic, with the colour coded stickers still on them. I could, if I had to, revisit them and do a new coding on them. There is no reason to horde data for forty years, but it is silly to destroy them too soon, and doctoral students should definitely keep all the raw data until they have graduated, and they have finished publishing from that fieldwork. The main reason for analysing data is, of course, to write about them, and that is the best bit of research.

The best bit

There is no point in doing research unless it is turned into a report, a thesis, an article, a set of papers, a book, or all five. There are three 'tricks': first, start 'writing up' from the very beginning, second accept the *pleasures* of drafting, and third write regularly. To take these in reverse order, I try to write 500 words every day of the week, and when I miss a day, I make it up as soon as possible. Writing means multiple drafts—but drafting, polishing, redrafting, scrapping rough bits are pleasures. Screwing up a piece of paper and throwing it away is fun. I write in biro on paper—and the amount in the waste paper basket—and I use a huge log basket as a waste paper basket—is an indication of the draft improving. Thirdly, thinking about the writing from the beginning is important. The Winnie the Pooh notebooks where I start putting possible titles, and the A5 notebooks where I put my ideas about what might be written (and in my case, journals where the writing might go) are vital parts of the research process.

This chapter is meant to be about observation, that is data collection, and only strays beyond that because the whole rationale of ethnography is that there are not discrete *stages*, but rather a continuous abductive, iterative process. As I stand in a corner of the gym in Fordhampton and watch Sicinnus teach I am not only doing fieldwork, I am also thinking about analysing the data and about what publications will emerge from the data collection.

Acknowledgements

Karen Chivers wordprocessed this paper for me with skill and accuracy: I am very grateful. The ESRC funded my St. Luke's research and the ORACLE project; the Welsh Education Office funded the study of mainstreaming. The *Capoeira* project is self-funded, the new project on vocal master classes is underpinned by money from Cardiff University.

I have been enormously privileged to watch Achilles teach one hundred and fifty lessons each of ninety minutes, and I have also seen thirty other people teach seventy other lessons of ninety or one hundred and twenty minutes. Achilles is one of the most inspiring teachers of anything I have ever seen, and all the *Capoeira* teachers I have met have been supportive and welcoming. There is a core of about fifty students who have been observed over one hundred times, and a further hundred who have tolerated me in their classes—I am very grateful to them too. Neil Stephens has been an excellent colleague, both in the classes and outside them, and Lunghri, Jagai, Mowgli, Raksha, Phao and Toomai have shown endless patience with my questions. Rodrigo Ribeiro has been invaluable, as an insightful social scientist and a Brazilian. My academic research has been helped by Matthias Rohrig Assuncâo, John Evans, Gary Alan Fine, J. Lowell Lewis and many Cardiff colleagues.

References

Atkinson, P. A., Coffey, A. and Delamont, S. (2003) *Key Themes in Qualitative Research.* Walnut Grove, CA: Alta Mira Press.
Becker, H. S., Geer, B., and Hughes, E. (1968) *Making the Grade*, Chicago: The University of Chicago Press.
Browning, B. (1995) *Samba*. Bloomington, Ind, Indiana University Press.
Coffey, A. and Atkinson, P. A. (1996) *Making Sense of Qualitative Data*, Thousand Oaks: CA, Sage.
Cusick, P. (1973) *Inside High School: the Students' World*, New York, Holt: Rinehart and Winston.
Delamont, S. (1984a) The old girl network: reflections on the fieldwork at St. Luke's in Burgess, R. G. (ed) *The Research Process in Educational Settings*, Brighton: Falmer Press.

Delamont, S. (1984b) Lessons from St Luke's: reflections on a study of Scottish classroom life, in Dockrell, B. (ed) *An Attitude of Mind*, Edinburgh: SCRE.
Delamont, S. (2002) *Fieldwork in Educational Settings: Methods, Pitfalls and Perspectives*, (2nd Edition), London: Falmer.
Delamont, S. (2004) Ethnography and participant observation in Seale, C. et al. (ed.) *Qualitative Research Practice*, London: Sage, 217-229.
Delamont, S. (2005a) Four Great Gates, *Research Papers in Education*, 20(1): 85-100.
Delamont, S. (2005b) No place for women among them? *Sport, Education and Society*, 10(3): 305-320.
Delamont, S. (2005c) Where the boys are? *Waikato Journal of Education*, 11(1): 7-26.
Delamont, S. (2006) The Smell of Sweat and Rum? *Ethnography and Education*, 1(2): 161-175.
Delamont, S. and Atkinson, P. (1995) *Fighting Familiarity: Essays in Ethnography and Education*, Cresskill, New Jersey: Hampton Books.
Delamont, S. and Galton, M. (1986) *Inside the Secondary Classroom*, London: Routledge and Kegan Paul.
de Marrais, K. B. (ed) *Inside Stories*, Mahwah, NJ: Erlbaum.
Downey, G. (2005) *Learning Capoeira*, New York: Oxford University Press.
Fielding, N. (2001) Computer applications in qualitative research, in Atkinson, P. A., Coffey,, A., Delamont, S., Lofland, J., and. Lofland, L. (eds.) *Handbook of Ethnography*, London: Sage.
Flecker, J. E. (1947) *Collected Poems*, London: Secker and Warburg.
Galton, M. and Delamont, S. (1985) Speaking with Forked Tongue? Two styles of observation in ORACLE Project, in Burgess, R. G. (ed.) *Field Methods in the Study of Education*. Lewes: Falmer.
Geer, B. (1964) First days in the field, in Hammond, P. (ed.) *Sociologists at Work*, New York: Anchor.
Landes, R. (1947) *City of Women*, New York: Macmillan.
Lewis, J. L. (1992) *Ring of Liberation*, Chicago: The University of Chicago Press.
Nordstrom, C. and Robben, A. C. G. M. (eds.) (1995) *Fieldwork Under Fire*, Berkeley: University of California Press.
Sampson, H. (2004) Navigating the waves, *Qualitative Research*, 4(3): 383-402.
Stephens, N. and Delamont, S. (2006a) Balancing the Berimbau, *Qualitative Inquiry*, 12(6): 316-339.
Stephens, N. and Delamont, S. (2006b) Samba no mar, in Vaninni, P. and Waskul, D. (eds.) *The Body and Symbolic Interactionism*, Aldershot: Ashgate.
Wacquant, L (2004) *Body and Soul: Notebooks of an apprentice boxer*, Oxford: Oxford University Press.

Chapter 4.

Ethnographic interviewing: from conversation to published text

Martin Forsey

We live in an 'interview society' (Silverman 1993, cited in Holstein and Gubrium 1995: 1), or at least those of us living in the so-called Western world do, where we are bombarded with various forms of interview as part of our news and entertainment. Not only that, the skills we acquire as interviewees impacts significantly on our ability to find meaningful work, acquire bank loans or welfare payments, and to negotiate the education maze (Briggs 1986: 1). Not surprisingly then, interviews also form the vast bulk of research data gathered in the name of qualitative studies in the social sciences (Briggs 1986: 1; Alvesson 2002). The strong trend towards interview-based studies bestows upon the main research instrument a taken-for-granted status, which means that the interview is often under-examined as 'a communicative event' in social science writing (Briggs 1986: 2).

In exploring the nature of ethnographic interviews as a tool of educational research, I continue the interrogation of the commonsense assumptions about research interviews instigated by the likes of Briggs and Alvesson. Like Briggs I want to think about the procedural implications of using the interview as a major means of coming to understand social reality, but I also want to widen the focus beyond the relationship between interviewer and interviewee to contemplate the interactions between researcher and reading audience. In other words I want to examine the ways in which we translate the interview into readable, communicative text—a task that Kvale (1996: 229-276) links to issues of validation and generalisation for qualitative research.

While I acknowledge that the ethnographic interview has some generalisable characteristics, I want to avoid a 'paint-by-numbers' approach to portraying this form of research—the vigilant reader can already find enough of these. There is a science to the methodology, but, as is the case with all good science, there is also an art to the process. As Alvesson (2002: 9) argues, 'referring to and following methodological guidelines is totally insufficient for good research … at least some of the complexities and uncertainties involved must be taken seriously'. In exploring some of these complexities, there are three main areas of interest in this chapter. (1) what it means to call an interview ethnographic; (2) the process of ethnographic interviewing; and (3) the ways in which ethnographic interviews are processed into transcript and then, hopefully, into published text. I will mainly use examples from my recently published ethnographic study of school reform (Forsey 2007) to illustrate the points being made. This school-based ethnography involved fifteen months of intensive fieldwork in the place I have come to call Ravina High. Conducted in the late 1990s, it is the result of many hours spent in classrooms, and staffrooms. I sat in on numerous lessons, as many meetings as I could get to, casual conversations in the staffroom and corridors of the school, as well as in bars frequented by the teachers and in the private homes of some of them. It also involved thirty-seven ethnographic interviews with the school staff, a research activity that I argue is part of the process of participant observation in an 'interview society'.

Interviewing ethnographically

What makes an interview ethnographic? I well remember asking a fellow novice researcher this question in 1998 as she headed out of the door of her office declaring she was 'off to do an ethnographic interview'. It was a genuine question and neither of us was particularly well equipped to address it at the time. Within the discipline that pioneered this methodological approach ethnography is often presented by anthropologists as intuitive, something one learns in the doing of it. Anthropological folklore is replete with stories of the neophyte ethnographer going to their supervisor for advice as they head off to the field and being told things like, 'buy a pencil and notebook', or 'go with the flow', and 'don't sleep with the natives'. A similar dynamic applies to the process of interviewing. Given that it is considered to be part of what one might do as an ethnographic fieldworker, it is not particularly surprising that the interview remains somewhat of a mystery in ethnographic work.

Qualitative interviews, which some might think of as ethnographic, have been variously described as 'a series of friendly conversations' (Spradley 1979: 58), naturalistic, informal, in-depth encounters between researcher and informants (Johnson 1990: 10), an 'unfolding, interpersonal drama with an unfolding plot' (Holstein and Gubrium 1995: 16), 'intersubjective interaction' (Kvale 1996: 66) and as an unstructured 'soaking and poking experience' where the very topic of conversation is subject to change as the interviewee wanders off in unexpected, and sometimes enlightening, directions (Leech 2002: 665). The ethnographic interview is aimed more at the gaining of insight about the human condition than it is at hypothesis testing, a reality that reflects the unique gift ethnographic research offers to the social sciences (Leech 2002: 665). As LeCompte and Goetz (1982: 32) put it, 'By admitting into the research frame the subjective experiences of both participants and investigator, ethnography may provide a depth of understanding lacking in other approaches to investigation'.

As one committed to the ethnographic pursuit of holism and depth, I find it useful to think about the ways in which interviews can be conducted with an ethnographic sensibility that aims at revealing the cultural context of individual lives through an engaged exploration of the beliefs, the values, the material conditions and structural forces underpinning the socially patterned behaviour of any individual. The questions we ask in an ethnographic interview should allow us to locate the biography of the individual in the broader cultural domains in which they live. Consequently we should be able to link aspects of their personal story to the issues we are seeking to describe and analyse in the formal write-ups of our research data.

There is some consensus that in order to be worthy of the additional title of *ethnographic*, interviews must be conducted within the context of the broader sorts of participant observer studies discussed elsewhere in this volume. Wolcott (1999: 44), in his useful overview of ethnographic processes as 'a way of seeing', alerts us to a dichotomy between those who conceptualise research interviews as part of the process of participant observation and those who view them as separate act where the interview is a supplement to, rather than a part of participant observation. Wolcott sympathies lie more with the latter view, and he is in good company (see for example Briggs 1984: 7,99; Spradley 1979: 32; Ortner 2003). The educational ethnographer John Devine (1996) is another who shares this perspective. In his fascinating study of violence in some of New York's inner city schools he draws upon Briggs's (1984) reappraisal of the interview process to suggest that formal or semi-formal interviews kill warmth and stifle spontaneity and, he advocates, at least when working among adolescents, that interviews should not be used in ethnographic study. Devine attributes greater levels of authenticity to participant observation, urging ethnographers to seek for the meanings arising 'on the edge of a remark' in ordinary conversation rather than the more contrived remarks arising out of interviews (1996: 65-66). But I beg to differ. To borrow Spradley's (1979) term, in a 'cultural scene' in which the interview is accepted as a normal enough speech event, and where those being researched may even expect the researcher to employ such a tool as part of the investigation, an interview becomes part of the act of participant observation.

This point is explored in greater depth below when thinking about how to select interviewees. Before contemplating how to do ethnographic interviews, however, it is useful to think about what we imagine we are doing in the first place. After all, imagination impacts profoundly on practice.

Imagining ethnographic interviews

In exploring the influence of the postmodern turn on research interview processes in general Alvesson (2002: 108-114) distinguishes between three current streams in interview-based research:

> *(1) Neopositivism*—aimed at capturing social reality by following research protocols that minimise researcher bias, and all other forms of 'contamination'.
> *(2) Romanticism*—aspires to explore the inner world of research participants and the social realities they perceive and experience by accentuating the need for 'genuine' human interaction established through the development of rapport, trust and commitment between interviewer and interviewee.
> *(3) Localism* – construes interviews as complex interactions that have little currency beyond the immediate environment of the interview space.

It is easy enough to imagine conducting a project based upon the imperatives of the first two research agendas. Indeed, many ethnographic researchers position themselves somewhere between the two. However, I find it difficult to conceive of conducting interviews producing data that cannot be understood or applied beyond the immediate locale of the interview. Of course all interviews produce a discourse peculiar to the time and place in which they are conducted, but the truth explored and sometimes uncovered in the dialogical, relational space of the interview is not simply 'contingent upon the specific situation', nor is it 'too local to be taken as reflections of how the interviewee thinks, feels, talks and acts in situations that are totally different to the interview situation' (Alvesson 2002: 115). Interviews allow participants to reflect upon the social realities that have simultaneously shaped them and been shaped by them. In my experience as both interviewee and interviewer respondents usually approach the event with a great deal of sincerity. They are keen to convey their memories and reflections as accurately as possible. What informants discuss is historically contingent.

A person's memory will be flawed and her/his ability to articulate what has happened always imperfect, but rarely is this absolute. Holstein and Gubrium (1995: 28) put it well when they point out that autobiographical narrators do not simply invent what they say at the point of contact with the interviewer:

> The improvisational narrative combines aspects of experience, emotion, opinion, and expectation connecting disparate parts into a coherent meaningful whole. The respondent does not just 'make things up' as much as he or she inventively, judiciously and purposefully fashions a story that is 'true to life'—faithful to subjectively meaningful experience—even as it is creatively, spontaneously rendered.

Alversson (2002) advocates a pragmatic response to the overly harsh postmodern critique of research interviews and argues for studies that are language sensitive, cognizant of the realities of fragmented subjects, but which also make judgements about external social realities and the meanings attributed to them by social actors (pp. 117-118). Clearly it is not enough to follow methodological guidelines. As has already been suggested, good research requires that we seriously engage with some of the complexities and uncertainties involved in the process, but not to the point where the insights arising out of this process are dismissed as locally obscure.

In his engaging and influential appraisal of qualitative research interviewing, Kvale (1996: 3-5) conceptualises two divergent metaphors of the interviewer—the miner and the traveller. The former has been used by a variety of scholars of qualitative methodology for different ends (McCracken 1988; Holstein and Gubrium 1995), but it is the latter metaphor to which Kvale is most drawn. While the miner digs for nuggets of objective facts, insights and meanings using methods 'unpolluted by any leading questions', the traveller is an interpreter of reality who seeks a level of engagement with the locals that is deep enough to allows the hosts to tell their own stories (pp. 3-4). The parallels with Alverssen's portrait of neo-positivist and romantic researchers are obvious, and as I have already suggested, many ethnographers position themselves somewhere between the two. We often seek to discover the meaning-making that is part of being human, and desire to do this in a manner which is personable, interactive, engaged, and perhaps even egalitarian. At the same time ethnographers are quite capable of worrying about how they might expose a relatively pure, rich ore body by digging into well-chosen, representative sites and samples. They are also concerned about devising correct interview schedules filled with valid, penetrating questions, but which are devoid of leading ones.

Who should we interview and how should we do it?

Appendix 1 contains a small excerpt from a transcript of an interview I conducted in June 1997 with Robert (not his real name). The semi-structured interview, which lasted a little over an hour, took place in a meeting room off the staffroom of the school I have come to call Ravina High. We sat across an elongated table with a tape recorder strategically positioned between us in such a way that the microphone pointed more towards Robert than it did towards me. As is usual with the many research interviews I have conducted over the past twelve years I began by asking Robert about the aspects of his life story that are pertinent to the issues being explored in the interview. Appendix 2 contains the schedule I developed for the interviews with teachers at Ravina High. It indicates that I first asked Robert to discuss his own educational background and how he became a teacher. From there we went on to discuss the various schools he had worked in. This led Robert to recall with a great deal of fondness the nine years he spent at a rural school nine hundred kilometres north of Perth.

The transcript picks up a section of the conversation shortly after Robert had spoken about his return to Perth and how he experienced this as a kind of social death. He returned to the city to take up an appointment at Ravina High. Robert walked into a school whose reputation as a 'good school' was under threat due to the closure of a nearby school that had caused a number of students deemed 'undesirable' by those responsible for running the school to enrol at Ravina High. According to Robert gangs and fighting had become commonplace during this period and he soon found himself in the role of acting deputy principal, which placed him in the thick of the struggles to turn the school around. As the transcript indicates, Robert believes that Ravina's reputation as a good school was restored due to the actions taken at that time.

The interview with Robert was the first of the many I conducted in 1998. I interviewed him mainly because he went on long-service-leave in the second half of that year, and I was worried about 'missing something'. While Robert had not been a particularly significant informant to that point of my research, the interview proved to be surprisingly important. The several lengthy segments from this conversation that I used in the final published monograph were far more than I used from any of the other interviews I did with Ravina High's teachers.

Reflecting on my experiences of this apprenticeship into ethnographic practice I sometimes think that I should have conducted fewer interviews. Consequently, I tend to caution postgraduate students against doing too many formal interviews. Anyone who has comprehensively transcribed thirty-seven interviews of at least forty-five minutes duration will understand why I issue this advice. Kvale (1996: 94) draws a similar conclusion in looking back at one of the more significant qualitative interview projects with which he was involved. However, I find it difficult to offer definitive advice about which people are important to interview and who should be avoided. Spradley (1978), who has had an enormous influence on several generations of ethnographic apprentices, asserts that one should seek out those who have worked in a place the longest as key informants: 'The more thoroughly enculturated an informant the better' (p. 48) he assures us. While I could easily have used this advice as a means of justifying my decision to interview Robert and many others at the school, I am also aware of how the perspectives of those who were new to the school offered an important contrast to the views of the well-enculturated informant. Neophytes see the cultural scene through fresher eyes and can sometimes raise the sorts of questions the 'old timers' have lost sight of through familiarity. Hard and fast rules rarely work in this business.

Looking back I can see why seasoned ethnographers advise neophytes to trust their judgement and to learn by experience. In the case of the interview with Robert, I could have easily found good reasons to not do it. I had not spent much time with him, it was early in the fieldwork period, and I was arguably not ready for it because I did not know what I wanted to know. Perhaps the main rationale for doing that particular interview at the time was as a pilot—a means of testing the waters and my skills as ethnographic interviewer. As it was, I took the opportunity to talk with a man who was in a senior position in the school and was going to be away for the rest of my fieldwork period. Doing this interview helped me to find what I needed to know. This interview alerted me to the period in Ravina High's history when 'the good school turned rough', which become a key theme of my research (Forsey 2007: 69). As I said earlier, the interview was very much a part of my participant observation, even if I was not aware of its significance at the time of doing it. As this volume suggests in a number of places, ethnography requires the researcher to trust its process as the stories and key themes unfold before us.

Questions of who to interview, where and how are never too far away from the ethnographic research project. Clearly they are important to address for the design of any research proposal. Commenting on the mystery that often surrounds what little discussion has been generated about the selection of research participants, Werner and Schoepfle (1987: 183) point to the opportunistic nature of ethnographic research and the fact that we ethnographers tend to interview 'whomever we are able to convince to cooperate'. But probably the question that is most immediate and vexing revolves around quantity—how many people do I need to interview for a valid study?

Quantitative concerns in qualitative research

Quantitative standards remain deeply embedded in the research agenda set by universities and it is very difficult to escape the effects of the tendency to judge qualitative research approaches according to quantitative standards (McCracken 1987: 18). As one who was trained in psychology, Steinar Kvale (1996) is well aware of the hegemonic status of quantitative methodology. His extensive survey of the number of interviews used in qualitative studies suggests that the standard number is 15 ± 10 (p. 102). The anthropologist Grant McCracken (1988: 17) argues that eight interviewees can be perfectly sufficient for many a research project. While readily acknowledging the difficulties this small sample space may pose for quantitatively trained researchers, he reminds us that the point of qualitative research is usually less about locating groups representing some part of the larger world and more about the opportunity to 'glimpse the complicated character, organisation and logic of culture'. Seven could suffice, as could nine or six, or even three. The point being that there is no magic number. One should aim to interview as many persons as necessary to answer the question one is addressing, or to find out what one needs to know (Kvale 1996: 101). This might involve capturing a pre-determined number of respondents, or interviewing until a saturation point is reached—when new interviews cease yielding fresh insights or new knowledge (Kvale 1996: 102).

Interviewing thirty-seven of Ravina High's teachers apparently went well above normal limits for a qualitative research project. I have already intimated that I felt the burden of this and would like to have reduced the numbers, or at least the work associated with them. Unlike Kvale (p. 94) in his reflections on an interview based study he conducted in the late 1970s into the educational effects of grading in Denmark, I do not believe my study would have benefited from 'fewer but longer, more intensive interviews'. For one thing, I doubt that many of Ravina High's teachers would have been willing to take still more extended periods of time out of their busy schedules. More significantly, positioning myself *amidst* the neo-positivist and the romantic projects, as both miner and traveller, I was not only eager to discover as much as I could about the inner world of the teachers in my fieldsite, I was also concerned about the representativeness of my sample.

When it came time to conduct the bulk of the interviews towards the end of my fieldwork period I wanted to ensure that I listened to the thoughts and experiences across a broad range of the teaching staff. My aim was to ensure that the sample I interviewed approximated the group's gender distribution, the age range and the subjects taught at the school. I was also keen to capitalise on the relationships I had developed with a number of teachers, but did not want to restrict my attention to those with whom I had already had ample time to discuss the matters of the school. Additionally there were key figures I had to interview—those who had played a key role in the reforms of which I eventually wrote and those who expressed obvious dissent towards these changes. But I was also conscious of not just discussing the restructuring with those who had a high profile in this regard. The thoughts and opinions of those with a more watchful, or disengaged response were also important to canvas. Conducting formal interviews across a range of the teaching population at Ravina High allowed me to capture something of the diversity of experiences and views of those who experienced what proved to be a tumultuous year in the life of the school. There was no magic number I could find, and I did not ever feel as though I reached saturation point in terms of the insights I gained through the interviews. Ethnography is rarely as neat as the methodological rubrics would want it to be. What I did was sample the range as comprehensively I could. I now realise that given the opportunity to do this research again I would still conduct approximately the same number of interviews, but I would not be as stringent in transcribing all of them more or less word for word. I would be more selective in this regard.

The conduct of ethnographic interviews

I agree with McCracken (1988: 41) that it is vastly preferable to audio record interviews. Taking notes does create an unnecessary distraction, and in my experience keeps the researcher more focused on the pen and paper than on those being interviewed. As has already been discussed, Appendix 2 shows the interview schedule developed for the Ravina High research. The schedule reiterates the point made earlier about opening interviews by exploring the pertinent aspects of an informant's life. Such questions are usually easy enough for people to answer; they signal an interest in the person and the stories they have to tell. They usually, but not always, help warm the interviewee to the topic and the process. More significantly, given that the interview is not primarily performed for the benefit or well being of the individual participant, such a line of questioning helps in achieving one of the major aims of ethnographic interviewing—locating individuals and the events of their lives in a broader socio-cultural context (Zaharlick 1992: 117).

Working with assumptions about human behaviour being culturally and contextually dependent, ethnographic interviews are at their most powerful when they help us to comprehend the beliefs and values, as well as the material and structural influences, underpinning and shaping a person's life course and their life chances. The questions we ask should allow us to locate the biography of the individual in the broader cultural domains in which their lives are operating. We should be able to articulate aspects of their personal story and their encounters with the issues we are seeking to describe and analyse in the formal write-ups of our research data.

Holstein and Gubrium (1995) argue convincingly against the positivist notion that in order for research interviews to yield valid, reliable information, they should be stripped of their interactional, 'biased' ingredients. Seeking acknowledgement that interviews are deeply social events, which are 'unavoidably implicated in creating meanings that ostensibly reside within respondents' (p. 3), they advocate for what they call the 'active interview'. Holstein and Gubrium emphasise the importance of striking a balance between the interactional, processual 'hows', and the content-focused, substance-seeking 'whats' of the interview practice: 'we think that understanding *how* the meaning-making process unfolds in the interview is as critical as apprehending *what* is substantively asked and conveyed' (p. 4).

In the spirit of understanding the world through the eyes of the informant, one of the most commonly agreed upon 'hows' of ethnographic interviewing is that the questions should be asked naïvely (Spradley 1979: 59). Given the almost universal experience of schooling and the fact that many of us who conduct research in the area have worked as educators, adopting such a stance can be difficult, and perhaps even disingenuous. But, no matter what the setting, it is always a *knowing* naïvety—or at least it should be. Understanding the local scene is an important aspect of asking good ethnographic questions and interpreting the answers (Holstein and Gubrium 1995: 45; Briggs 1986). In ethnographic contexts, a naïve question is really an invitation for the interviewee to share her or his expertise on the topic at hand in such a way that the knowledge of the interviewer is superfluous to the situation.

The schedule should guide rather than determine the overall shape of the interview. Where possible I like the opening and closing questions to be consistent, but all of the interviews I conducted at Ravina High went in different directions in getting from beginning to end. So much depended upon where the interviewee took me. But the interviews were never a complete free-for-all. Sensitive to the final product of the research that is evidenced in the recently published monograph, I ensured that the main questions, which were determined by the themes I aimed to follow in writing up the research, were always pursued.

Closing off an interview poses some interesting challenges. There is often more to say, but at about the ninety minute mark the energy levels of both interviewee and interviewer usually begin to flag. Referring to the interview schedule in Appendix 2, I found the question numbered 8, asking the participants to rate their experiences of teaching, to be the most useful way of drawing the conversation to a close. In practice it slipped to the bottom of the schedule. In fact the question listed at the end of the schedule asking teachers about their concept of culture, was not a well-chosen 'closer'. It was intended to take respondents away from the intensely personal focus of the interview, but it is too abstract. I also found that an anthropologist asking teachers about the culture concept was intimidating to some who worried about getting it wrong, and was most definitely not the way to close off this personal encounter.

What is the end of the process for the respondent, marks a new beginning for the interviewer as she/he processes the transcripts produced out of the intriguing conversations that make up the initial phase of the research project. Thinking briefly about the ways in which the thousand pages of transcript are turned into publishable text, marks the final section of this chapter.

From conversation to published text

McCracken (1988: 41-42) in his detailed account of how to perform 'long interviews', insists that the interviewer must not do the transcribing. Aside from the frustrations associated with the process, he argues that doing so creates a familiarity with the data that is counter-productive to later analysis. He is also adamant that transcripts must be verbatim records of the interview; summaries and excerpts are not permissible. Having already indicated my reluctance to set hard and fast rules regarding qualitative research, I take a far more pragmatic line than McCracken. There are advantages, and disadvantages, associated with whichever transcription path one takes. As a postgraduate student I did not have the resources to pay a professional typist to transcribe the many interviews I performed. Not only that, my apprenticeship into qualitative research was probably best served by my having to grapple with the enormous amount of data generated. How else would I have learned about the 'economy' of interview production?

More significantly, I do not share McCracken's sense of purity when it comes to analysing interview transcripts. When I transcribe the interview I come to know it far more thoroughly than I can by reading a verbatim transcript prepared by someone else. In my view, this assists rather than hinder analysis. It also allows me to summarise the interview more effectively than I might. One cannot possibly use all of the material generated. However, as a full time university teacher and researcher I find myself far more 'time poor' than I was a postgraduate student, and basically unable to transcribe interviews. Using the services of a professional typist is an efficient enough response to this dilemma, but it does create other forms of work. For instance one needs to listen to the interview wherever possible and to inject into the transcripts indicators that help capture the subtle nuances of language use, as well as the energy and emotional content of the interview. By their very nature open-ended interviews generate significant amounts of excess verbiage and one cannot ask a professional typist to cut this back in the way that the professional researcher might do if they transcribe the interview. This reality inevitably increases the reading load when one begins to process the transcripts done by professional typists.

There are a number of computer programmes available to assist with processing the interview transcripts (for reviews see for example Seale 2002; Welsh 2002; Barry 1998; Morrison and Moir 1998; Hinchcliffe et al. 1997; Kelle 1997). Such programmes have been used to good effect by many a qualitative researcher, but I have yet to find them particularly amiable or efficient. Along with many of my colleagues, I tend to use an electronic version of the 'cut and paste' approach to data analysis whereby I scour transcripts in search of key themes and drop the relevant sections of the interview into a separate file named after the identified theme. La Pelle (2004) offers some very useful advice to those who wish to avoid specific data processing packages by using standard word processing software.

No matter which methods one uses to process the transcripts, it is time consuming and requires careful attention to detail. One of the ways in which

I am trying to become more efficient in the processing of interview data is helped by keeping my mind firmly fixed on the end point of the process—the production of public documents in the form of reports, papers and monographs. In thinking briefly about the move from transcript to published document, I want to emphasise the importance of maintaining a focus on the social context of the lives we document when we conduct and process ethnographic interviews.

The 'rough' transcript of the segment of the interview with Robert contained in Appendix 1, is also accompanied by the final edited version of the interview that appears in the monograph reporting the research of which the interview was a part (Forsey 2007: 70). The comparison between the raw transcript and the final published product offers a means for reflecting upon the impact of preparing research data for re-presentation to an imagined audience. It should be obvious from comparing the two that the edited version smooths over some of the rougher sections of the interview, including a question that drew little by way of meaningful response from Robert. My aim in doing this editing was to give Robert's comments a stronger, more engaging narrative edge, while not losing the meaning or power of his comments. Clearly I do not subscribe to the view that we should not 'interfere' with our data in the move towards publication. Our readers, and the people we are representing to them, deserve better than this.

In their extensive and important research into school choice in England, which started to get published in the early 1990s, Bowe, Gewirtz and Ball (1994) highlight the importance of not wrenching people out of their social milieu in our written portrayals of them. This comment needs to be read in light of the ways in which research papers based on interview data are all too often characterised by a series of long, sometimes obtuse, quotes taken from various transcripts in a fragmentary manner (Kvale 1996: 254). Too many reports based on qualitative interviews are written in this rather tedious style. As Kvale puts it, 'the subjects' often exciting stories have—through the analysing and reporting stages—been butchered into atomistic quotes and isolated variables' (p. 254). Rarely do we get to meet the people behind the quotes, and, more importantly, we often do not come to appreciate the social context that shapes their discourse and lived realities. Ethnographic interviews should lead the researcher and her/his reader to appreciate the intricate stories that influence and shape individual choices people make, the complexities they face and the realities they help create. This is why I have moved towards the production of biographical summaries of each interview as a routine part of my research. Once the transcript has been read and coded I set myself, or my associates, the task of producing a short portrait of the interviewee(s). True to my ethnographic sensibilities, the aim is to locate the cultural context of the interviewee's life through the summary of the beliefs, the values, the material conditions and structural forces underpinning the socially patterned behaviour of the person that emerged in the interview. Key quotes from the interview are incorporated into these portraits to provide added texture.

I have yet to use one of these word sketches in a published paper, although my descriptions of Robert, among others, in *Challenging the System*, (Forsey 2007: 23-24) reflects my growing interest in developing these sorts of 'biopics'. They provide a vivid way of demonstrating the cultural influences and the structuring forces impacting on an individual's life, the goals they pursue and the choices they make. One cannot hope to put all of the portraits in one's collection on public display, but having some on display in a public gallery offers a reminder that these individual pictures are simultaneously idiosyncratic and reflective of the general patterns revealed through the research. The entire collection sits in our data files as a permanent, tangible, and accessible record of the overall project and we never know when we might want to dig them out again.

Conclusion

In suggesting that there can be no hard and fast rules on the road from 'conversation' to published text I am not advocating a free for all in the conduct of ethnographic interviews. Clearly I am arguing the need for these interviews to help reveal the structural and cultural patterns impacting the social trajectories of those we come to know through ethnographic research and for this to be done as systematically as possible. We should have an eye on validity and generalisability, the dominance of particular interpretations of what constitutes scientific research having such a dominant influence on funding almost demands that we do. But these realities should never compromise the sorts of in-depth of understanding of people as social and cultural beings that can only be generated by the ethnographic commitment to an open ended exploration of the human condition.

In an 'interview society' it is possible to start thinking about the research interview as a vital part of the participant observation process that is so essential to ethnographic research. Indeed, I am starting to form a view that interviews that seeks to document and analyse the impact of the social and cultural realities of an interviewee's life story might in some instances be the only way that we can conduct a study approximating an ethnographic approach. But that is another argument that I would like to pursue at another time. For now it is sufficient to repeat my call for ethnographers whose research is significantly enhanced by conducting formal interviews to continue pursuing an engaged exploration of an individual's beliefs, and values juxtaposing these with the material and structural conditions underpinning the socially patterned practice of the interviewee. For those who have not tried this form of research yet, I can recommend it as a powerful human encounter that not only expands the knowledge of the researcher, but also can enrich the interviewee's self understanding, or at least that is what they often tell me and who am I to doubt them?

Appendix 1
Transcript of interview with robert and published Version

Transcript

Robert: So it was, it slowly changed, it slowly changed. We had parents, really very good parents, they got in here and they rang up every parent talked about uniform er, we had a very good principal, not that we haven't now, but we had a very good principal then, he bore the brunt of it, he was amazing and he just drew the line and he said if you step over that line we have to act (at this point he hit the table which gave me quite a shock through the headphones). And yet he still worked at it from the other side of things too, to try and keep the kids, get the kids a reasonable amount of education, a reasonable amount of happy education, more than anything else. He said if you walk over that line, (again hitting the table), expectations and everything else, you know, he was very consistent. And I think that those two things, the parents working with the parents and he being consistent.

Martin—and was this specifically the parents of the new students?

Robert—er, … I don't know about that. I reckon it's a bit hard to say. There's just simply, I must admit that anyone who did this (again striking the table and laughing) you got suspended or you whatever the particular punishment was. But the kids seemed to respond to that, they then knew this is what happened. There were still people who tried things out, but in general it slowly died away, got back into a reasonable routine. And the next year, I couldn't believe the difference. The kids all came along in their uniform, no skull and cross-bones, you know, sort of … (the idea tailed away)

Published version

We had very good parents. They got in here and they rang up every parent and talked about uniform. We had a very good Principal. He bore the brunt of it. He was amazing and he just drew the line and said (hitting the table with a loud thump) 'if you step over that line we have to act'.

And yet he still worked at it from the other side of things too, to try and keep the kids and get the kids a reasonable amount of education, a reasonable amount of happy education, more than anything else. He said if you walk over that line, (again hitting the table), we have these expectations and everything else, you know. He was very consistent. And I think that those two things, the parents working with the parents and he being consistent.

Anyone who did this (again striking the table and laughing) got suspended, or whatever the particular punishment was. And the kids seemed to respond to that; they then knew this is what happened. There were still people who tried things out, but in general it slowly died away, got back into a reasonable routine. And the next year, I couldn't believe the difference. The kids all came along in their uniform, no skull and cross-bones, you know!

Appendix 2
Interview schedule for staff at Ravina High, Sept. 1998

The aim of the interviews is twofold:
1. Explore motivations—why are people teachers, what led them to the work and what sustains them in their work?
2. Understand their views of the current work place—of the students, parents, administrators and their fellow teachers

So that

I will be able to write from the perspective of teachers about the complex world of teaching, its joys and frustrations, as well as of what the work entails, its opportunities and challenges.

I will be able to say something about how teachers position themselves in relation to the various sections that impact on them—the central administration, the school based administration, the students as well of course as their fellow teachers. (Perhaps even the wider society).

With that in mind, these are the questions I want to ask

1. Please tell me a little about yourself, where you were born, grew up, went to school. Your memories of school?
2. How did you get to be a teacher, what was your path to teaching?
   Why did you choose to work in the Government School system?
   Do you think government schools share a distinctive culture?
   Bob Connell, a sociologist, describes government school education as working class education, what do you think of this idea? How would you describe the role of government schools?
3. And your path to here, to Ravina High, where have you taught or worked previously?
4. Tell me about Ravina, you started here in _____
   What were your first impressions of the place
5. Tell me about your experience of the place, what has happened to you since joining the staff of Ravina. What stories stand out in your memory?
6. What have you noticed about the students at Ravina? How would you describe them?
7. What has your contact with the parents been like? Are there any stories you could relate about encounters with parents at Ravina?
8. What about the teachers, how would you describe them?

And the administration?

9   What does being a teacher mean to you? Can you imagine not being a teacher and what life would be like? What I am getting at is asking you to think about how important a part of your identity is your work as a teacher? When you meet people for the first time how do you introduce yourself?

10 How do you think teachers are regarded in Australian society? How have you reached these conclusions? What influences your thinking about teaching? Personal conversations? Media? Whatever? How significant an aspect of your identity is teaching? Your work as a teacher how important is it to you

11 Teaching, would you recommend it as a line of work for others to take up?

    What are the best things about being a teacher? What are the challenging aspects?

    Do you see yourself still teaching in ten years time? If so where do you think you will be and what do you hope to be doing? If not, what would you rather be doing?

12. One final set of questions, about culture, what do you understand this term to mean?

    What do you think culture is? Do schools have a distinctive culture? Is it a useful concept to help us understand what schools do, how they operate? Do schools share a culture, does it make sense to study life in a school in terms of culture?

References

Alvesson, M. (2002) *Postmodernism and Social Research*, Buckingham: Open University Press.

Barry, C. (1998) Choosing qualitative data analysis software: Atlas/ti and NUD.IST compared, *Sociological Research Online*. 3(3), available at www.socresonline.org.uk/socresonline/3/3/4.

Bowe, R., Gewirtz, S., and Ball, S. (1994) Captured by the discourse? Issues and concerns in researching parental choice, *British Journal of Sociology of Education*. 15(1):63-78.

Briggs, C. (1986) *Learning How to Ask: A Sociolinguistic Appraisal of the Role of the Interview in Social Science Research*, Cambridge: Cambridge University Press.

Devine, J. (1996) *Maximum Security: The culture of violence in inner-city schools*, Chicago: University of Chicago Press.

Forsey, M. (2007) *Challenging the System? A Dramatic Tale of Neoliberal Reform in an Australian High School*, Charlotte: Information Age Publishing.

Hinchcliffe, S. J., Crang, M. A., Reimer, S. M., and Hudson, A. C. (1997) Software for qualitative research: Some thought on aiding analysis, *Environment and Planning A*, 29:1109-1124.

Holstein, J., and Gubrium, J. (1995) *The Active Interview*, Thousand Oaks: Sage.

Johnson, J. (1990) *Selecting Ethnographic Informants*, Newbury Park: Sage.

Kelle, U. (1997) Theory building in qualitative research and computer programmes for the management of textual data, *Sociological Research Online*. 2(2), available at www.socresonline.org.uk/socresonline/2/2/1.html

Kvale, S. (1996) *InterViews: An Introduction to Qualitative Research Interviewing*, Thousand Oaks: Sage.

La Pelle, N. (2004) Simplifying qualitative data analysis using general purpose software tools, *Field Methods*, 16(1):85-108.

Leech, B. (2002) Asking questions: Techniques for semistructured interviews, *PS: Political Science and Politics*, 35(4): 665-668.

LeCompte, M., and Preissle Goetz, J. (1982) Problems of reliability and validity in ethnographic research, *Review of Educational Research*, 52(1): 31-60.

McCracken, G. (1988) *The Long Interview*, Newbury Park: Sage.

Morrison, M., and Moir, J. (1998) The role of computer software in the analysis of qualitative data: Efficient clerk, research assistant or Trojan Horse? *Journal of Advanced Nursing*, 28(1) 106-116.

Ortner, S. (2003) *New Jersey Dreaming: Capital, Culture, and the Class of '58*, Durham, NC: Duke University Press.

Seale, C. (2002) Computer assisted analysis of qualitative data, in Denzin, N. and Lincoln, Y. (eds.) *Handbook of Qualitative Research*, 2nd ed. pp. 273-285, Thousand Oaks: Sage.

Silverman, D. (1993) *Kundera's Immortality and Field Research: Uncovering the Romantic Impulse*, unpublished manuscript, Department of Sociology, Goldsmith's College, University of London.

Spradley, J. (1979) *The Ethnographic Interview*, New York: Holt, Rinehart and Wilson.

Welsh, E. (2002) Dealing with data: Using NVivo in the qualitative data analysis process, *Forum Qualitative Social Research*. 3(2), www.qualitative-research.net.fqs.

Werner, O. and Schoepfle, G. M. (1987) *Systematic Fieldwork: Volume 1 Foundations of Ethnography and Interviewing*, Newbury Park: Sage.

Wolcott, H. (1999) *Ethnography: A Way of Seeing*, Walnut Creek, AltaMira Press.

Zaharlick, A. (1992) Ethnography in anthropology and its value for education, *Theory into Practice*, 31(2):116-125.

Chapter 5.

Video-enabled ethnographic research: A microethnographic perspective

W. Douglas Baker, Judith L. Green and Audra Skukauskaite

This chapter presents ethnography as a philosophy of inquiry and explores how video enables particular ways of systematically recording and analysing patterns and practices of everyday life in classrooms and other educational settings. Throughout this chapter, we explore how video enables a broad range of theoretically driven actions that support ethnographers in collecting, archiving, retrieving, and analysing ethnographic records to construct accounts of everyday life in classrooms. As part of the discussion we show how philosophical and theoretical orientations guide the ways in which ethnographers form partnerships with video to explore and report the patterned ways of knowing, being, and doing that constitute cultural knowledge of a social group (Heath, 1982).

To illustrate what video enables, we present a study from an ongoing ethnographic program of research that we undertook for this chapter. In presenting the decisions we made throughout this study, we show how video enables explorations of social life within an intergenerational Studio Art class (Baker, 2001), in which new members entered each year and others continued with the class across a three-year period (grades 10-12 in the US). By unfolding the levels of analysis needed to understand what was recorded on video, we make visible different ways in which video served as an *anchor* for analysis, how video archives provided a resource for more complex levels of analysis across recorded events, and how an ethnographic corpus with multiple sources of records was necessary to construct warranted accounts about factors that supported and constrained student learning.

The discussion of how video enters into and enables particular forms of ethnographic work is presented in three parts, and describes briefly ways video enters into partnership with ethnographers across phases of the research. In the first, we make visible the ways in which video is used as a recording device, becomes an artifact of the decisions ethnographers make throughout an ethnographic project, and provides a basis for analysing and representing life recorded on video (for example, analog or digital files).

The second section presents principles and theories guiding ethnographic research in education in general and then describes principles and theories guiding, *Interactional Ethnography*, our ethnographic approach to the study of the consequential nature of everyday life in classrooms and other social settings (e.g., Collins and Green, 1992; Dixon and Green, 2005; Rex, 2006; Santa Barbara Classroom Discourse Group, 1992a). The goal of this section is to make visible what is meant by the claim that ethnography is a theoretically driven approach to the study of life within in social groups. By highlighting *Interactional Ethnography* we present an *illustrative case of theory-method relationships* (Mitchell, 1984) central to understanding what counts as video-enabled ethnography. Through this case, we illustrate how the decisions we make about when to use video, for what purposes, in what ways, in relationship to what other artifacts, shape what can be learned from any particular study.

In the third part we present an illustrative case of how video records can be used to anchor a new analysis within an ethnographic program of research. The study is the third in a chain of studies on what counts as studio art in an intergenerational class (Baker, 2001; Baker and Green, 2007). Through this case, we make visible the ways in which constructing warranted accounts about what students were learning in this class required a series of decisions about analyses at multiple levels of analytic scale. In this case we examine *what counts as knowledge* of studio art at both the individual and collective levels across a three-month period. In this way, we demonstrate how video is more than a tool, or a neutral recording device (Erickson, 2006); that is, we make visible how video is a dynamic resource with which the ethnographer forms partnerships to accomplish different dimensions of the inquiry process (e.g., Baker and Green, 2007; Goldman-Segall, 1998).

A brief overview of ways ethnographers partner with video

In this section, we present a series of partnerships with video that ethnographers have created across different phases of their studies. In presenting these partnerships, we initiate an exploration of what counts as video at different points in a research study—from the beginning moments of formulating a study through constructing ethnographic accounts. This discussion lays a foundation for the second and third sections of this chapter about how the decision to use video at different points in a study in particular ways shapes, and is shaped by, the theoretical perspective(s) guiding researchers' decisions.

The partnerships that follow are illustrative of ones that we, and colleagues who share a *microethnographic perspective* (Bloome et al., 2005; Martin-Jones and Jones, 2000), have constructed during our ethnographic work in classrooms and other social settings. Microethnographic work differs from other forms of video-based research—and other forms of ethnography—in that it focuses on language or discourse-in-use and on how life in social groups and institutional settings is constituted in and through discourse (e.g., Bloome et al., 2005; Cook-Gumperz, 2006; Edwards and Mercer, 1987; Erickson, 1986; Erickson and Shultz, 1981; Green and Wallat, 1981; Gumperz, 1986; Hymes, 1996; Hornberger and Corson, 1997; Martin-Jones and Jones, 2000; Mehan, 1979; Rex, 2006). Therefore, in microethnographic research, video is a central partner, one that enables the researcher to record segments of life in classrooms and other social groups in which members discursively construct events, identities, and academic content, among other social accomplishments.

Our goal in drawing attention to the range of partnerships with video that microethnographers have constructed is two-fold: 1) to make visible ways in which video joins with the ethnographer at different points in a study to support particular forms of data (re)collection and analysis within and across times, actors, and events; and 2) to foreshadow the ways in which video, combined with other sources of data (for example, interviews, artifacts, including written records) enhances the microethnographers' ability to provide warranted claims about the consequential and constructed nature of everyday life in classrooms and other social settings.

The following partnerships represent the range of decisions from initiating a study through reporting accounts constructed across phases of the research:

* *proposing to potential participants, Institutional Review Board(s) of a school system and university* (or other institutional reviewing agency) the role of video, including the ethical and human subject issues of its use as a partner in the research from entry to conclusion of the research project (e.g., see Chandler in Zaharlick and Green, 1991, p. 214);
* *introducing and entering video as a partner in the site* for collecting particular types of information about the everyday life of the group (Corsaro, 1985; Kantor and Fernie, 2003);
* *collecting (recording) relevant streams* of life within the group (e.g., Corsaro, 1985; Erickson, 1986; Green, 1983; Green, Dixon and Zaharlick, 2003);
* *sharing the records with members* of the site, and through these interactions

grounding interviews in the record, or permitting participants to revisit recorded events for their own purposes (for example, instructing, or representing to others, as a form of scholarship (Yeager, Floriani and Green, 1998));
- *archiving the recorded bits of life* (and related artifacts) for analysis during and following field work (Baker and Green, 2007; see Erickson et al. and Merritt and Humphey as cited Green, 1983);
- *searching for, selecting, and retrieving particular segments of life for analysis* during the study, or for a new study that (re)examines particular bits of social or academic life—these studies can be undertaken by the primary ethnographer, or by others (with permission) not present during the original study (e.g., Baker and Green, 2007; Castanheira, Crawford, Dixon and Green, 2000; Goldman, Pea, Barron and Derry, 2007; Skukauskaite, Liu and Green, 2007);
- *using video records as an anchor for analyses at different levels of analytic scale—* exploring micro/macro relationships between and among events of life within the group and among other dimensions of human activity (e.g., Baker and Green, 2007; Bloome and Egan-Robertson, 1993; Dixon and Green, 2005; Putney et al., 1998; Skukauskaite, et al., 2007; West, 2007);
- *identifying themes, actions, and practices* through contrastive and over-time analyses of what members construct together and how the moment-by-moment interactions make visible what members signal to each other and how these interactions are socially and academically significant (e.g., Barr, 1987; Bloome et al., 2005; Bloome and Carter, 2006; Cochran-Smith, 1984; Cochran-Smith, Kahn and Paris, 1991; Cook-Gumperz, 1986; 2006; Gilmore and Glatthorn, 1982; Green and Wallat, 1981; Green, Harker and Golden, 1986; Kelly and Chen, 1999; Lemke, 1990; Willett, Solsken, and Wilson-Keenan, 1998; Wilson-Keenan, Solsken, Willett, 2001; Tuyay, Jennings and Dixon, 1995);
- *constructing and presenting (writing) warranted accounts of social life* through triangulating perspectives, methods, theories, and forms of data (e.g., Tusting and Barton, 2005; Bloome et al., 2005; Anderson-Levitt, 2006; Athanases and Heath, 1995; Corsaro, 1981; Erickson, 1986; Gee and Green, 1998; Heap, 1980; 1991; Heath, 1982; MacBeth, 2003; Mehan, 1979; Mishler, 1979; 1984);
- *using video as a form of published work* that represents particular dimensions of social life studied (e.g., Goldman-Segall, 1998; Levien, 2006).

Although the list presented appears linear, in the remaining sections of this chapter we make visible ways in which partnerships with video are (re)formulated in response to new questions that arise based on what members in the recorded events are doing and on ethnographers' understandings of what is significant or occurring across phases of ethnographic work. Viewed in this way, partnerships are part of the interactive and responsive nature of ethnographic inquiry. Furthermore, we make visible how understanding theory-method relationships are critical, since the nature of the partnerships is more than pragmatic: they are related to and shaped by theories guiding researchers' choices and actions (Birdwhistell, 1977).

What counts as video-enabled ethnography in education: ethnography as a philosophy of inquiry

Today, many disciplines in social science and humanities have taken an *ethnographic turn* to explore questions of interest to members of a discipline (for example, anthropology, art, education, history, literature, media studies, social psychology and sociology). Given the widespread use of ethnography in a variety of disciplines, ethnography, or rather, what counts as ethnography, is situated within particular traditions and their questions of interest (e.g., Smith, 1978; Ellen, 1984; Green, Dixon and Zaharlick, 2003). To help frame this discussion as it relates to video-enabled ethnography in education, we draw on three conceptual arguments that are central to the discussion of *what video is* and *what it enables*. As we demonstrate, each argument implicates a general principle of inquiry, and we identify the principle related to each argument. Throughout this discussion, we make visible how these principles provide a coherent framework (Heap, 1995) for each new study of social life within and across social groups (for example, a classroom, a school, a family, a community centre).

The first argument relates to issues of theory-method relationships. To address these relationships and to make visible a principle that guides our ethnographic work, we build on Bateson's and Birdwhistell's (Birdwhistell, 1977, p. 114) argument about *methodology as theory and theory as methodology*, thus implicating particular forms of methodology, which in turn, are tied to and guided by particular theories. Thus, how video is used and video records constructed are of theoretical concern and what is recorded (or collected through other methods) is a theoretically driven inscription of the bit of life recorded on the video (or other recording devices). Such records make possible particular ways of analysing and theorising patterns of life recorded on video (e.g. Birdwhistell,

1977), an issue discussed and researched across disciplines for the past three decades (e.g., Green and Harker, 1988; Grimshaw, 1994;Goldman, Pea, Barron and Derry, 2006; Koschmann, 1999; Green and Dixon, 2002; Rampton et al., 2002). Therefore, the issue that must be addressed by those seeking to (re)analyse ethnographically framed video records is captured in the question *what is the video a record of?*

The second principle further elaborates this argument about theory-method relationships. Anderson-Levitt (2006) argued that *ethnography is a philosophy of research rather than a specific method* (p. 279). Guided by this principle, we argue that an ethnographer constructs a logic of inquiry, not a method (c.f., Birdwhistell, 1977). Central to this argument is a view of video records as a type of fieldnote on which the ethnographer records particular dimensions of social life, not the whole of life of a social group. In discussing written fieldnotes, Geertz (1973) captures this issue succinctly: '[t]he ethnographer 'inscribes' social discourse; he writes it down. In so doing, he turns it from a passing event, which exists only in its own moment of occurrence, into an account, which exists in its inscriptions and can be reconsulted' (p. 19).

Drawing on this definition of *what a fieldnote is a record of*, we argue that a video record of an event represents not the event in its complexity, but rather, it is an inscription of how the ethnographer chose to focus the camera. As a fieldnote, therefore, the video (re)presents an event selected by the ethnographer, making available for analysis a particular range of discourse and actions among members. From this perspective, video and fieldnote records are ways of (re)presenting culture, not of finding culture. The constructed nature of video and fieldnotes is captured by Goldman-Segall (1998):

Geertz reminds us that 'what we can construct, if we keep notes and survive, are hindsight accounts of the connectedness of things that seem to have happened: pieced together patternings, after the fact.' 'After the fact' means after the event, but it also means we are now beyond the belief that 'facts' are anything more than social constructions. The ethnographer who does not use film or video to record events has to reconstruct the story from fieldnotes or audiotapes. The video ethnographer is at an advantage; she can concentrate fully on the person and on the subtleties of the conversation without having to worry about remembering every detail. (p. 34)

This view of the relationship between the study of culture and work of ethnographers implicates particular ways of collecting and analysing culture as local knowledge, which Geertz (1983) and others (i.e., microethnographers) view as visible in discourse (signifying and symbolizing actions) of a social group. From this perspective, cultural practices, meanings and processes are visible in what members propose, recognise and act on, socially accomplish, and signify as socially significant (Bloome and Egan-Robertson, 1993; Bloome et al., 2005). Thus, the ethnographer in selecting particular segments of life to record in particular ways creates particular possibilities for making visible and interpreting cultural patterns and practices after leaving the field. The ethnographer, therefore, inscribes a particular view of culture through the records collected and constructed. (Similar arguments about inscription of theories of cultural processes and practices have been made for transcribing, e.g., Green, Franquiz, and Dixon, 1997; Ochs, 1979; Roberts, 1997, as well as writing ethnographic fieldnotes, e.g., Emerson, Fretz and Shaw, 1995; Nespor, 2006 and ethnographic accounts in education, Atkinson, 1990; Heath, 1983; Walford, 1991; Van Maanen, 1995; Spindler and Hammond, 2006; Zaharlick and Green, 1991).

The third principle draws on Walford's argument that *objectivity in ethnography is an illusion* (Walford, 1991) and further extends the above discussion about the work of ethnographers, and once again raises the question about how to understand what a video is record of. If objectivity is an illusion, then ethnographers need to make transparent the *logics of inquiry* guiding their work, from its initial formulation as something appropriate to study ethnographically to the construction of ethnographic accounts. In framing this principle, we contribute to arguments about the need for transparency in ethnographic and other forms of research discussed nationally and internationally (e.g., AERA, 2006; ESRC, 2005). The third principle, therefore, can be thought of as a *principle of transparency*, in which ethnographers make visible theory-method relationships guiding, and deriving from, the logic of inquiry constructed for particular studies.

These three principles, and the arguments that frame them, constitute a way of understanding what counts as ethnography-in-education across disciplines, traditions and national borders. However, a comprehensive examination of how these principles apply to all forms of video-enabled ethnographic work is not possible. Therefore, we foreground one particular perspective: Interactional Ethnography, a microethnographic approach to video-enabled ethnography.

An ethnographic imagination as logic of inquiry: a microethnographic approach to video-enabled research

To illustrate how an ethnographic imagination (Atkinson, 1990) guides (re)formulations of partnerships with video across phases of our microethnographic work, we present a new analysis of what counts as Studio Art, grounded in a two-year collection of ethnographic records by Baker (2001). This analysis, guided by an Interactional Ethnographic framework, constitutes an orienting logic of inquiry for members of our research community, the Santa Barbara Classroom Discourse Group (1992 a; b; Green and Dixon, 1993).

Interactional Ethnography as a philosophy of inquiry draws on theories from anthropology, cognitive science, education, linguistics, and sociology in order to explore discursive and social constructions of everyday life and make visible local theories and situated knowledge(s) that members construct in social groups. Underlying this perspective is a view of social groups as inscribing local and situated ways of knowing, being and doing through face-to-face interactions within and across events, as well as in their writings and other artifacts (for example, documents, photographs, among others). Drawing on theories of social and discursive construction of everyday life as an overarching framework, we view life in classrooms as, *as discursively constructed, socially accomplished*, and as *developing a particular set of linguistic, cultural and social resources that are socially and academically significant* (e.g., Cazden, John and Hymes, 1972; Cazden, 1988; Collins and Green, 1992; Erickson, 1986; Green and Wallat, 1979; 1981; Cook-Gumperz, 1986; Gumperz, 1986; Smith, 1987; Bloome et al., 2005; Rex, 2006).

From this perspective, members (re)formulate and construct texts of everyday life and through discursive and social processes establish norms and expectations about how life will be conducted as well as roles and relationships that members draw on to participate in as they construct subsequent academic or social events (e.g., Bloome et al., 2005; Athanases and Heath, 1995; Green, 1983). Furthermore, through these interactions, members construct referential systems (e.g., Castanheira, Crawford, Green and Dixon, 2000; Lin, 1993) and common knowledge (Edwards and Mercer, 1987) that they draw on as they engage in new opportunities for learning across times and events (e.g., Collins and Green, 1990; Heras, 1993; Lin, 1993; Putney et al., 2000; Santa Barbara Classroom Discourse Group, 1992a; Yeager, Floriani and Green, 1998).

These principles lead interactional ethnographers to ask overarching questions as they enter a social group to collect and analyse video records of life:

What counts as knowing, being and doing in this social group?

How are processes, practices, referential systems, academic content(s), common knowledge(s), identities, roles and relationships as well as norms and expectations of everyday life discursively and interactionally constructed?

Who has access to these processes, practices, identities and other social constructions, when and where, under what conditions, in what ways, for what purpose(s)?

What are outcomes or consequences for students and teachers across times and events and how do these shape repertoires for learning that students (and teachers) have available to guide their actions and interpretations in other events, groups or disciplines?

We ask these and related questions, whether entering a classroom or other social setting, exploring social and discursive activity recorded on video records, or engaging with or interpreting other types of artifacts socially constructed or used by members of a particular social group (for example, written texts, drawings, and physical objects) (Castanheira, Crawford, Dixon and Green, 2000). Through these questions, we engage in an interactive-responsive process of analysis of video and related records that focus on the discourse-in-use among members and that follow the trail of what members are proposing, constructing and accomplishing, (Agar, 1994).

Video records, therefore, make it possible to (re)consult the work among members recorded on video and to examine how, through this work, members signal to each other what is socially and academically significant for individuals as well as the collective. They permit exploration of the work of members at multiple levels of analytic scale—including individual and collective actions, actions across times and events, including historical information referentially presented and future actions referentially signaled, among others. From this perspective, archives of video records that are systematically collected and indexed make it possible to use one event or observed pattern of practice as an anchor and then search for the roots and routes of the event. In this way, ethnographers identify a new data set consisting of a key event (Gumperz, 1986) and related events (processes, practices and content) occurring on other days (e.g., Baker and Green, 2007; Bloome and Egan-Robertson, 1993).

Anchoring, therefore, constitutes a key concept in analysis of video grounded in a process of making visible ties across times, events and actors (e.g., Bloome and Bailey, 1992; Bloome and Egan-Robertson, 1993; Floriani, 1993; Heras,

1993: Green and Meyer, 1991). It implicates a broad range of theoretical partnerships with video records, ones that begin with creating a new data set related to the anchor video and proceeds through a range of methodological decisions related to goals of a particular analysis—for example, transcribing a segment of life, creating events maps of particular events as they are developing, and examining chains of coordinated actions and what is being discursively and interactionally accomplished (e.g., Baker and Green, 2007; Castanheira, Crawford, Dixon, and Green, 2000; Dixon and Green, 2005; Green and Meyer, 1991; Green, Harker and Golden, 1986). In this way, theory-method relationships are not static but are a resource for further theorising and for identifying methodological principles of action guided by particular theories.

What counts as studio art? An illustrative example of a logic of inquiry

In this section, you will see, at times, a shift in our writing voice in order to invite you on an analytic journey into layers of ongoing ethnographic work on construction of disciplinary knowledge in an intergenerational Studio Art class (Baker, 2001; Baker and Green, 2007). In taking you on this analytic journey, we make visible how ethnographic research often supports multiple studies, drawing on records in a video-based archive, and how interrelated studies form an ongoing program of research in which the ethnographer (with colleagues) continues to uncover new questions whose exploration is supported by the existing archive.

Our goal in describing the decisions made for the new studies is four-fold: 1) to help you explore how an interactional ethnographic approach constitutes a *philosophy of inquiry*, 2) to demonstrate how the principle of *theory as method and method as theory* informs our work, 3) to illustrate how we graphically (re)present analyses that serve as the basis for constructing *warranted accounts* about the consequential ongoing nature of life in the group the ethnographer is entering, and 4) to illustrate how a theoretically driven process of inquiry is needed to analyse video records, creating an interactive and generative approach to ethnographic research. We encourage you to ask yourself questions about how you might (or might not) use the principles, practices and actions that we make transparent to inform your work as video-enabled ethnographers. As you reflect on connections with your potential research with video, examine how our logic of inquiry unfolds and permits us to develop warranted accounts of learning of studio art in this particular social group.

How to begin: Entering and positioning the video recording device and ethnographer within the social world

Once you have constructed a conceptual framework for the study; negotiated support of the teacher and school to engage in an ethnographic project; been approved by teachers, students, parents, administrators, and review boards at university, district and school level, your next phase of the journey is to enter the classroom. Given that the current study builds on and uses video records and other artifacts from Baker's (2001) archive, we begin by reconstructing his decisions about how and why he entered the Studio Art class. Therefore, given our argument that video records are a type of fieldnote and are selective angles of vision (e.g., Goldman-Segall, 1998), knowledge about the complex phases of Doug's entry is critical since his entry process shaped the kinds of records and artifacts we were able to *interrogate* (Heap, 1995) and analyse.

Doug's first point of entry into the class came from a professional development experience (in summer 1998) that he shared with the Studio Art teacher and one of her colleagues. Following this, he and the Studio Art teacher engaged in a series of discussions about common interests in exploring how disciplinary knowledge is constructed, and how her goals and practices help students develop as studio artists. These discussions led to an agreement to work collaboratively to record and explore what counts as Studio Art in her class, a collaboration that involved a two-year process of entering and collecting ethnographic records in the class (1998-2000).

When Doug entered with the video camera on the first day of school, he asked the teacher where she would like him to position himself and the video camera (they had negotiated the use of one camera). The teacher requested that the camera remain stationary and that Doug limit his movements in the classroom, since she viewed an ethnographer as a *fly on the wall* (her metaphor). Doug honoured the decisions of the teacher and placed (with her approval) the camera either at the back left or side left of the classroom; however, as the year progressed, informal discussions with students about art and the class became part of the ethnographic process, with implicit and explicit agreement of the teacher.

In honouring the teacher's decisions about where to place the camera and ethnographer movements, Doug created a *negotiated social contract with the teacher*, which limited his position and movement for observing. The social contract meant that certain actions and related angles of vision would not be possible to record either on video or in fieldnotes (for example, small group interactions).

This limited the potential range of questions and information available to him through direct observation, as well as on video records. However, since the teacher—particularly her public discourse and actions—was a focal point of his research, the placement of the camera at this point allowed him to 'capture' (record) what was publicly available to students, i.e., discourse that could be heard in the public space and actions that could be viewed from his *angle of vision* or *point of viewing* (Goldman-Segull, 1998). He also considered the height of the camera to capture the students' angle of vision.

From this perspective, video recording is not an objective process in which you, the ethnographer, frame a question, select an angle of viewing, and then move the camera when phenomena you are exploring changes. Rather, the ethnographer, who is *a professional stranger* (Agar, 1996), participates in dynamic relationships with members of the class bound by the (re)developing social contract with teacher and students. These relationships, therefore, shape, and are in turn shaped by, what can be seen and thus learned through this process during the study and in subsequent research using archived records.

(Re)entering the video record: decisions related to analysis of archived ethnographic data

Central to analysis of video-based ethnographic records is ethnomethologist James Heap's (1995) argument that regardless of the question that initiated the research, when we leave the field, whether for a brief time or permanently, we must *interrogate* the archived video records (a type of fieldnote) to identify what questions and analyses are possible. Thus, the next phase of our ethnographic journey involves interrogating archived records (Baker, 2001; Baker and Green, 2007) in order to construct a *data set* that can be used to address our questions for the current study. In taking these actions, we engaged in a process that ethnographers refer to as *following the actions of the actors* (Spradley, 1980), or in other words, what is situationally or locally relevant (Gee and Green, 1998; Geertz, 1983; Hymes, 1974).

Our goal in drawing attention to the new analysis is to demonstrate how the principle of *ethnography as a philosophy of inquiry* (Anderson-Levitt, 2006) guides our analysis as well as collection of ethnographic records from an archive. The questions for the current inquiry were originally raised by Baker (2001) at the conclusion of his study. He identified individual performances on a common task as a topic for further research, and this area of interest led to two additional studies. The first study involved a contrast of performances across generations, with special focus on differences in performance between a second and a third-year student (Baker and Green, 2007); the second, the current study, examines the performances within a generation, with a focus on two first-year students.

Each study involved a shift from Doug's original focus on opportunities for learning within the whole group (the collective) to our focus on individual performances within the public critique event and factors that supported and constrained these performances across and within generations. How and why we arrived at the need for this shift is made visible in the following sections as we *trace* the *decision trail* from Baker's original study to the current study, examining the roots and routes of individual performance within a generation of students.

Identifying a key event as a boundary for the current study

Baker (2001) explored ways in which discursive and social actions of the teacher and students *talked-into-being* a local and situated *culture-in-the-making* of Studio Art (Green and Dixon, 1993; Dixon and Green, 2005). His analysis created accounts of both *opportunities for learning* (Tuyay, Jennings and Dixon, 1995) constructed at the collective level of scale across the year and at the level of individual performances that crossed generations. Through the collective and *contrastive analysis* of individual performances during a key event, *public critique*, Baker identified the following local principles of Studio Art practices: 1) that studio art involves particular ways of talking about the work of each artist, 2) that studio art is a publicly assessed activity at particular points in artists' work, and 3) what counts as knowledge about studio art processes and practices becomes common knowledge within generations, but not necessarily across generations of students given the differences in opportunities for learning associated with time in the class.

His analysis demonstrated the centrality of *public critique* in learning to be studio artists, and how examining individual performances during this event made visible differences in first-year through third-year students' understanding of studio art. In deciding where to begin our new study, we used Baker's (and Baker and Green's, see below) analysis to inform us about where to look in the archive. We decided to begin our journey of creating a new data set by using this event as one boundary point for our analysis of individual student work. We then searched records preceding this event to identify related events that also involved forms of public critique.

Performance differences across student generations: A contrastive analysis

Baker and Green's (2007) analysis across generations provided contextual information to construct the new data set. This study sought to address an unresolved question in Baker's original study: *How and in what ways were different times of entry into the class consequential for what different generations of students took up, used and exhibited in their individual performances?* This question led to a contrastive analysis of performances of four students with different amounts of time in the class—from first through third year, with special attention given to a second and third-year students. It explored ways in which the more experienced students were able to (re)formulate and extend their understandings as they engaged in recurring events.

The *cross-generation analysis* made visible how length of time in this intergenerational class led to differences in performance and limits to certainty in interpretation. In taking this action, we created a *rich point* (Agar, 1994) for learning about cultural patterns and practices available to students (and ethnographer), and how interpretations and warrants for claims of observed actions and discourse are sensitive to differences in time in the class for both student and ethnographer (two years for Baker). This analysis framed a direction for the current study: *the need to explore further the impact of time and opportunities for learning by examining the performances of two first-year students during public critique.* Thus, our journey to identifying an appropriate data set for this study involved reading historical documents, both those archived during data collection and published reports generated from the analysis (e.g., Baker and Green, 2007). Our goal in taking these actions was to build a web of related work across studies, one that added depth of knowledge to our growing understanding of what members of the Studio Art class needed to produce, predict, interpret and evaluate the social significance of (Heath, 1982) if they were to take appropriate cultural actions as artists in this class.

Performance differences within a generation: Constructing a new study

Having described the history of our journey that led to the current study, we now describe steps we took in analysing the relationship in performances of James and Maya, two first-year students who entered the class at different points (September and October, respectively). Through these steps, we make visible the multiple levels of analytic scale needed to identify and create warranted accounts of the roots and routes James and Maya took from entry into the class to performance in public critique. This analysis demonstrates how in seeking the roots and routes for differences in performances, we created a potential rich point for learning about the ways in which *opportunities for learning*, not merely 'artistic ability' of students, shaped Maya's and James' performances in this key event.

The next phase of our journey in constructing the data set involved a reformulation of the question raised by Baker and Green: *How and in what ways were different times of entry into the class consequential for what students within a generation took up and exhibited in their individual performances?* As we present steps that followed from this decision, we make transparent the logic of inquiry guiding decisions within this study, and how the decisions we made at different points created boundaries of units at different levels of analytic scale. As part of this discussion we make visible theory-method relationships that shaped what we were able to learn about factors supporting and constraining Maya's and James' performances.

Constructing a data set: (Re)entering the ethnographic archive

In constructing a *data set* that would permit us to explore factors relevant to the impact of entry time on student performance, we faced a series of complex decisions, including framing a coherent set of questions that would enable us to trace the roots and routes of opportunities for learning afforded James and Maya, interrogating and identifying records available for analysis, and theoretically selecting records necessary to address the question(s) posed. This interrogation of archived video records involved examining who could be seen (or heard), doing what, in which events and locating relevant artifacts (for example, student work and interviews with teacher and students).

As in Baker and Green (2007), we examined both collective activity within and across events and individual performances in *public critique*; therefore, to construct the data set we (re)consulted the index of fieldnote and video records between the first day of school, when James entered, to student performances in the public critique event in November, just over a month after Maya entered. This *constructed boundary* represents the time period for James and includes the entry point for Maya. Selecting video and other archival records also involved, for example, (re)analysing previously constructed transcripts of public critique performances and identifying key artifacts related to the questions that arose across previous studies.

Table 1 represents the relationships between this new data set and the 1999-2000 archive (part of the ethnographic corpus, 1998-2001) and shows the questions guiding the current study and data selected.

The choice of relevant records (for example, fieldnotes, videos, and artifacts) as a starting point was guided by three questions. The first question (middle column, Table 1), *How does students' public discourse make visible norms and expectations for publicly presenting Studio Art?*, focused on how each of the two first-year students displayed (or did not display) principles and practices for performance constructed in *cycles of activity* (Green and Meyer, 1991) preceding the *public critique* event. The first question, therefore, led us to existing video records and transcripts of the *public critique* event (11/16-19), which in turn led us to (re)consult a particular video record (11/17) and (re)analyse the transcripts to identify differences in the ways that James and Maya referenced the processes and practices of studio art. Informed by Baker's (2001) findings, this interactive-responsive process led us to construct a warranted account of James' performance as typical of a first-year student and Maya's as atypical, which will be discussed further in relationship to Table 2.

The second question in Table 1 (middle column) focused on ways the teacher discursively initiated the class and began the process of defining what counts as studio art. Central to this process was a developing *language of* the class (Lin, 1993) that formulated local and situated meanings of studio art. Analysis of discourse on video records of the first two days of school, in which James was present, showed the teacher initiating the process of referentially inscribing a language of the class (Lin, 1993) and formulating (Vygotsky in Reiber and Carton, 1987) principles and practices needed to act as studio artists. Furthermore the analysis foreshadowed events that students would undertake as studio artists, including *public critique*.

The goal of this analysis was to identify when principles and practices referenced by students and teacher during public critique were introduced, and to trace their use and development across times and events. This process of *forward and backward mapping* (e.g., Green and Meyer, 1991; McDonnell and Elmore, 1987) laid the foundation for addressing the third question (middle column): *What counted overtime as discourse and practices of studio artists?* The outcome of this mapping process was the identification of cycles of activity related to public critique that preceded the November performances and event. In the sections that follow, we present a chain of analyses that move from contrastive analysis of

Table 1: Current Data Set

Sub-Archive (Year Two: 1999-2000)	Guiding Research Questions for Current Study	Data Selected from Archive for Current Study
Recordings • Fieldnotes (57 class periods) • Videotapes (58 class periods) • Audio and Videotaped interviews (students and teacher) Artifacts (partial list) • Transcripts (previously constructed) • Class handouts, e.g., rubric for critique • Frame grab of student drawing • Teacher lesson plans (first two months)	How does students' public discourse make visible norms and expectations for publicly presenting 'Studio Art'? Contrastive Analysis of Anchored Event: Public Discourse and Actions of Two First-Year Seniors: • Maya (entered class around 10/11) • James (entered class on Day One, 9/2)	Videotapes: • 'Public Critique'—'Figure Drawing Unit' ('Bug Art') • November 16-19: Maya and James (Nov. 17) Related artifacts: • Transcripts (complete)—Nov. 17 • Handout: 'Rubric for Critique' (Nov. 16)
	How did teacher initiate classroom and Studio Art practices, including 'public critique'? Analysis of First Days of Class: 9/2-9/3	Videotapes: • Days 1-2—Initiation of Studio Art and class (and first assignment leading to first cycle of critique—first mentioned on 9/2) Related artifacts: • Transcripts (complete)—Sept. 2-3 • Letters from past students (in transcripts, 9/2)
	What counted overtime as discourse and practices of studio artists? Analysis of cycles of critique and related discourse and classroom practices	Videotapes: • 'Sharing'—Sept. 9-10 ("Common material") • 'Gentle Critique'—Sept. 22-24 ("Synectic Art") • 'Public Critique' ('Bug Art')—Nov. 16-19 Related artifacts: • Transcripts of critique; • Constructed list of literate practices observed, including drawing techniques and materials

* Quotation marks signal folk, or insider, term used by the teacher and students.

the performance of public critique by the two first-year students to increasingly greater levels of analytic scale (as represented in Figure 1).

Constructing representations of James' and Maya's performance of public critique

To understand this next phase of the journey and logic of inquiry that guided it, we make visible how we constructed a graphic representation, Table 2, to address the first question, *How does students' public discourse make visible norms and expectations for publicly presenting Studio Art?* The process of constructing a graphic representation, a table or a figure, is central to our approach, since it serves as a means of exploring different kinds of figure-ground relationships, for example, representing the contributions of particular actors to a developing event.

The elements in Table 2, therefore, represent a logic of analysis for the multiple levels of scale of information about patterns of interaction and content presented for the public critique event for Maya and for James. For example, since Maya's and James' performances are the centre of the current contrastive analysis, we use their turns at public critique as anchors for data representation and analysis. We use the concept of *turn-at-performing-public-critique* since each turn as an analytic unit involved both their individual performances and responses from teacher and students.

In Table 2, we represented what occurred during their turn in three ways. First, we located representative dimensions of studio art in the discourse of the teacher in the framing event for public critique (*In Rubric Provided*, introduced on 11/16), the initiating phase in which the teacher framed the day by providing students with what she called a *rubric*. We also reconsulted previous analysis to identify additional dimensions and to confirm the significance of the ones represented (Baker, 2001; Baker and Green, 2007). The representative dimensions selected are represented in the left column entitled, *what counts as studio art referentially signalled by teacher.*

Second, we made a decision to represent Maya's and James' *take up of public critique* in two ways. The first involved constructing two columns that display excerpts of transcripts of the students' performances (columns: *Maya and James*), which are example representations of their discourse during critique. By displaying segments of the transcript we show how the students inscribed ways of working as studio artists; additionally, the inscriptions demonstrate the need for us to examine how prior experiences (or lack of) led to the observed differences in the discourse.

Table 2: Contrastive analysis of what Maya and James discursively referenced as studio art during public critique

(transcript excerpts from 11/17)

What counts as studio art referentially signaled by teacher	Maya (first-year senior: entered after Oct. 11)			Responses to Maya-James		James (first-year senior: entered Sept. 2)		
In rubric provided	Obs.	Transcript excerpt				Transcript excerpt		Obs.
Purpose/Questions	X	I guess my drawings will help me with shape and color (483-86)		T*	S/T	I wanted to like express/how life is everywhere (1075-76)		X
Approach/Selection	X	[selected the idea of] the beast in *Lord of the Flies* (497)		T	S/T	I wanted to look at the whole (1091)		X
Evolution/Process	X	[implicit, although does not mention process]		T	T/S	It's a long process/like I worked on this for …/five/six/seven days straight (1128-32)		X
Technique	X	I just practiced with/like dark lines/ and shading/and stuff (508-11); mosaic (535)		T/S*	S/T	I started out/like with just ink/just black ink (1077-79)		X
Outcome/Presentation	X	I don't know if I/succeeded…but I tried …who's to say (574-95)				It [the daily work and details] all adds up at the end (1142)		X
About representative principles referentially constructed across prior events								
Process: Idea development	X	my first thought/when I got this idea (488-89); I don't know if I succeeded (575-77)		T/S	S/T	I wanted to like express/how life is everywhere (1075-76); long process (1128)		X
Process: Technique	X	I just practiced with/like dark lines/ and shading/and stuff (508-11)		T/S*	S/T	You can't just draw the whole thing all at once (1102)		X
Time required: Developing idea	X	[implicit: M states that she began with an idea and explains evolution of it]		T	T	It's a long process/like I worked on this for …/five/six/seven days straight (1128-32)		X
In representative practices referentially constructed across prior events								

'Seeing' (9/30-10/1)					You need to examine every single part and see how they relate/to each other (1099-00)	X
Layering sequence (10/5-8)					You can't just draw the whole thing all at once (1102)	X
continuous line					I started out/like with just ink/.../and drew the whole butterfly (1077-80)	X
texture				T/S	But it doesn't look/like textured (1108-09)	X
shape	X	I guess my drawings will help me with shape and color (483-86)		T/S	[implicit:] I drew the whole butterfly (1077-80)	X

*T Teacher responds to a different aspect of Maya's drawing, 'spatially she's created tension' (992). Maya depicted a fly that is either flying up the side of a tree trunk or is flying over the tree, yet she is non-committal about her intentions. Another student (a third-year) initiated the discussion of this tension, and she and the teacher publicly discussed the apparently unintended ambiguity of the image.

Video-enabled ethnographic research: A microethnographic perspective 97

The second way we elected to represent their take up of public critique involved identifying and marking with an 'X' in the Obs. (observed) column the existence in their discourse of the particular dimensions listed. Thus, the transcript segments illustrate how each talked about particular elements of dimensions of studio art and whether or not these were referenced during the presentation of their drawings. This process supported analysis of different levels of information, for example, existence/non-existence of a particular dimension and way of inscribing work of studio artists.

Since Maya and James were presenting to an audience, we chose to represent response patterns of the teacher and students (columns: *Responses to Maya* in column to right of Maya's discourse; and *Responses to James* in column to left of discourse) to examine who responded, to what, and for what purposes and how these responses laid a foundation for triangulation of what counted as studio art in this class. The inclusion of the responses (centre columns) enabled us to contrast another level of activity within the event, thus providing multiple readings of the different types of information provided.

In describing how the table was constructed and the ways in which we brought together different kinds of data, we made visible how graphic representation of patterns involves an interactive-responsive process and how these can be used for complex levels of analysis—not simply for data reduction. The levels of analysis reported for this table demonstrate why the logic guiding our decisions must be transparent to readers, if they are to interpret the information in ways consistent with the account that we construct based on these data.

Reading table 2: Interpreting data and (re)constructing accounts

In this section, we present three levels of accounts grounded in information represented in Table 2: 1) an account of James, 2) an account of Maya, and 3) an account of the differences in performance. We began by constructing an account of James because he represented first-year students who had been present from the first day. Our next decision entailed deciding on what 'bit of information' represented in the table would serve as a starting point in constructing our account of what James knew about studio art. For this illustrative analysis, we selected the dimension *ideas* within the section on *Representative principles referentially constructed across prior events*.

In reconsulting the video in relationship to the data represented in Table 2, we observed James presenting these segments of discourse in the opening moments of his presentation during public critique. He states that he 'wanted to like express/how life is everywhere' (lines 1075-1076), and describes the process of drawing the image as a 'long process' (line 1128), one that he 'worked on … for five/six/seven days straight' (lines 1128-1132). James, therefore, draws attention in his talk that process and time spent with the work are critical parts of being an artist and inscribes a practice he used across time, one that Baker (2001) identified as a developing theme in the class. The way in which James presented a critique of his work is representative of the ways in which first and second-year students talked about their art and represented discourse of practices and principles that the teacher had introduced to the group across time, which we discuss more in relationship to Figure 1.

Analysis of Maya's transcripts and related video shows a markedly different way of talking, one that did not represent the common language of principles and practices of studio art identified in James' presentation, or in the everyday discourse of the teacher and students about art. Maya begins, like James (and other students), by explaining how she got an idea for a drawing, in her case linking a personal experience (a nightmare) and an aspect of a novel (the beast in *The Lord of the Flies* by William Golding). However, what happened next deviated from the expected pattern: she wondered aloud about the success of her final drawing, 'I don't know if I succeeded' (lines 575-577). She focused on whether or not the representation of the planned image was a success, although who would assess it was ambiguous.

This type of discourse of success or failure was unexpected; as James' discourse showed, what was expected was a self-analysis of process involved in constructing the representation of the idea. Although Maya recounts her attempt to draw something 'massive/and dark' (lines 495-496), she is unable to and decides to 'just … make it/like/three dimensional' (lines 568-570). In describing the evolution of the idea into image, she represented process in a way that was unexpected because her explanation referred to what she had attempted to present, not what she had drawn. What she said next made visible the tension of her analysis: she posed a rhetorical question as a concluding statement about the final drawing that signalled that she did not acknowledge potential for common agreement (among members of this studio art class) about process or practice. In Maya's final comments about her attempt at constructing an image of the beast, she says, 'who's to say/what it's supposed to be [the image of the beast]/it could have been/something a little less/overbearing/but still capture your eye' (lines 594-600).

Maya's statement makes visible a limited understanding of what counted as appropriate practice when we placed it in the context of Baker's (2001) over time analysis of the principles of practices in the studio art class, presented previously:

1) *that studio art involves particular ways of talking about the work each artist was doing;*
2) *that studio art is a publicly assessed activity at particular points in artists' work; and*
3) *what counts as knowledge about studio art processes and practices becomes common knowledge within generations, but not necessarily across generations of students given the differences in opportunities for learning associated with time in the class.*

The juxtaposition represented here provided the basis for an emerging hypothesis about what Maya knew, or did not know, and led us to a phase of triangulating data as well as perspectives to seek further evidence to confirm or disconfirm our emerging account.

Seeking confirming/disconfirming evidence through contrastive analysis

To further understand how Maya's discourse differed from what was expected, we explored responses to her work by the teacher and students (represented in column, *response to Maya*). Following Maya's presentation the teacher opened the response period with a statement that she had 'a couple of things to say' but wanted to give students a chance to respond first. Only one student responded and asked a personal question about the origins of her name, which Maya answered. The teacher then began her comments by making a public statement directed to the students:

> I think we should congratulate Maya/for being/first up/in critique/and never having critiqued with us before/that took a lot of courage/and you ah/feel really comfortable/up there/and that's nice to see/ why do you/uh/couple of questions/one/uh/you were talking about/during the warm-up series/you had already started to think about the Lord of the Flies/so/…/you were/practicing/um/thick lines/and dark shading/…/ so the ideas started to percolate/even before you knew/that there would be a final/ (lines 624-664).

In this statement the teacher positions Maya as someone new to the class who had not been present for previous critiques. Her delivery is marked with hesitation markers (uh's) that she rarely inserted when responding to the presented processes of other students. Given that this statement was addressed to students who would soon give their presentations, and who had been in the class over a longer period of time, her comments may be viewed as acknowledging Maya's limited time in the class and signalling that Maya had not had opportunities to learn the principles of practices associated with public critique, which was becoming a pattern and common knowledge in this class.

To identify if and how the teacher's response was socially significant and culturally appropriate, we contrasted it with the response pattern to James, (and other students). For James, the teacher's response followed an extended period of comments and questions from students about the drawings, a pattern identified as common across the public critique event. The teacher then addressed the class about a question raised by James during his presentation:

> but I want to challenge you [the class]/he's [James] asking you/does it [the drawing] move/and you all said yes/tell him/how/you know that it moves/visually/what is he doing in there/to help you understand/that it moves/(1351-1362).

This challenge to the class (not to James) led to a discussion between one student and the teacher about James' use of colour and how he used it to create movement in the drawing.

These two contrastive segments make visible differences in the ways in which the teacher engaged the two students. In Maya's case, the teacher engaged Maya directly and used questions to reconstruct what Maya had presented, while tying it to what she had observed Maya doing in the class since her entry; the teacher did not encourage a direct response to Maya's drawings. In contrast, in responding to James, the teacher did not immediately engage James about his presentation; rather, she handed the discussion over (Edwards and Mercer, 1987) to students by *challenging* them to answer a question that James had asked of the students.

The difference in the teacher's response pattern to Maya and James, along with her statement to the class about Maya's inexperience with public critique, became a rich point around which we wove our interpretation of Maya as having limited *insider knowledge* and James being an *insider* in the class and in the practice of public critique. That she did not engage James directly but handed over the opportunity for discussion to students through her challenge, the teacher provided evidence that public critique was not a critique by the teacher but a community event in which those responding, not just the artist, were responsible for providing evidence of the processes of interpretation, which included taking up through discourse the principles and practices constructed over time in the cycles of critique identified in Figure 1. Her actions, therefore, signalled that there was a process for answering Maya's statement—*who's to say*.

The analysis in Table 2 provided an anchor for us in that it made visible key segments of life that when juxtaposed with other sources of data and perspectives provided a context for interpretation of a particular moment in time. However, these forms and levels of analysis were incomplete in that they did not represent the history of the opportunities afforded members of the class that were referentially signalled by the teacher in her response to Maya.

To construct a more textured and layered account of the differences and what they signalled, we undertook analysis at multiple levels of time scale to retrieve historical information that the teacher signalled in her talk. Therefore, findings of the contrastive analysis served as an anchor for a series of analyses undertaken to make visible the importance of time and opportunity for learning in this class and how these opportunities (or missed opportunities) contributed to the identified differences in presentations of James and Maya, and in the teacher's and students' responses. The following questions were generated for the new analyses:

- *How did the teacher initiate and develop a discourse, a set of practices, and principles of practice about what is involved in being studio artists?*
- *What opportunities were afforded James (by entering on Day One) that Maya missed by entering the class one month into the school year?*
- *And how were differences in experience identified through the mapping processes visible in Maya's and James' performance of public critique?*

Tracing the roots and routes to performance in public critique

These questions initiated a series of analyses that focused on identifying historical influences relevant to the differences in the social, linguistic and academic texts that James and Maya had opportunities to construct with class members, and to take up across times and events prior to public critique. To identify information needed to interpret these differences, we engaged in *backward mapping* (Green and Meyer, 1991; McDonnell and Elmore, 1987), a process that involved

102 How to do educational ethnography

Figure 1: Timelines leading to cycles of activity of *public critique*

Life history of class: timeline of intergenerational studio art class (1997-2000)

Teacher—	1996-1997	1997-1998	1998-1999	1999-2000
29 years of teaching	(5% of students enter)	(12% of students enter)	(35% of students enter)	(53% of students enter)

Entering the field: Timeline of the ethnography 1998-2000

Academic Year One (1998-1999)	Academic Year Two (1999-2000)

9/2 First Day Of School: Initiating Cycles

Clock Time (Videotape time)	Running Record of Phases (**phase numbers on left**)	Running Record of Events (line numbers)
9: 09-9: 18 (00: 00: 01-00: 10: 01)	1. T preparing (talks to researcher) 2. T explaining letters from past students to present students	1. T preparing before students arrive (1-79)
9: 18-9: 22 (00: 10: 02-00: 13: 56)	1. T talking about class preparation 2. T instructing students to pick up two index cards and select a workbench	2. Students arriving; T greeting students at door (80-134)
9: 22-9: 30 (00: 13: 57-00: 21: 04)	1. Students writing two questions, etc. 2. T giving each student an envelope 3. Students passing back index cards	3. T taking roll and initiating 'index card activity' (134-235)
9: 30-9: 44 (00: 22: 32-00: 36: 14)	1. *T presenting overview day and program 2. Introducing Disney video 3. Playing Disney video 4. Explaining links with video	*T initiates cycles of friendly sharing; 'tomorrow I'll have a short activity that's kind of a creative activity' (lines 332-334) (occurs on 9/3)	4. T welcoming, presenting agenda and introducing self and program (236-686)

Video-enabled ethnographic research: A microethnographic perspective

6 min. (00: 28: 28-00: 34: 28)		4a. Disney video (442-621
9: 44-9: 55 (00: 36: 15-00: 47: 24)	1. T reading letters from: D, M, A, C 2. T explaining connections	5. T reading and commenting on excerpts from letters of past students (687-1063)
9: 55-10: 00 (00: 47: 26-53: 01)	1. T assigning letter of intent 2. Handout; quoting Z. Hurston 3. 'Student agendas'	6. T assigning: Read letter from past student and write letter of intent (1064-1243)
10: 00-10: 09 (00: 53: 03-01: 01: 40)	1. T introducing sketchbooks 2. Notebooks: connection to AP and areas of concentration 3. Folders: Value of handouts 4. Fee: Cost of some of the materials	7. T presenting four needs for class (1234-1568)
10: 09-10: 15 (01: 02: 04-01: 08: 18)	1. Mini-chalk festival with kids 2. Visit from superintendent 3. Presentations from students who attended art summer school 4. 'Film Festival'; 5. 'Breakfast Club'; 6. 'Fashion Show'	8. T discussing 'Highlights' of upcoming year (1569-1792)

Cycles of critique

Framing class 9/2; James enters	Friendly Sharing 9/10, 13	Gentle Critique 9/22-24	Maya enters 10/11	Deep Critique 11/16-19

examining video records, available transcripts—or constructing transcripts, fieldnotes and written records. We selected records that would support an in-depth examination of ways in which the teacher initiated local and situated views of studio art on the first day of school.

The next steps involved *forward mapping*, a process that entailed following the events referenced in the daily work of the teacher and students (available on video records) to identify tied cycles of activity that preceded public critique, and the developing principles and practices of each cycle. In this way, we traced the referential content to identify principles, practices, and discourse that were signalled as important for doing studio art as well as developing as studio artists.

Figure 1 represents these multiple layers of analysis using a format we call *swing out charts* (Castanheira et al., 2000; Kelly and Chen, 1999). This format allows us to represent *part-whole relationships* that were visible across events recorded on video and to move between micro-macro relationships for different purposes. For the present analysis, we begin with a time line that represents the history with the class of the teacher, students and ethnographer, and in the second table we locate the three-month cycle that includes the public critique event of the current study within the time line of the ethnography. In the third table of Figure 1 we represent the discourse and what was accomplished through the discourse on the first day of school. Finally, in the fourth table we present the cycles of activity (and James' and Maya's entries) identified through forward mapping, ones that were referentially foreshadowed by the teacher across time from the first day of school to Maya's and James' performance. These different levels of analytic scale provide different texts that foreground particular data that we used to explore the questions raised in the previous section.

As indicated in Figure 1, the members of the class were an intergenerational group with different histories with, and times in, the class. In an interview, the teacher explained that students could take Advanced Placement Studio Art multiple times; however, since it was an elective course and because of other academic requirements, many students chose to take the class only once or twice. Therefore, the core group of students (and ethnographer) represents 1-2 years of experience with the content, processes and practices, further supporting the analysis of times for learning that has emerged across the three studies and is the focus of the within-generation analysis of the current study. The ethnographer (Baker) entered the class in 1998-1999, suggesting that he was in some ways a second-year member, which Baker and Green (2007) demonstrated limited his (and other students') understandings, based on observations alone, of what members need to know, do, understand, predict and produce (Green, Dixon and Zaharlick, 2003; Heath, 1982). This latter finding from Baker and Green guided our search for multiple sources of evidence to support each account we constructed about life and learning in this class.

The third table in Figure 1 represents an *event map* (Green and Wallat, 1981) of the first day of school, signalling the constructed actions of the day, including the teacher's initiation of an activity that led to the first cycle of public critique ('Friendly Sharing'). The event map was constructed by first identifying the clock time that marked the on-set of each shift of events (left column), and then the chains of actions that constituted the events. The middle column presents a *running record* of the chains of actions members engaged in to construct events, and the right column represents those events. In representing the chains of actions that led to the particular events first, we represent the developing and constructed nature of classroom life (Green, 1983; Green and Dixon, 1993; Green and Wallat, 1981; Santa Barbara Classroom Discourse Group, 1992).

Because members of a class through discourse and interactions construct the chains of activity bit-by-bit, we organised the event map to represent the bit-by-bit construction of the content, practices, and coordinated activity of members across time from the first day of school—once again demonstrating theory-method relationships. This map, therefore, profiles, what Giddens (1984) calls, the flow of conduct through which members structure their worlds. Furthermore, the map allows us to identify and represent the initiation of particular cycles of activity.

Analysis of the running record dimension of this table enabled us to identify one particular event that foreshadowed public critique (event 4, phase 1). In this event the teacher introduced the activity that initiated the cycle of *friendly sharing*: 'tomorrow I'll have a short activity that's kind of a creative activity' (lines 332-334). Analysis of the video and transcripts of the next day (9/3) indicated that this activity did take place, initiating the first cycle of critique, which occurred on 9/10 and 9/13 (see last time line of Figure 1).

Furthermore, on this day the teacher invokes the voices of former students by reading letters written by them to current students. By reading excerpts from the letters (and inserting oral comments) the teacher highlights embedded principles and practices experienced by those students and foreshadows ways of working in the class. In another event, through showing a brief video that celebrates an award given to the teacher by Disney Corporation, the teacher shows work of the class through classroom interactions depicted on the video, and she further inserts comments about how the class will work. In this way she introduces multiple levels of text and demonstrates a relationship between visual and other forms of meaning construction—and her actions represent a metaphor for the type of work that students will do as artists, constructing layers of studio art.

The brief analysis of this day demonstrates how Figures, like the tables presented previously, are written-in-to-being and do not speak for themselves. Our journey showed how we moved between different levels of analysis, video records, and the histories of analysis that Baker, as a member of the writing team, represents. In this way, we made visible how layers of data and evidence are needed to construct warranted accounts of what members are constructing and how one bit of life is consequential for other bits and thus how life is referentially intertextual, consequential, and non-linear (past, present and future are signalled), although chronological time is present in the history of any given day (Adam, 1990). The final analysis makes this point.

When we listen to the discourse on one video record (rather than watch all video records—approximately thirty between 9/2 and 11/17) and examine past referents (for example, as in *warm-up; yesterday*) and the use of past tense (for example, *we already worked on this*), we are able to identify potential records to search and (re)consult ones that were tied to the event under construction. In this way, we move between one referent and another, one event and another, and one video record (or other artifact) and another, by *following what actors signal is socially, culturally and academically relevant*. The final table in Figure 1 shows the three cycles of public critique that James had an opportunity to experience, contribute to and learn through. As indicated in this table, critique as an overall process began with an event called (using the teacher's names, or *folk terms*, for the events) *Friendly Sharing*, moved to *Gentle Critique*, and then to *Deep Critique*—each cycle reflects the name of the core event. The *consequential progression* (Putney, et al., 2000) across cycles indicates how the teacher helped students develop *public texts* (Kelly, Crawford and Green, 2001) for critique that became more focused across different levels of presenting, discussing, and examining students' art.

The part-whole representation in Figure 1 provides a context for understanding the significance of the teacher's comments presented in the account we constructed using Table 2 as an anchor source of evidence. We ended the contrastive analysis discussion with a hypothesis about the consequential nature of the missed opportunities for Maya, opportunities that the teacher signalled in her response to Maya's performance. When the generated account of the difference in Maya's and James' performance on 11/17 (Table 2) is examined in light of the layers of analyses represented in Figure 1, the hypothesis of the consequential nature of the missed opportunities was confirmed.

The multi-level, across time analysis showed that what Maya had available to guide her were the experiences of the one month in the Studio Art class, previous educational and life experiences, and the rubric as a guide that the teacher presented to the class the day prior to the public critique event. Furthermore, the analysis of the first day, in the context of missed opportunities, showed that the language of Studio Art was an historical language that linked generations of students, was a situated construction, and foreshadowed, named and initiated an intertextual world of work of studio artists. Therefore, Maya's entry provided her with partial access to the language, practices, and experiences that were part of the repertoires for performance of public critique of other class members. Furthermore, the differences that James' represented indicated that this knowledge developed from the first moments of the class, not just across generations as Baker and Green (2007) made visible in their exploration of second and third-year students.

Making visible the invisible: video and contrastive analyses in microethnographic research

The illustrative cases presented in this chapter provided a grounded means of demonstrating the multiple ways in which video played a central role in our ethnographic work, enabling multiple levels of analytic scale across times, events, and actors. From these analyses we constructed a series of warranted accounts about what counted as studio art and how time in the class was consequential for members as they constructed the events of classroom life and learned from these events. Furthermore, the analysis of Maya and James showed that to construct an account of individual student performance involved an interactive and responsive exploration of what the group as a whole was doing and how individuals, for example, Maya and James, contributed to what was being socially constructed. Thus, the contrastive analysis of individual student performance served as an anchor for subsequent historical analysis of work leading to the observed moment.

In unfolding the multiple layers of analysis needed to construct a warranted account of what contributed to the differences in performance, we illustrated how ethnography is a philosophy of inquiry, one reflected in the ethnographers' decisions. Furthermore, we illustrated why an over-time analysis was needed to *construct an explanation* of the differences in Maya's and James' performances. Therefore, in describing our logic of inquiry, we made visible why and how we constructed different forms of graphic representations and multiple levels of analysis.

In presenting the chains of logic guiding each phase, we made transparent the basis for the claims we are making about the importance of examining the history of the opportunities for learning afforded to and taken up by students, rather than assessing individual performance based solely on observed behaviours or performance on a single task. Moreover, the microethnographic analysis, with its focus on discourse, showed why a close examination of discourse and what is constructed through it is critical in understanding what it means to claim that classrooms are cultures-in-the-making and that individual performance must be examined within the collective history. We also demonstrated that without the historical archive, we would not have been able to trace the roots of particular practices or the routes that individual students took. Without multiple records (video and other), each of which provided particular inscriptions of the world of the classroom, we would not have been able to triangulate information obtained from one analysis with subsequent analyses. Finally, without historical published records, with their varied levels of analysis and different foci, we would not have been able to locate public critique, time in class (generation), or individual-collective actions and opportunities for learning as key areas to begin a new exploration.

Some final thoughts

In the beginning of the chapter we asked two key questions, *what is a video a record of* and *what do we mean by the concept of video-enabled ethnography*. The answer to these questions, as we made visible in this chapter, is complex and depends on the range of decisions ethnographers make as well as the theories guiding their work—at all levels of the research process. Although we presented an illustrative case of one approach to video-enabled ethnography, the practices and processes we identified are not limited to this approach. Therefore, if you agree that video is more than a tool, you will want to consider: In what ways will you create partnerships with video? What theories will guide your decisions? How will you archive the video and other artifacts? What logic will guide your search and retrieval of archive records and artifacts? And how will you represent your analyses to create warranted accounts and claims from your data?

References

Adam, B. (1990) *Time and social theory,* Philadelphia: Temple University Press.

American Educational Research Association. (2006) *Standards for reporting on empirical social science research in AERA publications*, retrieved December 12, 2006 from www.aera.net/opportunities/?id1480.

Agar, M. (1994) *Language shock: Understanding the culture of conversation*, New York: William Morrow.

Agar, M. (1996) *The professional stranger, 2nd ed.*, New York: Academic Press.

Anderson-Levitt, K. M. (2006) Ethnography, in Green, J., Camilli, G. and Elmore, P. (eds.) *Handbook of Complementary Methods in Education Research):* 279-295, Mahwah, NJ: Lawrence Earlbaum Associates.

Athanases, S., and Heath, S. B. (1995) Ethnography in the study of teaching and learning of English, *Research in the Teaching of English*, 29(3): 263-287.

Atkinson, P. (1990) *The ethnographic imagination: Textual constructions of reality*, London: Routledge.

Bahktin, M. M. (1986) *Speech genres and other late essays*, Austin: University of Texas Press.

Baker, W. D. (2001). *Artists in the making: An ethnographic investigation of discourse and literate practices as disciplinary processes in a high school, advanced placement studio art classroom*, unpublished doctoral dissertation, University of California, Santa Barbara.

Baker, W. D., and Green, J. L. (2007) Limits to certainty in interpreting video data: Interactional ethnography and disciplinary knowledge, *Pedagogies*, 2(3): 191-204.

Barr, R. (1987) Classroom interaction and curricular content. In D. Bloome (ed.) *Literacy and schooling.* Norwood, NJ: Ablex.

Birdwhistell, R. (1977) Some discussion of ethnography, theory, and method, in Brockman, J. (ed.) *About Bateson: Essays on Gregory Bateson*, pp. 103-144, New York: Dutton.

Bloome, D., and Bailey, F. (1992) Studying language and literacy through events, particularity, and intertextuality, in Beach, R., Green, J., Kamil, M. and Shanahan, T. (eds.) *Multidisciplinary Perspectives on Literacy Research)*, pp. 181-209, IL: NCTE.

Bloome, D., and Carter, C. (2006) Discourse-in-use, in Green, J., Camilli, G., and Elmore, P. (eds.) *Handbook of Complementary Methods in Education Research)*, pp. 227-241. Mahwah, NJ: Lawrence Earlbaum Associates.

Bloome, D., Carter, S., Christian, B. M., Otto, S., and Shuart-Faris, N. (2005) *Discourse analysis and the study of language and literacy events: A microethnographic perspective,* Mahwah, NJ: Lawrence Earlbaum Associates.

Bloome, D., and Egan-Robertson, A. (1993) The social construction of intertextuality in classroom reading and writing lessons, *Reading Research Quarterly*, 28(4): 305-333.

Castenheira, M. L., Crawford, T., Dixon, C., and Green, J. (2000) Interactional ethnography: An approach to studying the social construction of literate practices, *Linguistics and Education: Analysing the Discourse Demands of the Curriculum,* 11(4): 353-400.

Cazden, C. B. (1988) *Classroom discourse: The language of teaching and learning*, 2nd ed. London: Heinemann.

Cazden, C. B., John, V., and Hymes, D. (1972) *Functions of language in the classroom*, New York: Teachers College Press.

Cochran-Smith, M. (1984) *The making of a reader*, Norwood, NJ: Ablex.

Cochran-Smith, M., Kahn, J. L., and Paris, C. L. (1991) *Learning to write differently*, Norwood, NJ: Ablex.

Collins, E.C., and Green, J. L. (1990) Metaphors: The construction of a perspective, *Theory into Practice*, 29(2): 71-77.

Collins, E., and Green, J.L. (1992) Learning in classroom settings: Making or breaking a culture, in Marshall, H. H. (ed.) *Redefining Student Learning*, pp. 59-85, Norwood, NJ: Ablex.

Cook-Gumperz, J. (1986) *The social construction of literacy*, Cambridge: Cambridge University Press.

Cook-Gumperz, J. (2006) *The social construction of literacy*, 2nd ed, Cambridge: Cambridge University Press.

Corsaro, W. (1981) Entering the child's world: Research strategies for field entry and data collection in a pre-school, in Green, J. L. and Wallat, C. (eds.) *Ethnography and language in school settings*, 117-146. Norwood, NJ: Ablex.

Corsaro, W. (1985) *Friendship and peer culture of the young child*, Norwood, NJ: Ablex.

Dixon, C., and Green, J. L. (2005) Studying the discursive construction of texts in classrooms through interactional ethnography, in Beach, R., Green, J., Kamil, M. and Shanahan, T. (eds.), *Multidisciplinary Perspectives on Literacy Research*): 349-390, Cresskill, NJ: Hampton.

Economic and Social Research Council (ESRC). (2005) *Research ethics framework*, retrieved May 12, 2007 from www.esrcsocietytoday.ac.uk/ESRCInfoCentre/opportunities/research_ethics_framework/?data%2fFrXH.

Edwards, A. D., and Mercer, N. (1987) *Common knowledge*, London: Methuen.

Ellen, R. F. (1984) *Ethnographic research: A guide to general conduct*, New York: Academic Press.

Emerson, R. M., Fretz, R. I., and Shaw, L. L. (1995) *Writing ethnographic fieldnotes*, Chicago: University of Chicago Press.

Erickson, F. (2006) Definition and analysis of data from videotape: Some research procedures and their rationales, in Green, J., Camilli, G., and Elmore, P. (eds.) *Handbook of Complementary Methods in Education Research*, 177-191. Mahwah, NJ: Lawrence Earlbaum Associates.

Erickson, F., and Shultz, J. (1981) When is a context? Some issues and methods in the analysis of social competence, in Green, J. L. and Wallat C. (eds.) *Ethnography and language in educational settings*, pp. 147-160. Norwood, NJ: Ablex.

Erickson, F. (1986) Qualitative research, in Wittrock, M. (ed.) *The Third Handbook for Research on Teaching*, pp. 119-161. New York: Macmillan.

Floriani, A. (1993) Negotiating what counts: Roles and relationships, content and meaning, texts and context, *Linguistics and Education*, 5(3 and 4): 241-274.

Gee, J., and Green, J. (1998) Discourse analysis, learning, and social practice: A methodological study, *Review of Research in Education*, 23: 119-170.

Geertz, C. (1973) *Interpretation of cultures*, New York: Harper Collins.

Geertz, C. (1983) *Local knowledge: Further essays in interpretative anthropology*, New York: Basic Books.

Giddens, A. (1984) *The construction of society: Outline of the theory of structuration*, Berkeley: University of California Press.
Gilmore, P. , and Glatthorn, A. A. (1982) *Children in and out of school: Ethnography and education*, Washington, D.C.: Center for Applied Linguistics.
Goldman-Segall, R. (1998) *Points of viewing children's thinking: A digital ethnographer's journey*, Mahwah, NJ: Lawrence Earlbaum Associates.
Goldman, R., Pea, R., Barron, B., and Derry, S. (2007) *Video research in the learning sciences*. Mahwah, NJ: Lawrence Earlbaum Associates.
Green, J.L. (1983) Context in classrooms: A sociolinguistic perspective, *New York University Education Quarterly*, 14, (2): 6-12.
Green, J.L., and Dixon, C.N. (1993) Talking knowledge into being: Discursive and social practices in classrooms, *Linguistics and Education*, 5: 231-239.
Green, J. L., and Dixon, C. N. (2002) Exploring differences in perspectives on microanalysis of classroom discourse: Contributions and concerns, *Applied Linguistics*, 23(3): 393-406.
Green, J., Dixon, C., and Zaharlick, A. (2003) Ethnography as a logic of inquiry, in Flood, J., Lapp, D. and Squire, J. (eds.) *The Handbook for Research in the Teaching of the English Language Arts*, Mahwah, NJ: Lawrence Earlbaum Associates.
Green, J., Franquiz, M., and Dixon, C. (1997) The myth of the objective transcript, *TESOL Quarterly*, 31(1): 172-176.
Green, J. L., and Harker, J. 0. (1988) *Multiple perspective analyses of classroom discourse*. Norwood, NJ: Ablex.
Green, J. L., Harker and Golden, J. (1986) Lesson construction: Differing views, in Noblit, G. and Pink, W. (eds.) *Schooling in social context: Qualitative studies*), pp. 46-77. Norwood, NJ: Ablex.
Green, J. L., and Meyer, L. A. (1991) The embeddedness of reading in classroom life, in Baker, C., and Luke, A. (eds.) *Towards a critical sociology of reading pedagogy*), pp. 141-160. Philadelphia, John Benjamins.
Green, J. L., and Wallat, C. (1979) What is an instructional context? An exploratory analysis of conversational shifts across time, in Garnica, O. and King, M. (eds.) *Language, Children and Society*), pp. 159-174, New York: Pergamon.
Green, J. L., and Wallat, C. (eds.). (1981) *Ethnography and language in educational settings*, Norwood, N J, Ablex Publishing Corporation.
Grimshaw, A. et al. (1994) *What's going on here? Complementary studies of professional talk (Volume Two of the Multiple Analysis Project)*, Norwood, NJ: Ablex.
Gumperz, J. (1986) Interactive sociolinguistics on the study of schooling, in Cook-Gumperz, J.(ed.). *The Social Construction of Literacy)*, pp. 45-6, Cambridge: Cambridge University Press.
Gumperz, J. J. (1992) Contextualization and understanding, in A. Duranti and C. Goodwin (eds.) *Rethinking context: Language as an interactive phenomenon*), pp. 229-252, Cambridge: Cambridge University Press.
Gumperz, J. J., and Herasimchuk, E. (1973) The conversational analysis of social meaning: A study of classroom interaction, in Shuy, R. (ed.) *Sociolinguistics: Current trends and prospects* (Monograph Series on Language and Linguistics, 23rd Annual Roundtable Vol. 25), Washington DC: Georgetown University Press.
Heap, J. L. (1980) What counts as reading? Limits to certainty in assessment, *Curriculum Inquiry*, 10(3): 265-292.

Heap, J. L. (1991) A situated perspective on what counts as reading, in Baker, C. and Luke, A. (eds.) *Towards a critical sociology of reading pedagogy*), pp. 103-139. Philadelphia: John Benjamins.

Heap, J. L. (1995) The status of claims in 'qualitative' educational research, *Curriculum Inquiry*, 25(3): 271-292.

Heath, S. B. (1982) Ethnography in education: Defining the essentials, in Gilmore, P. and Glatthorn, A. A. (eds.) *Children in and out of school: Ethnography and education*): 33-55. Washington, DC: Center for Applied Linguistics.

Heath, S. B. (1983) *Ways with words: Language, life, and work in communities and classrooms*, Cambridge: Cambridge University Press.

Heras, A. I. (1993) The construction of understanding in a sixth grade bilingual classroom. *Linguistics and Education*, 5(3 and 4): 275-300.

Hornberger, N., and Corson, D. (1997) *Research methods in language and education*. Boston, MA: Kluwer.

Hymes, D. (1974) *Foundations in sociolinguistics*, Philadelphia, University of Pennsylvania Press.

Hymes, D. (1996) *Ethnography, linguistics, narrative inequality: Toward an understanding of voice*, London: Taylor and Francis.

Kantor, R., and Fernie, D. (2003) *Early childhood classroom processes*, Cresskills, NJ: Hampton Press.

Kelly, G. J., and Chen, C. (1999) The sound of music: constructing science as sociocultural practices through oral and written discourse, *Journal of Research in Science Teaching*, 36(8): 883-915.

Kelly, G. J., Crawford, T., and Green, J. L. (2001) Common task and uncommon knowledge: dissenting voices in the discursive construction of physics across small laboratory groups, *Linguistics and Education*, 12(2): 135-174.

Koschmann, T.(1999) Meaning making, *Discourse Processes*, 27:2.

Lakoff, G., and Johnson, M. (1980) *Metaphors we live by*, Chicago: University of Chicago Press.

Lemke, J. (1990) *Talking science: Language, learning and values*, Norwood, NJ: Ablex.

Levien, P. (2006) Retrieved January 21, 2007 from quest.carnegiefoundation.org/~dpointer/phillevien/archive.htm.

Lin, L. (1993) Language of and in the classroom: Constructing the patterns of social life, *Linguistics and Education*, 5(3 and 4): 367-410.

Martin-Jones, M., and Jones, K. (2000) *Multilingual literacies*, Philadelphia, John Benjamins.

MacBeth, D. (2003) Hugh Mehan's 'Learning Lessons' reconsidered: On the difference between the naturalistic and critical analysis of classroom discourse, *American Educational Research Journal*, 40: 239-280.

McDonnell, L. M., and Elmore, R. F. (1987) Getting the job done: Alternative policy instruments, *Educational Evaluation and Policy Analysis*, 9(2): 133-152.

Mehan, H. (1979) *Learning lessons*, Cambridge, MA, Harvard University.

Mishler, E. G. (1979) Meaning in context: Is there any other kind, *Harvard Educational Review*, 49: 1-19.

Mishler, E. G. (1984) *The discourse of medicine: Dialectics of medical interviews*, Norwood, NJ: Ablex.

Mitchell, J.C. (1984) Typicality and the case study, in Ellen, R. F. (ed.) *Ethnographic research: A guide to general conduct*, pp. 238-241, New York: Academic Press.

Nespor, J. (2006). Finding patterns with field notes. In Green, J., Camilli, G., and Elmore, P. (eds.), *Handbook of Complementary Methods in Education Research*, pp. 297-308, Mahwah, NJ: Lawrence Earlbaum Associates.

Ochs, E. (1979) Transcription as theory, in Ochs, E. and Schieffelin, B. (eds.) *Developmental Pragmatics*, pp. 43-72, New York: Academic Press.

Putney, L., Green, J., Dixon, C., Durán, R. and Yeager, B. (2000) Consequential progressions: Exploring collective-individual development in a bilingual classroom, in Smagorinsky, P. and Lee, C. (eds.) *Constructing meaning through collaborative inquiry: Vygotskian perspectives on literacy research*), pp. 86-126, Cambridge: Cambridge University Press.

Rampton, B., Roberts, C., Leung, C., and Harris, R. (2002) Methodology in the analysis of classroom discourse, *Applied Linguistics*, 23(3): 373-392.

Reiber, R. W., and Carton, A. S. (1987) *The collected works of L. S. Vygotsky, Vol. 1*, New York, Plenum Press.

Rex, L. A. (2006)(ed.) *Discourse of opportunity, How talk in learning situations creates and constrains*, Cresskill, NJ: Hampton.

Roberts, C. (1997) Transcribing talk: Issues of representation, *TESOL Quarterly*, 31(1): 167-172.

Santa Barbara Classroom Discourse Group (1992a) Constructing literacy in classrooms: Literate action as social accomplishment, in H.H. Marshall (ed.) *Redefining student learning*), pp. 119-150. Norwood, NJ: Ablex.

Santa Barbara Classroom Discourse Group (1992b) Do you see what I see? The referential and intertextual nature of classroom life, *Journal of Classroom Interaction*, 27:29-36.

Skukauskaite, A., Liu and Green, J. L. (2007) Logics of inquiry for the analysis of video artefacts: Researching the construction of disciplinary knowledge in classrooms, *Pedagogies*, 2(3): 131-137.

Smith, D. (1987) *The everyday world as problematic: A feminist sociology*, Toronto: University of Toronto Press.

Smith, L. M. (1978) An evolving logic of participant observation, educational ethnography, and other case studies, *Review of Research in Education*, 6: 316-377.

Spindler, G., and Hammond, L. (2006) *Innovations in educational ethnography: Theories, methods and results*, Mahwah, NJ: Lawrence Earlbaum Associates.

Spradley, J. P. (1980) *Participant observation*. New York: Holt, Rinehart and Winston.

Tusting, K., and Barton, D. (2005) Communities-based local literacies research, in Beach, R. et al. (eds.) *Multidisciplinary perspectives on literacy research, 2nd ed.*), pp. 243-263, Cresskill, NJ: Hampton.

Tuyay, S., Jennings, L., and Dixon, C. (1995) Classroom discourse and opportunities to learn: An ethnographic study of knowledge construction in a bilingual third-grade classroom, *Discourse Processes*, 19: 75-110.

Van Maanen, J. (1995) *Representation in ethnography*, Thousand Oaks, CA: Sage.

Walford, G. (1991)(ed.) *Doing educational research*. London: Routledge.

West, T. (2007) Multi-layered analysis of teacher-student interactions: Concepts and perspectives guiding video analysis with tattoo, the analytic transcription tool, *Pedagogies*, 2(3): 135-150.

Willett, J., Solsken, J., and Wilson-Keenan, J. (1998) The (im)possibilities of constructing multicultural language practices in research and pedagogy, *Linguistics and Education*, 10(2): 165-218.

Wilson-Keenan, J., Solsken, J., and Willett, J. (2001) Troubling stories: Valuing productive tensions in collaborating with families, *Language Arts*, 78(6): 520-28.

Yeager, E., Floriani, A., and Green, J. L. (1998) Learning to see in the classroom: Developing an ethnographic perspective, in Egan-Robertson, A. and Bloome, D. (eds.) *Students as researchers of culture and language in their own communities)*, pp. 115-140, Cresskill, New Jersey: Hampton Press.

Zaharlick, A., and Green, J. (1991) Ethnographic research, in Flood, J. L., Jensen, J., Lapp, D. and Squire, J. (eds.) *Handbook on Teaching and Reading the English Language Arts)*, pp. 205-225, New York: Macmillan.

Chapter 6.

Bypass surgery: Rerouting theory to ethnographic study

Mats Trondman

Prologue

The arteries that bring blood to the heart can become clogged by plaque. Fat, cholesterol and other substances can slow or stop the blood flow through the vessels leading to the heart. Chest pain or heart attack can be the outcome. But pain can be relieved and the risk of heart attack reduced if the blood flow to the heart is increased. By using a segment of a healthy blood vessel from another part of the patient's body the surgeon reroutes blood around clogged arteries. This is called bypass surgery. It saves lives.[1]

This contribution, of course, is not really about heart, blood, plaque and bypass surgery. It is about the *need, meaning and use of theory in ethnographic study*. However, bypass surgery is a metaphor for what I will do.

The actors

I will play the role of the *surgeon*. I will also be responsible for making the roles of others. The same goes for the line of arguments to be laid out. And I cannot be but honest: there will be no new discoveries launched. I will only refer to old, sometimes very old, arguments for a *theoretically informed methodology for ethnography* (Willis and Trondman, 2000: 11-14).

The role of *heart* is of course played by ethnographic study. That is, ways of collecting and contextualising data. Hence, heart is method. The role of *blood*—the carrying of oxygen to the heart muscle, so that it can be pumped to other parts of the body, is played by theory. Then the tricky one, the one to be bypassed by surgery: the role of *plaque*, which is played by no less than three narrowed down characters, or, rather, ideal types.[2] I name them 'the good', 'the bad' and 'the ugly'.

---

1 The information on bypass surgery is taken from www.americanheart.org/presenter.jhtml?identifier=4484
2 According to Talcott Parsons, explaining Max Weber's classical concept, such types do 'not formulate the actual concrete meaning of an action but an extreme limiting case, in which certain elements were stated in their logically pure form and others intentionally neglected' (1948/1966: 248). Hence, an ideal type is 'a particular character of abstraction in a special direction' (ibid.). Rather than concrete actions it describes 'the normative patterns which may be considered binding on the actors' (ibid.).

The first type of plaque argues that ethnography should be about what vulnerable ethnographers feel when they study themselves while being in the field studying others. This is the regretful and self-loathing ethnographer afraid of using others for their own purposes. This is 'the good' distrusting the possibility of really being good. The second type, which also concerns ethnographers studying ethnographers, is a Janus-faced type. With one mask on, it is practicing self-critical reflexivity with the intention of revealing its own biased representations of the worlds of others. This not-enough-self-reflexive ethnographer finds her- or himself not to be trusted. With the other mask on, the second type deconstruct other ethnographer's ways of writing culture. It then finds other ethnographers not to be trusted, because the not-to-be-trusted-enough ethnographer represents the world of others in such a way that misrecognitions of it is written into layers of text. According to the scroll these two masks go as one type called 'the bad'. The third type finds itself living in the ruins of the whole modern scientific enterprise. It has designed for itself a lived culture characterised by the non-possibilities of reason, truthfulness and enlightenment. It completely distrusts the possibility to describe, explain and interpret others and their worlds. This ethnographer so deeply mistrusts studies of lived realities that she or he has decided to give it up. Besides a strong belief in the possibility of representing the ruins of science this type finds that epistemology is not to be trusted. This is, of course, 'the ugly'. However, like an enlightener, it has got a mission of its own: to preach and practice ruins.

The chapter

This chapter deals with three things. In the first part I will determine the meaning and importance of the heart. That is, ethnography. In the second part I will do the same thing with theory, that is, blood. I will also reason about why heart and blood should be considered as two 'unavoidables', informing each other through the whole research process. This means theory as a 'pre-cursor, medium and outcome' (Willis and Trondman, 2000: 7) to surprise the ethnographic data *and* to be surprised by data (since theory can never fully cover and know the empirical world) (Willis 1980, Trondman 1997). Hence, the empirical is dependent on theory, but is not completely determined by it (Trondman, 1999: 68-70). 'Experience has', as William James (1842-1910) put it, 'a way of *boiling over*, and making us correct our present formulas' (1978: 106), while 'reason', in my case theory, is carrying, quoting Martha C. Nussbaum, a 'special dignity that lifts it above the play of forces' (1997: 38).

The third, and last, part takes on plaque, and plaque related issues. Why are 'the good', 'the bad' and 'the ugly' there clogging the arteries? How is plaque production related to what I consider to be a too vague theoretical awareness in ethnographic study? What is wrong with these plaque types? Should they really be bypassed? Maybe, somehow, we need to communicate with them?

Part I. Ethnography as the heart

In the editorial introduction to *Handbook of Ethnography*[3] Paul Atkinson et al. describe ethnography through its 'common features' (2001: 4). Of course there are differences and tensions, but, I agree, most ethnographers tend to share a common ground. Despite 'the manifest diversity', Atkinson et al. write, 'there remain the core achievement of ethnographic research over the best part of a century' (ibid.: 6). Hence, the *Handbook* editors are men and women with a mission, because 'equally', they tell the reader, 'we seek to reclaim a tradition' (ibid.). I agree with that mission.

Being there in settings

What, then, are these common features to be reclaimed? I name the first and most precious one *being there*. It means, as the editors of the *Handbook* define it, 'a commitment to the first hand experience and exploration of a particular social and cultural setting on the basis of (though not exclusively by) participant observation' (Atkinson et al., 2001: 4). Or as John Van Maanen formulates it: 'Fieldwork usually means living with (…) those who are studied' (1988: 2). It demands, he adds, 'the full time involvement of a researcher over a lengthy period of time (typically unspecified) and consists mostly of ongoing interaction with the human target of study on their home ground' (ibid.: 2). In other words, 'participation' and 'observation' are 'the characteristic features of the ethnographic approach' (ibid.: 4-5). 'There is no substitute', writes Harry F. Wolcott, 'for 'being there' and 'doing it'' (1999: 16). Accordingly, ethnographers, irrespective of home discipline and empirical research interests, will hang around at street corners, sit at restaurant tables, inhabit class rooms, academies for ballet dancers or locker rooms, watch soap-operas with viewers in their living rooms, follow football crowds to away games, stray with hobos or stay with scientists in laboratories, live with people in small rural villages or with crack-dealers in urban ghetto-environments, hustle among hustlers, or spend time with doormen, teachers, mental patients, dishwashers, or air hostages.

---

3 The *Handbook* is, according to the editors, 'authoritative in that we chose contributors who are leading scholars' (2007: 1). They are, again according to the editors, of 'international excellence' and 'scope' (ibid.: 2).

So, 'being there', now moving to the second feature, is always being there in a particular and strategically chosen *setting* in which ethnographers try to move with what moves these lived cultures. Basically ethnographers will ask themselves and others 'what is going on here?' (Wolcott 1999: 279). They might choose to spend a lot of time teasing out the meaning of only one setting. They might want to experience being-there in several, more or less, diverse settings and thereby be able to make comparisons between them. Or they might want to follow the same group of people around, experiencing many different settings. But whatever choice of methodological design the ethnographer cannot do without the being there in these setting(s). These features are the stuff that the heart of ethnography is made off.

Additional devices

In most cases ethnographers would not only be there to observe and take part. They will also talk to people under study. In other words, they would not only watch people doing things and talking, they would also want to know how actors understand and explain themselves and others. As in Paul Willis' modern classic *Learning to Labour* (1977), they might ask: What meaning-making of their own made them feel they were doing the right thing leaving school to become shop-floor workers? For remember, social and cultural worlds are, to quote Andrew Abbott, 'made by activity in structure', that is, 'with social activity in its immediate contexts of social time and place, (1999: 3). Other sources of information, like visual and textual materials, also come to hand in the ethnographer's openness to 'thickets of detail, copses of complexity, and virtual forests of facts' (ibid.). The ethnographic demand on being there in settings does not exclude the use of other research methods and strategies.

These very useful and often needed *additional devices* make the third feature in what defines ethnography as heart. But these devices cannot determine ethnography. They are not as decisive as the being there and the setting. So, once more, I agree with Atkinson et al. (2001) that ethnographer's sometimes conflate in-depth interviews, focus groups or loads of textual materials with ethnography, but they can only be ethnographic if they are embedded in the socio-cultural settings in which they are used and should only be used additionally. As Alfred A. Young Junior put it in his study *The Minds of Marginalised Black Men* (2004), 'a proper cultural analysis of low-income men must (…) thoroughly interrogate how these men formulate world views, ideologies, and belief systems regarding their life circumstances and possible futures' (ibid.: 18). It is not enough to focus 'certain behaviours' that only 'serve to reinforce the already problematic social predicament of black men' (ibid.).

Young Junior's study of black marginalised men constitutes a fine example of why additional devices, mainly conversations, should belong to the core characteristics of ethnography. But as Martin Forsey (2008) remarks in this volume: 'to be worthy of the additional title of *ethnographic*, interviews must be conducted within the context of broader sorts of participant observer studies discussed elsewhere'. To sum up: ethnography as the *heart* is about *being there in strategically chosen settings with useful additional devices*.[4]

Theoretical absence and theory as fashion

I identify with ethnographic analysis that relates what people do and say to specific settings *and* to wider structures in which these settings are located and lived. However, I do *not* identify with how theory tends to be disconnected from how ethnography all too often is determined. And, as I will later make explicit by examples, it is the absence of theory or, rather, to be more precise without being contradictory, its *implicit being there-ness*, that not only increases the risk of getting arteries clogged by plaque but also, again, turns the practice of ethnography into an oxymoron: a heart that ticks without blood. So, at the same time as ethnographic study needs its more *empirical socio-cultural embeddedness*—its being there-ness in social settings with additional devices with an aim of making connections within as well as outside the setting—it cannot do without a *theoretical informed-ness*. The interconnection between the embedded empirical and the theoretically informed constitute the two 'unavoidables' in ethnographic study.

When Atkinson et al. at the end of their editorial introduction to the *Handbook of Ethnography* conclude by saying that 'the ethnographic gift' it is not 'just a romantic device' but 'the *heart* of the ethnographic enterprise', I agree. But when this justification and protection of the heart of ethnography is set up against what the editors calls 'the fashion of theory', I find it very problematic. Of course there are 'theoretical fashions'—theory as the sign of the times, like

---

4 Of course, ethnography can be defined in a variety of ways and still have about the same meaning. In *Manifesto for Ethnography* Willis and Trondman defined it as follows: 'What is ethnography for us? Most importantly it is a family of methods involving direct and sustaining social contacts with agents, and of richly writing up the encounter, respecting, recording, representing at least partly in its own terms, the irreducibility of human experiences. Ethnography is the disciplined and deliberate witness-cum-recording of human events. As arguable the first ethnographer, Herotodus, said in arguably the first ethnography, *The History*, 'So far it is my eyes, my judgment, and my searching that speaks these words to you' (1987: 171).'This-ness' and 'lived-out-ness' is essential to the ethnographic account: a unique sense of embodied existence and consciousness (…)' (2000: 1).

pop music to ears informed by a required *habitus* in specific zones, or fields (Bourdieu 1990), of alternative possibilities—for instance postmodern 'ruins' (Lather 2001).

But just because there are theoretical fashions we do not have to reject theory. Obviously, the editors operate with a half-house-logic. First, fashions are not *per se* bad just by being fashion. Some fashions might by well informed and, hence, needed. And 'old' still analytically productive theories might once have been fashionable. Secondly, even if we find all fashion bad it does not rule out the use of theory because all theories cannot be reduced to fashion. And also, I do *not* think Atkinson et al. would want to argue that we ought to give up the 'ethnographical enterprise' because there are people who only do interviews and call their work ethnographical. So, yes, we have a conflation here. Theory is needed though it can be fashion, because it cannot be reduced to fashion only. Ethnography is needed despite the fact that all that is called ethnography might not properly be it. However, the need, meaning and use of theory have to be taken further. Simply being there in settings, as Wolcott argues, 'is not enough to guarantee results', because 'if it were', he continues, 'we would be doing ethnography all the time' (1999: 16). It also demands a specific 'way of seeing' (ibid.: 70) informed by the insight that a way of seeing is also, at the same time, as Kenneth Burke once so cleverly put it, 'a way of *not* seeing' (1935: 70, my italics). And both an explicit way of seeing and an awareness of its limitations is what the work of theory ought to be about. Yes, we do need blood. So, what is the meaning of theory, and how can it be used?

Part II. What is blood?

'To understand', writes Isaiah Berlin in an essay on Giambattisa Vico (1668-1744)[5], 'is to enter into the outlook of those who speak to others, and whom we too can overhear (2000: 62)', that is, 'to see the world as they saw it, and then, only then, will their poetry, their myths, their institutions, their rites, their entire societies, whence we ourselves originated, become intelligible to us' (ibid.: 61-62). This is part of what we could call an allegory on theory. Theories, quoting Sherry Ortner (2006: 90), are to 'describe, explain, and represent how the social and cultural world is put together, and why things are the way they are and not otherwise'. Blood really needs heart; heart needs blood.

---

5   Berlin considered Giambattista Vico (1668-1744) to be 'the true father' of 'sociology of culture' (2000: 66). See also Trondman 2002: 47-48.

The importance of theory

Why, then, is theorising, besides describing, explaining and representing social and cultural worlds, of such an importance? I think it is because it makes possible the seeing of oneself as signifying someone which one does not easily recognise in ones own everyday life struggle—that is, the other, which is also me, but seen from another perspective, through another language. I do believe this seeing of oneself as a conditioned 'other' (or others as their conditioned 'selves') through the language of theory can contribute to better citizenship. It can carry social hope also towards the need and possibilities of others. It is a way of owning rather than disowning knowledge. One could become like Fleda in the Henry James' novel *The Spoils of Poynton* (1897), 'She could at a stretch imagine people not 'having', but she couldn't imagine their not wanting and not missing'.[7] In theory, hopefully, we can come to recognise our own and others rejected thoughts and longings. To paraphrase Ralph Waldo Emerson on the work of great artists: 'they come back to us with a certain alienated majesty', and, hence, 'tomorrow a stranger will say with masterly good sense precisely what we have thought and felt all the time, and we shall be forced to take with shame our own opinion from another' (quoted from Cavell, 2004: 19). The outcome of the work of theory on ethnographic data can most certainly have 'aha-effects' which 'fuse old experiences with new ones, thus opening the reader's minds toward new horizons' (Willis and Trondman 2000: 12).

The use of theory

If we agree with Ortner (2006) and Alexander (1995), which I do, we would not be doing theory by just describing teachers in the classroom. However, if the teacher's doings and sayings are approached as signifying practices in search of a legitimate ground for adult authority *vis-à-vis* children in a society characterised by increasing social differentiation, inequality, lack of trust in social institutions and rates of precocious 'tweens',[7] we would be using theoretical thinking on several analytic levels, but also, of course, empirical knowledge. Alternatively, we would also be practising theory if football player's goal gestures were interpreted as cases of individualisation, that is, meaning-making, in a global football economy. I am thinking about individual players who after scoring a goal, run away to perform their own individual gesture, before being caught up by the celebrating herd of more or less scattered teammates.

---

6   Quoted from Cavell, 2005: 236.
7   Basically children with a child's body but a teenager's mind and practices.

But, seeing it just like that, 'individualisation' is quite 'collective'. All goal scorers seem to be doing the same thing in their own way. Individual expressions might be (slightly) different, but the *cultural* (the expression as a phenomenon), the *social* (the getting away from team mates) and the *economic* (the player as a commodity in the global market place) *logics* are basically the same. In both these cases, teachers and footballers, we are, following Alexander (1995), 'abstracting from concrete cases' and making connections between different levels of analysis—individual, interactional, group, institutional and societal/structural—to deal with the symbolic, social and material aspects of human conditions of existence (Trondman 1999). Hence, a setting, as pointed out above, could not be understood as an isolated or free-floating island. It might have some logics of its own. Teachers would not normally do individual goal gestures if their skills in human relations establish legitimate authority *vis-à-vis* children in the classroom. However, they would probably feel good and think they picked the right vocation. They might also think that some of their colleagues did not. But there are not only differences. There is also sameness. To become a vehicle for meaning making, both the teachers and footballers need to, to paraphrase Clifford Geertz, construct 'a poetry', or 'a voice', 'out of the voices that surrounds it' (1983: 117). Because the actor, in all arts, 'works with his (sic) audience's capacities—capacities to see, or hear, or touch, sometimes even to taste and smell, with understanding' (ibid.: 118). This is also what contemporary teachers and footballers must get right when practising their arts in specific settings. Understanding this is also a case of generalised abstraction from particulars (Alexander), a way of seeing (Wolcott), and describing, explaining and representing how the social and cultural world is put together (Ortner). At the same time it is a very well needed theoretical insight made for human use and the enlargement of life (Keke 2006).[8]

Thus having been there in specific settings with additional devices, ethnographers then try to analyse collected data 'as something', as 'thick' descriptions (Geertz 1973: 6-10) regarding, for instance, 'class', 'reproduction', 'mobility', 'nobility', 'identity', 'authority' or 'individualisation'. We would then have had practiced theory the way Alexander and Ortner want us to, that is, separated abstractions from particulars with the aim of describing, explaining and interpreting. We would also have understood that ethnographer's particulars—multidimensional and non-reductive empirical specifications of strategically

---

8 I am here, following Keke, thinking about theoretical imagination: 'The work of the imagination', writes Keke, 'is thus the enlargement of life by the enlargement of its possibilities' (2006: 15).

chosen settings, humans and their lived cultures—are unavoidable in the construction of theoretical abstractions or ways of seeing and not seeing.

The unavoidable theory

Why, then, do we need to use theory and data as just suggested? What is, following Alexander's line of arguments, the significance of theory? Why can we not be without it? One way to answer these questions is to transform them into another one, namely, 'how are theories produced'? (Alexander 1987: 5) Are theories to be induced from data, from empirical facts? If this is the case the ethnographers just need to be there in the setting to record theoretical answers from more or less given and self-illuminating truth-patterns existing within the data itself. As if data were ready-made truths just lying around waiting to be discovered and re-told by an ethnographer. This was the botanist Carl von Linnaeus (1707-1778) self-understanding of his life-project. What God already had created, Linnaeus, with the help of his apostles, organised and gave names. Everything was, from the beginning to end, created by and, hence, in the hands of God (Sörlin, Fagerstedt, 2004) Oh, hark! I hear an inductive ethnographers monstrous little voice! 'Oh, all you data in the classroom', he or she solemnly speaks, 'just stand and unfold yourself, blow thy truths in forms of ready-made patterns on me. I will do nothing but to record the already given self-explained truths that are already lodged within thee. Names I will give thee, only names of the truth-pattern already there, given and laid out as it is, before my pure recording, mirroring and re-telling existence'.

This 'notion of induction', Alexander argues, 'is simply untrue' (1987: 5). For certain, 'theory can not be built without facts', *but* 'it cannot be built on them only either' (ibid.). This careful using of facts but not facts only was exactly what Linnaeus, despite his own self-understanding, did in practice. According to his lectures on *Fundamenta Botanica*, held in 1748, he was not satisfied with what he named the *Descriptores*, those florists who would only work out descriptions of different seeds (2007: 75). Neither was he satisfied with those he called the *Philosophi* (ibid.: 83). They put forward rules and axioms built on pure reason and confined experiences only. These philosophers reminded Linnaeus of 'a skipper on the wild ocean without compass and nautical chart' (ibid.). It is to the position of that kind of '*Philosophi*' I now turn. Because being against induction, we might want to argue that 'theory precedes any attempt at generalisation' and that we ought to 'go out into the world of facts armed with theory' (1987: 5). But still we would have a problem. How can we 'use a-theoretical facts to verify or falsify our general theoretical concepts' (1987: 5)? This According to Alexander this means that theories 'cannot finally and conclusively be tested by facts, even though a reference to facts is a vital part of every theoretical test' (ibid.). Overall I find his arguments well grounded and indisputable. At least I am not informed by better arguments.

How, then, are theories produced? Is there a position beyond a haphazard and pointless collection of facts *and* complex speculative theories made out of nothing? If it is, how can such a theoretical and empirical work be legitimated? Continuing Alexander's line of arguments, these works are being generated 'as much by the non-factual or non-empirical processes that precede scientific contact with the real world as they are by this 'real world' structure' (1987: 6). We should not forget, he emphasises, that 'the real world puts terrible strict limits on our theorising' (ibid.). '

This position is also the one that Linnaeus took more than 250 years ago. Out of his long experiences of the world of seeds *and* his broad readings of other botanist's work he came to generate a theoretical understanding of his own on how plant species could best be studied, defined, and organised. Hence, he was not a pure empirical describer. Neither was he a pure theoretical philosopher. Rather he was, in his own words from the *Botanica*, a scientist who 'distributes with the help of the sex' (ibid.: 95). He was, again in his own words, a *'sexualist'* (ibid.).

I do not think that the theoretical and empirical logic of Emile Durkheim's understanding of how a science of education ought to be determined differs from Linnaeus's, or Alexander's, or Ortner's understandings of the relation of theory and data in research. A science of education is possible, Durkheim stated, but education in itself is not that science (1970: 1, see also Trondman, 2007).[9] Again, the lived, empirical world of education would not speak its, using Durkheim's words, 'role' and 'nature' by itself. That speaking needed to be informed by theoretical and historical understanding of education as a specific phenomena, and it is that specific form of understanding that makes a science of education possible (1956: 61-90).[10]

Accordingly, quoting Alexander, 'there is, then, a double-sided relation between theories and facts' (1987: 6). At the same time as we as ethnographers need to be committed to rigorous empirical work—being there in settings with additional devices for a longer (or shorter) period—we also need to accept that the rationality of science depends heavily on theoretical understandings

9   It might also need an explicit normative grounding on what education is, what it should do and why (Trondman, 2007).

belonging to institutionalised academic traditions.[11] And these, 'old' or 'new', theoretical traditions are 'the a priori element' (ibid.) of the ethnographic practice. Since data can, on one hand, not speak for itself, and theory, on the other hand, cannot, as precursor, medium or outcome, be proved by data as if it was a last God-like first and last instance. To be aware of that, and spell it out, I think, is as good as the scientific ethnographic enterprise can get. This does not mean that 'anything goes'. It means that we as rationally and explicitly as possible tell our readers why, how and under what circumstances our theoretical informedness is sound, and how the empirical world of human agencies and contexts where collected and analysed as 'surprises' and 'proofs'. This is truth, or rather truthfulness, as good as it can get. 'Truthfulness implies', Bernard Williams explains, 'a respect for truth' (2002: 11). To him that demands 'Accuracy' and 'Sincerity' that is, 'you do the best you can to acquire true beliefs, and what you say reveals what you believe' (ibid.). 'The authority of academics', he continues, 'must be rooted in their truthfulness in both these respects: they take care, and they do not lie' (ibid.).

Understanding the theoretical and the empirical aspects of ethnography in this way does not mean that a theoretically informed ethnographic study can stand alone as an invulnerable, self-enclosed and self-correcting truth practice. It only means that this whole demonstration both prepares and justifies it with all its informed weaknesses. Hence, how we can make truthful claims about how we made that particular ethnographic study in which we have been seeing something as something—for instance, goal gestures as cases of a critically examined individualisation in the world of global football. That is, a meaning-making not reducible to the logic of capitalism only. It is *also*, at its creative and playful best, like the work of Shakespeare, Coltrane or Hewitt, a vibrant expression of cultural autonomy within or beyond traditions that represent humans and their lived culture(s) non-reductively and in a multidimensional way within a 'social imaginary' (Taylor 2004) of deep-working, socio-historically constructed, traditions making validity claims, grounded and contested truths, as truthful as these truths can become among humans in cultures allowing and making them possible.[12]

---

11 For a very interesting and clear historical analysis of how 'new' perspectives and 'old' traditions can clash and struggle against each other, see Strenksi 2007. His example is Durkheim and the Durkheimians struggle for a more theoretically informed sociology of religion at a time when science of religion in France was dominated by empiricism.

12 This is how Taylor begins his understanding of 'the social imaginary' that I refer to: 'My basic hypothesis is that central to Western modernity is a new conception of the moral order of society. This was at first

Thus the ethnographical enterprise—its contribution—vitally depends on these here collected and interrelated insights. As noted by Kirsten Hastrup being informed by Pierre Bourdieu, 'progress in knowledge in the social sciences implies progress in our knowledge of the conditions of knowledge' (1995: 8)[13] To me it means, to let Alexander conclude, that 'all scientific development is a two-tiered process, propelled as much by theoretical as by empirical argument' (1983: 30). This means, following Alexander, referring to the philosopher of science Imre Lakatos, that '*all scientific data are theoretically informed*'. (ibid.) The problem is not whether we should stick to data or theory. We must critically engage with both.

Raymond Aron (1905-1983) wisely warns us from 'the temptation to seek absolute objectivity through empirical moderation', because 'to recognise the impossibility of demonstrating an axiom system (…) is not a defeat of mind, but the recall of the mind itself' (quoted from Alexander, 1983: 33). Blaise Pascal (1623-1662) warns us, Bourdieu writes, against 'two extremes: to exclude reason, to admit reason only' (1999: 72). Pascal was known for letting his arguments 'play brilliantly, on the emotions as much as they do on the intellect—on our longing for self-knowledge, justice and happiness' (Rogers, 1998: 13). Hence, he spoke, to 'his readers heart as well as their heads' (ibid.). Well-informed on 'doctrinal conflicts' he turned to the profane world of pagan thinkers and played them off against the scholastics (ibid.). Obviously the theoretically informed ethnographic gift, in its struggle for multidimensionality, has been there, even if not so labelled, for quite a long time.

Part III. Types of plaque

Since the theoretical awareness of the ethnographic enterprise is all too often implicit and under-argued I need to do two more things. First, I will try to make the reader more concretely aware of the implicit being there-ness of theory in ethnography. It is, I believe, this in-articulation that opens up for too much plaque production and, hence, makes it hard, sometimes impossible, for the blood to reach the heart. Next, I will deal with plaque and plaque-related issues.

---

just an idea in the minds of some influential thinkers, but it later came to shape the social imaginary of large strata, and then eventually whole societies. It has now become so self-evident to us that we have trouble seeing it as one possible conception among others. The mutation of this view of moral order into our social imaginary is the coming to be of certain social forms, which are those essentially characterising Western modernity: the market economy, the public sphere, and self-governing people, among others' (2004: 2).
13 See Bourdieu 1990: 1.

The in-articulate speech of the heart

The literal meaning of ethnography is written accounts of people's ways of life. This understanding, freed from the urgencies of theoretical work, seems to have its own inertia. However, even if theory is not a constitutive part of how ethnography is defined literally it still has a way of being there when established ethnographers try to determine it. The same goes for how the ethnographic research process is understood. Few, if any, experienced ethnographers preparing less experienced ones before entering the field would be satisfied with Robert Park's advice to Nels Anderson in the early 1920s: 'Write down what you see and hear; you know, like a newspaper reporter' (quoted from Van Maanen 1988: 18). The struggle with determining ethnography and the decisive parts of its research process, that is, how data ought to be collected, analysed and presented, holds, as pointed out above, an implicit being there-ness of theory. It is asked for, or even demanded, without being spoken of in explicit and rationalised terms. Blood seems to be the inarticulate speech of the ethnographic heart.

'Ethnography is the result of fieldwork', Van Maanen writes, but a 'written report' that 'represent culture', is, he concludes, 'not the fieldwork itself' (1988: 4). Peter K. Manning states that ethnography 'provides the context within which signs, symbolic forms and content are joined with meaning' (2001: 148). Hence, the acts of interpretation and writing are singled out as something different from, but still related to, fieldwork. To me this is nothing but the heart asking for blood without using its real name. Van Maanen in the quote above is focusing 'narrative conventions', that is, ways of presenting written accounts of ethnography (1988: 1), and Manning is launching a semiotic perspective (2007). So, I am dealing with, I know, quite well informed cases. That is the reason I find it so hard to grasp why they are not more explicit about theory in determining ethnography. None of them supports an inductive or a grounded theory approach to qualitative analysis of data. But neither did Barney G. Glazer and Anselm L. Strauss, that is, the discoverers of grounded theory.[14]

Van Maanen writes that theory 'can' but must not always be, 'a formidable task-master' or 'may provide an illuminating reading' of 'data' (1988: 130, my italics). He hesitates about general use of theory however, because he is afraid of it as 'sovereign' (ibid.: 131). Like Atkinson et al. (2001) he conflates fashion,

---

14 In his book *Qualitative Analysis For Social Scientists* Strauss writes: 'Because of our earlier writings in *Discovery* (1967) where we attacked speculative theory–quite ungrounded in bodies of data–many people mistakenly refer to grounded theory as 'inductive theory' in order to contrast it with, say, Parsons or Blau. But as we have indicated, all three aspects of inquiry (induction, deduction, and verification) are absolutely essential' (1987: 12).

or, with Van Maanens own words, 'the ideological rule' (ibid.) of the day, with sound theoretical work even though, at the same time, he argues that 'culture is not itself visible, but is made visible only through its representation' (ibid.: 3). Better then, again, to have an explicit theoretical informed representation of that culture, than to say that you cannot always trust theory. Ethnographers at their writing tables cannot escape being informed by something while constructing understandings of other's lived cultural forms. So how can interpretation and explanation be something other than an explicit use of theory? As Hastrup argues, 'we cannot write real cultures without experience of other worlds' (1995: 17), but 'observation is never neutral' (ibid.: 4) and 'there is no way of speaking from nowhere' (ibid.: 13). The ethnographer needs to take the responsibility for 'the process of theorising' (ibid.: 7). And this cannot mean but making explicit theoretically informed meanings out of other peoples meaning-making: blood reaching the heart through open vessels. It also means that I have to become suspicious when Bourdieu (1996) recommends that theory should be used without being seen.[15]

The implicit being there-ness of theory also tends to characterise ethnographer's methodological advice on how data should be conducted. 'Fieldnotes', Robert M. Emerson et al. emphasise, 'are a form of *representation*, that is, a way of reducing just-observed events, persons and places to written accounts' (2001: 353). Accordingly, observations are 'selective', and these selections 'frame the events and objects written about' (Van Maanen 1988: 5). And since, recalling Hastrup, 'observation is never neutral' (ibid.: 4) and 'there is no way of speaking from nowhere' (1995: 13), the most rational strategy must be to let a theoretical framework inform the selective seeing and hearing. At the same time the use of theory must be open to, as pointed out by James, empirical boiling over and correction of previous formulas. Let theory surprise data, and data surprise theory (Willis and Trondman 2000), and let that shuttle process be in search for multidimensionality in both ways. Collected data cannot fully speak for itself. It needs to be analysed by ways of seeing and not seeing.

Accordingly, it must be the responsibility of the ethnographer to do the needed interpretations and explanations of people's doings and sayings, that is, to try to, informed by theory and surprised by data, tease out underlying logics,

15 It was my colleague and sociologist Ola Agevall who made me aware of this aristocratic dimension of Bourdieu's point of view of the use of theory. In *The Rules of Art* Bourdieu writes that 'to the same degree as I dislike those pretentious professions of faith by pretenders eager to sit down at the table of 'founding fathers', so do I delight in those books in which theory, because it is the air one breathes, is everywhere and nowhere–in the detour of a note, in the commentary on an old text, or in the very structure of interpretative discourse' (1996: 178).

depth of grammars and disowned knowledges. Hence, the ethnographer will fly close to the ground and imaginatively produce contextualised meanings of how and why people, as examples, 'buy and sell, christen their children and bury their dead, place bets and fall into trances and so on' (Faubion 2001: 44). I am in full agreement with Hastrup that theoretical analysis, at its best, represents 'a new reality', one that 'takes shape as it is conceptualised' (1995: 24). Because 'life has to be recreated in a separate language in order to be comprehended' (ibid.: 22). Accordingly, 'a theoretical project' is a project that 'sets itself apart from the practical project of living' (ibid.: 5). It is not the same as how 'the realities of other people' are told by themselves in their own 'local language' (ibid.). At its best, truthfully and evocative, it contributes to, as mentioned earlier, 'aha-effects' (Willis and Trondman 2000). In *The Weight of the World* (1999) Bourdieu formulates the job that needs to be done:

> Attempting to situate oneself in the place the interviewees occupy in the social space in order to understand them as *necessarily what they are*, by questioning them from that point of view, and to some degree to *take that part* (in the sense that the poet Francis Ponge, in the title of his collection, *Le Parti pris des choses*, implies taking part or 'side' of things) is not to effect the phenomenologists' – 'projection of oneself into the other'. Rather, it is to give oneself a *generic and genetic comprehension* of who these individuals are, based on (theoretical or practical) grasp on the social conditions of which they are a product: this means a grasp of the circumstances of life and the social mechanisms that effect the entire category to which any individual belongs (high school students, skilled workers, magistrates, whatever) and a grasp of conditions, inseparably psychological and social, associated with a given position and trajectory ins social space. Against the old distinction made by Wilhelm Dilthey, we must posit that *understanding and explaining are one*.
> (Bourdieu, 1999: 613)

To make this research process happen the ethnographer, following Bourdieu, must 'help to create the conditions for an extra-ordinary discourse, which might never have been spoken, but which was already there, merely awaiting the conditions for its actualisation' (ibid.: 614). It means at least two things, from the perspective of the ethnographer, 'a sort of *intellectual love*' for the whole enterprise and its aims, and, from the perspective of those under study, the possibility 'to make themselves heard, to carry their experience over from the private to the public sphere; an opportunity also to *explain themselves* in the fullest sense of the term, that is, to construct their own point of view both about themselves and about the world and to bring into the open the point within this world from which they see themselves and the world, become comprehensible, and justified, not least for themselves' (ibid.: 615). And the logic of a theoretically informed methodology for ethnographic study makes it possible: 'this kind of match achieved between the researcher's precaution or attentiveness and the respondent's expectation based on practical mastery of the social logic by which these data are constructed' (ibid.: 617-618).

This 'effort' will 'bring to light these things buried deep within the people who experience them—people who are both unaware of these things and, in another sense, know them better than anyone' (Ibid.: 621). And, again, to do this demands a specific way of seeing and not seeing. It demands, following Bourdieu, 'breaking with the spontaneistic illusion of a discourse that 'speaks for itself' (ibid.: 621-622). In other words, the ethnographer in deep contact with other people's forms of self-understanding needs to retell those forms in another language. Yes, theory is 'rupture', that is, 'a way of breaking the continuities of the empirical world' (Hastrup, 1995: 3). It means that theory is more about interpretation and explanation, seeing something as something, rather than corresponding to or mirroring 'reality'.

In the double sense of being surprised by data and theoretically informing the meaning of data the ethnographer can be understood as 'the radical interpreter', that is, one who, as formulated by Donald Davidson, 'provides an understanding that is not given by the object, but which emerges in the process of theorising' (1984: 128). So, a reclaimed tradition of ethnography, talking about the need of interpretation, is nothing but a demand for theoretical work. That is, a responsible ethnographer talking back in her or his own theoretically informed right: a belief in letting blood make the heart beat in a specific way.

The ethnographer's interpretation of culture must also be presented to readers of articles, reports and monographs, or to lay people in the wider public sphere. To me this is writing (or talking) culture but it is not to be conflated with epistemology, that is, with how truthful knowledge is to be produced. Writing is rather a rhetorical device for the evocative representation of theoretically informed ethnographic studies. Hence, we should not collapse writing into epistemology. Neither should we deny the use of rhetorical skills for persuasion

16 For a wonderful account of this issue, on how to 'instruct the listener as to what is right and wrong' (scientific knowledge) and 'the power to convince by your words' (rhetoric), see Cormack, 2002: 18-23.

of truthful representations of others.[16] Do not forget that culture is, as Hastrup formulates it, 'not only written stuff, it is lives people are living' (1995: 46), lives that the radical interpreter has understood and explained from a specific theoretical angle, an angle, of course, also influenced by the language of people's lived cultures. Thus people's lives cannot be reduced to literary genres and styles of representations. Neither can truthfulness be told without written, more or less evocative, accounts. Thus writing is the practice of truthful representations of lived realities interpreted through the use of theory: as pre-cursor, medium and outcome. Life might be messy, but neither the theoretically informed ethnography nor its mode of, using a Van Maanen term, 'cultural portraiture' (1998: 1) must by necessity be messy too. Ethnographers who think that life is messy and that therefore also written accounts of culture must be messy are often quite clear when they explain the meaning of messiness. I prefer, without denying that life could be messy, to learn from the latter.

Ethnography is and cannot be other than a means of representation. But only thanks to theoretical work we can avoid both the implicit being there-ness of theory and conflating writing with epistemology. We can also avoid messy analysis and writings. However, the inarticulate speech of the heart is not the only alternative to a theoretically informed methodology for ethnographic study. Other solutions, or modes of doing ethnography, can easily follow from that in-articulation. Hence, we now turn to the plaque stuffing the vessels leading to the heart, the last of my points.

'The good', 'the bad' and 'the ugly' revisited

I will first recall the core position of the three ideal plaque types. The focus will be on what they distrust in ethnographic practices. I will then critically examine the different logics of this distrust: to what extent are these logics to be trusted? As will be known in more detail, I find 'the good' much easier to like than 'the bad'. I like the first mask of 'the bad' better than the second one. And I definitely like 'the bad' much better than 'the ugly'. Undoubtedly there is a hierarchy of liking involved in my examination of these plaque types. It also needs to be said that even if all three types will be bypassed, I do think that theoretically informed ethnographers at times ought to hang around with them in the clogged areas were they dwell. If we can avoid the temptation to be glued there forever, we can learn from doing it. Accordingly I will consider the plaque types as more or less important sidekicks for the theoretically informed ethnography laid out in the two previous acts. In other words, my critique of 'the good', 'the bad' and 'the ugly' need to be understood in relation to that very ethnography here taken for granted. But while 'the good' is warm-hearted and 'the bad' is, at least seemingly, smart-headed, the ugly, unfortunately, is quite hopeless- and ruin-minded. As will be argued, it is only possible to hang around with 'the ugly' if seen as a jester at the court of plaque.

'The good' represents the vulnerable ethnographer. Like a seismograph this ideal type records the movements of its own emotions while 'being there' studying others. Having a strong, sometimes over-explicit, belief in being too cold and distanced 'the good' can easily turn regretful and self-loathing. Am I not just using others for my own purposes? Who am I to poke around in their world? Despite, or maybe due to, a strong awareness of the need of others 'the good' distrusts its own goodness.

In principle I identify with this struggle for goodness. But I do think that it has too much of finality about it. Only if it were differently accentuated could I find its logic to be trusted. I agree with Nussbaum saying that emotions 'involve judgments about important things' (2001: 19). Emotions embody 'ways of seeing' (ibid.: 27) and are 'concerned with value and importance' (ibid.: 30). Emotions are informed by 'beliefs' (ibid.: 28) and they 'fit the world', because they concern 'events that really do take place' and they 'seek to get an appropriate view of what matters' (ibid.: 48).

In terms of all these interrelated meanings the strivings of 'the good' is to be admired. However, even if belief, value and perception play a large role in emotions, they are 'not', as Nussbaum wisely points out, 'identical with them' (ibid.: 33). We need to reason about, not only feel, the way things really are: to ask ourselves what feelings mean in particular settings and what we need to do about them and ourselves. As ethnographers we should, of course, be informed by a rational awareness of emotions, but we cannot turn the whole ethnographic enterprise into finding out weather we should trust or distrust our emotional goodness.

Hence there are severe risks involved in being 'the good' distrusting goodness. One risk is to be too sensitive. To be overwhelmed by misguided and self-occupied empathy. The ethnographer would then be reduced to a self-loathing character dwelling upon a desire for emotional self-distrust. Another risk would be to deny the need for radical interpretation. In other words to hinder those being studied from the possibilities of seeing themselves in another light, that is, recalling Davidson, to deny the provision of an understanding 'that is not given by the object, but which emerges in the process of theorising' (1984: 128).

I find Bourdieu very reasonable, even wise, on this issue. 'Producing awareness of these mechanisms that make life painful, even unlivable', he states, 'does not neutralise them; bringing contradictions to light does not necessarily resolve them' (1999: 629), but is rather about 'allowing those who suffer to find out that their suffering can be imputed to social cause and thus to feel exonerated' (ibid.). Hence, it must be the task of the ethnographer, to make generally known 'the social origin, collectively hidden, of unhappiness in all its forms, including the most intimate, the most secret' (ibid.). And in order to do that work ethnographers cannot drown themselves in self-loathing distrustfulness. Rather, we must trust what I would like to call 'a double sense of goodness', to be emotional about ourselves and other peoples struggles in life, *and* to represent, with theoretically informed interpretations, the conditions of those struggles and the forms of lived cultures they produce, reproduce or/and transform.

'The bad' is the Janus-faced type with two intermediated logics of distrust. With one mask on it represents ethnographers who do not trust their own intellectual devices when conceiving and representing worlds of others. Too easily they will be engulfed in endless talks of the weaknesses of their self-reflective capacities. Sooner or later every effort to understand other's lived cultures, due to these ethnographers biased world views, turn into missions of the impossible. In the end they become unable to unleash themselves from this vicious never-ending reflexive self-occupation. However, deep inside and against the grain of their postmodern *Zeitgeist* they still long for truthful representation of others.

Undoubtedly so, they must have a strong and, hence, an admirable, belief in the development of modern scientific knowledge. Why would they otherwise put so much time and energy into trying to clean up what they understand as their murky ways of seeing and representing the world of others? If we could only be more reflexive, their cognitive unconscious must keep telling them, there might be a solution.

The bearers of the first mask also carry the burden of an implicit being there-ness. In this case a belief in scientific practices. That is, to objectify oneself and others, to start the thinking not as free but as conditioned. Why, then, this in-articulation? Basically, I think, because these bad ethnographers do not want to be considered as representatives of rude 'scientism'. At the same time, when at their very best, they have, as just mentioned, a strong drive for scientific seriousness and truthfulness. If asked they would probably support the belief that, as earlier pointed out, progress of knowledge in social sciences implies progress in our knowledge of the condition of knowledge (Bourdieu 1990: 1).

But, again, this very insight does not break through. Accordingly, 'the bad', just as 'the good', lock themselves up. Self-occupied by their own knowledge-power discourses they will never be able to see the light it really craves. They cannot really get into themselves because they cannot really get out of themselves. Therefore it all ends up with the too precious self-determination of the not-enough-self-reflexive ethnographer. Yet another type, or rather, half-a-type, caught in the self-ascribed logic of distrust. Plaque is gathering in the vessels. The blood cannot come through. The heart of ethnography is aching for the theoretical informed-ness it cannot beat without. But do not worry. This play is not, even if it might easily seem so now, a tragedy.

Enter so 'the bad' with the other mask on. With the aim of escaping the weight of its own world, that is, its seemingly non-escapable power-knowledge existence, it turns its intellectual devices towards the outcomes of other ethnographer's practices. That is, the research of the latter, or, rather, their soon to be discovered bad representations of others. Hence, with the second mask on 'the bad' is under the spell of a particular desire: to reveal how other ethnographers representing others are occupied by a non-reflexive-enough being there-ness in biased discourse or grammar. And therefore the outcome cannot but be the misrecognition and subordination of others. Thus, with the second mask on these deconstructing ethnographers, or, rather, critical reviewers, can slip away from the intellectual weaknesses of the bearers of the first mask. The latter's wrongly ground ways of seeing and writing others has now disappeared. By deconstructing ethnographers of the first mask, the ethnographers of the second mask become non-biased constructers of worlds of others—that is, other ethnographers—*per se*. Or rather, to be more cynically subversive, they get away from being deconstructed themselves.

This is the very trick. The second mask can supposedly do what the first mask cannot. While the first mask comes up with nothing but misrecognitions of others whilst studying them, the second mask walks free by hiding their construction of other first-mask-ethnographers under the banal banner of deconstruction. *Voilá!* Such a compelling act of self-forgetfulness! And of course, 'the good', the one studying itself while being in the field studying others, is not available in the mindset of the bad of the second mask. The latter do not have any doubts about whether she or he is using others for own purposes. While studying other's misrecognitions of other's suffering they need the cool distance. Just like me laying out my point of views of the point of views of others in ideal type form.

How, then, can the second mask of the bad be essentially different from the first one? Are not both constructing others? Well, there is a decisive difference already touched upon. The ethnographers of the second mask do not need to operate with the first mask's under-mining reflexivity at work. The second mask is only successful because it forgets to use the self-critical devices of the first. And thus the first mask survives as canon fodder for the second. But what would happen if ethnographers of the second mask put the first mask on top of their precious second? Would not that immediately turn out to be devastating? Had I been an ethnographer with belief in action research I would have had tried to intervene and help the ethnographers of the first mask to critically deconstruct how they are fooled by the trick of the bearers of the second. I can see two possible outcomes. Either the bad with the first mask would stop being bad and accept a theoretically informed methodology for ethnographic study *or* be bad enough to throw the first mask away and only play the trick of the second. There is, of course, also a third trick—and, thus, a third, (post-post-mask—to deconstruct those that have been deconstructing us. To do onto others what others have done unto us. In one sense it would definitely be much safer. They could stop having second-mask-thoughts about their own biased intellectual devices.

There are few ways out of the paradoxical solution of 'the bad'. One would be to withdraw and start to believe in plain induction. The truth is waiting out there. Forget theory. Forget 'the good' and 'the bad'. Just go and get it. Be like a journalist, or a travel writer. Another would be my recommendation, that is, a theoretically informed methodology for ethnographic study: to accept the need for bypass surgery and hence reroute theory to ethnography by ways of 'old' arguments discussed earlier. However, there is also yet another way out, or, rather, trick to deal with. It is to reach the conclusion that we are living in the ruins of the whole modern enterprise. This is the role played by 'the ugly' who completely distrust studies of lived realities and fitly have decided to give it up. There are no longer any lived logics, grammars and disowned knowledges to tease out. What is left is to represent ruins, which must be impossible since the pre-suppositional starting-point for the logic of 'the ugly' is that nothing can any longer be represented. If 'the ugly' thinks that so has always been the case, that is, if it is considered to be a universal truth claim, or whether if it is something that just happens to happen in post-post moderns times, and hence can change again with changing times, she or he does not say. However, with 'the ugly' we are supposed to acknowledge a new 'first', lasting or not, philosophy: nothing can be represented but the ruins. This is, assuredly so, an ugly trick. Basically a clean-cut case of anomaly, or, rather, oxymoron: the only thing to be trusted in the total ruins of representation is the trustworthy representation of ruins. Thus this truth claim completely distrusts the possibilities of epistemological reason *and* creates a remarkable self-assured epistemology of its own kind. In other words, 'the ugly' distrusts everything but itself. If find such ethnographers not to be trusted. This is the definite postmodern desolation row of ethnographic study.

According to the *Longman Dictionary of Contemporary English* a 'sidekick' is 'someone who spends time with or helps another person, especially when that person is more important than they are' (1995: 1332). I consider 'the good', 'the bad' and 'the ugly' to be, yes, well-needed sidekicks for ethnography. *Not* its core and main occupation. I find it commendable for theoretically informed ethnographers to hang around with these types in the clogged areas where they prefer to dwell. If we see them occasionally I am convinced that we can really learn something from them. And when seeing them, try to be kind. Remember that everyone you'll ever meet is fighting a hard battle. And that 'everyone' includes 'the good', 'the bad', and 'the ugly' too. Try to take it in that our intellectual devices can let ourselves as well as others down. Learn that we can improve the way knowledge is produced. As a part of the work with improving your theoretical informed-ness, try to deconstruct your own becoming constructions of selves and others. We can learn from our biased mistakes. However, we should definitely not accept lives in ruins only. We should continue to continue the needed and useful work of theoretically informed ethnographic studies. Do not let yourself down by taking for granted the normality of 'the good', 'the bad' and 'the ugly'.

What then about the ugly dwelling in desolation. Do I really mean that we ought to hang around with those representatives of ruins? I do not think we should do that if we are supposed to take their propositions seriously. So, how then do we deal with 'the ugly' in a social-liberal and pluralistic world of opportunities? They do exist, and sometimes, when I am in good mood, I do admit, I find it quite fun to hang around with them. My suggestion is that we think of the representatives of 'the ugly' as jesters rather than villains. 'Clowns and fools', writes John Southwork, 'have been a feature of virtually ever recorded culture in the history of civilizations and have made significant contributions to the development of early theatre and literary drama' (2003: 1). So why not, I think, 'late' ethnography. And remember that the jester's historically gained identity in his or her relation to 'the master' (ibid.: 2).

Yes, I can hear the jesters coming now, with their pointed shoes and bells. They are coming right out of clogged vessels and alleyways singing chimes of ruins. After spending some time in the alternative world of conceptual art, we can, I belief, safely return home. We are, accompanied by our theoretically informed reason, good enough, not that bad, and quite beautiful.

References

Abbott, A. (1999) *Department and Discipline. Chicago Sociology at One Hundred*, Chicago: University of Chicago Press.

Abbott, A. (2001) *Time Matters. On Theory and Method.* Chicago: University of Chicago Press.

Alexander, J. (1982) *Theoretical Logic in Sociology, Volume One: Positivism, Presuppositions, and Current Controversies*, London: Routledge and Kegan Paul.

Alexander, J. (1987) *Twenty Lectures. Sociological Theory Since World War II*, New York: Columbia University Press.

Alexander, J. (1995) *Fin-de-siecle Social Theory*, London: Verso.

Alexander, J. (2006) *The Civil Sphere*, Oxford: Oxford University Press.

Aron, R. (1949) Max Weber and Polanyi, in Shils, E. and Finch, H. (eds.) *The Methodology of the Social Sciences: Max Weber*, New York: Routledge.

Atkinson, P., Coffey, A., Delamont, S., Lofland, J. and Lofland, L.H. (2001) Editorial Introduction, in Atkinson, P., Coffey, A., Delamont, S., Lofland, J. and Lofland, L.H. (eds.) *Handbook of Ethnography*, London: Sage Publications.

Berlin, I. (2000) *The Power of Ideas*. Princeton, NJ: Princeton University Press.

Billig, M. (1995) *Banal Nationalism,* London: Sage Publications.

Bourdieu, P. (1990) *The Logic of Practice*, Cambridge: Cambridge University Press.

Bourdieu, P. (1996) *The Rules of Art. Genesis and Structure of the Literary Field*, Cambridge: Polity.

Bourdieu, P. et al. (1999) *The Weight of the World. Social Suffering in Contemporary Society*, Cambridge: Polity.

Burke, K. (1935) *Permanence and Change*. New York, New Republic.

Cavell. S. (2004) *Cities of Words. Pedagogical Letters On A Register of the Moral Life*, Cambridge, MA: The Belknap Press of Harvard University Press.

Cavell, S. (2005) *Philosophy The Day After Tomorrow*, Cambridge, MA: The Belknap Press of Harvard University Press.

Cormack, P. (2002) *Sociology and Mass Culture. Durkheim, Mills, and Baudrillard*, Toronto: University of Toronto Press.

Comaroff, J. and Comaroff, J (1992) *Ethnography and the Historical Imagination*, Boulder CO: Westview Press.

Crick, M. (1982) Anthropological Fieldwork, Meaning Creation and Knowledge Construction, in Parkin, D. (editor) *Semantic Anthropology*, London: Academic Press.

Davidson, D. (1984) *Essays on Actions and Events*, Oxford: Clarendon Press.

Davis, C. (1999) *Reflexive Ethnography. A Guide to Researching Selves and Others*, London: Routledge.

Dictionary of Contemporary English (1995), Harlow: Longman.

Durkheim, E. (1971) *Moral Education. A Study in the Theory and Application of the Sociology of Education*, New York: Free Press.

Durkheim, E (1915) *The Elementary Forms of Religious Life*, Trans. Joseph Ward Swain, London: George Allan and Unwin.
Dylan, B. (2005) *Chronicles. Volume One*, London: Simon and Schuster.
Emerson, R. M., Fretz, R. I. and Shaw, L. L. (1995) *Writing Ethnographic Fieldnotes*, Chicago: University of Chicago Press.
Emerson, R. M., Fretz, R. I. and Shaw, L. L. (2001) Participant Observation and Fieldnotes, in Atkinson, P., Coffey, A., Delamont, S., Lofland, J. and Lofland, L.H. (eds.) *Handbook of Ethnography*, London: Sage.
Faubion, J.D. (2001) Currents of Cultural Fieldwork, in Atkinson, P., Coffey, A., Delamont, S., Lofland, J. and Lofland, L.H. (eds.) *Handbook of Ethnography*, London: Sage.
Forsey, M. (2008) Ethnographic interviewing: From conversation to published text, in Walford, (ed.) *How to Do Educational Ethnography*, London: the Tufnell Press.
Geertz, C. (1968) Thinking as Moral Act: Ethical Dimensions of Anthropological Field Work in the New States, *Antioch Review* 28(2): 34-59.
Geertz, C. (1973) *The Interpretation of Cultures*, London: Fontana Press.
Geertz, C. (1983) *Local Knowledge. Further Essays in Interpretative Anthropology*, New York: Basic Books.
Glaser, B. and Strauss, A. (1967) *The Discovery of Grounded Theory: Strategies for Qualitative Research*, New York: Aldine.
Hastrup, K. (1995) *A Passage to Anthropology. Between experience and theory*, London: Routledge.
James, W. (1978) *Pragmatism and the Meaning of Truth*, Cambridge, MA: Harvard University Press.
Keke, J. (2006) *The Enlargement of Life. Moral Imagination at Work*, Ithaca, NY: Cornell University Press.
Lather, P. (2001) Postmodernism, Post-structuralism and Post(Critical) Ethnography: Of Ruins, Aporias and Angels, in Atkinson, P. Coffey, A., Delamont, S., Lofland, J. and Lofland, L.H. (eds.) *Handbook of Ethnography*, London: Sage.
Lyndon-Gee, C. (2003) Notes on George Rochberg, from the sleeve of the CD Georg Rochberg, Symphony No. 5, Black Sounds, Transcendental Variations: Naxos.
Manning, P. (2001) Semiotics, Semantics and Ethnography, in Atkinson, P., Coffey, A., Delamont, S., Lofland, J. and Lofland, L.H. (eds.) *Handbook of Ethnography*, London: Sage.
Nussbaum, M. (1999) *Sex and Social Justice*, Oxford: Oxford University Press.
Nussbaum, M. (2001) *The Upheavals of Thought. The Intelligence of Emotions*, Cambridge: Cambridge University Press.
Ortner, S. (2006) *Anthropology and Social Theory. Culture, Power, and the Acting Subject*, Durham: Duke University Press.
Parsons, T. (1948/1966) Max Weber's Sociological Analysis of Capitalism and Modern Institutions, in Barnes, H. E. *The History of Sociology*, Chicago: University of Chicago Press.
Rogers, B. (1998) *Pascal. In Praise of Vanity*, London: Phoenix.
Sennet, R. and Cobb, J. (1973) *The Hidden Injury of Class*, New York: Vintage Books.
Southworth, J. (2003) *Fools and Jesters at the English Court*, Stroud, Gloucestershire: Sutton Publishing.
Strauss, A. (1987) *Qualitative Analysis For Social Scientists*, Cambridge: Cambridge University Press.

Sörlin, S. and Fagerstedt, O (2004) *Linné och hans apostlar*, Stockholm: Natur och kultur.
Taylor, C. (2004) *Modern Social Imaginaries*, Durham: Duke University Press.
Trondman, M. (1994) *Bilden av en klassresa*, Stockholm: Carlsons Förlag.
Trondman, M. (1997) Some Remarks on a Theoretically Informed 'Empirical Return', in Fornäs, J. (ed.) *Advancing Cultural Studies*, Department of Journalism, Media and Communication, Stockholm: Stockholm University.
Trondman, M. (1999) *Kultursociologi i praktiken*. Lund: Studentlitteratur.
Trondman, M (2004), Fantasia: En essä om Gianbattista Vico och kultursociologin, in *Idrott, kultur, fantasi och historia, Rapportserien Centrum för kulturforskning*, 2004(1), Växjö: Växjö universitet.
Trondman, M. (2006) Disowning Knowledge: To be or not to be 'the immigrant' in Sweden, *Ethnic and Racial Studies*, 29(3): 431-451.
Trondman, M. (2007) Emile Durkheims utbildningsvetenskap: Ett försök till rekonstruktion, in Sanding, B. and Säljö, R. (eds.) *Utbildningsvetenskap. Ett kunskapsfält i formering*, Stockholm: Carlsons förlag.
Van Maanen, J. (1988) *Tales of the Field. On Writing Ethnography*. Chicago: University of Chicago Press.
Von Linnaeus, C. (1735-1736/2007) *Fundamenta Botanica*. (Om botanikens grunder. Ett 1700-talsmanuskript sammanställt av Lars Bergquist), Stockholm: Atlantis.
Williams, B. (2002) *Truth and Truthfulness*, Princeton: Princeton University Press.
Willis, P. (1977) *Learning to Labour: How working Class Kids get Working Class Jobs*, Farnborough: Saxon House.
Willis, P. (1980) Notes on Method, in Hall, S., Hobson, D., Lowe, A. and Willis, P. (eds.) *Culture, Media, Language*, London: Hutchinson.
Willis, P. and Trondman, M. (2000) Manifesto for Ethnography, *Ethnography*, 1(1): 5-16.
Wolcott, H. F. (1999) *Ethnography. A Way of Seeing*, Walnut Creek, CA: Altamira Press.
Young, A. (2004) *The Minds of Marginalised Black Men. Making Sense of Mobility, Opportunity, and Future Life Chances*, Princeton, NJ: Princeton University Press.
Zagorin, P. (1998) *Francis Bacon*. Princeton, NJ: Princeton University Press.

Chapter 7.

Characterising social settings as the basis for qualitative research in ethnography

Bob Jeffrey

Introduction

Ethnographic research includes involvement, immersion and empathy on the one hand and distance, scientific appraisal and objectivity on the other. It is a focus on natural settings, an interest in meanings, an emphasis on process, inductive analysis and grounded theory (Hammersley, 1993). The researcher is there to get to the bottom of things, to analyse, advance explanations and represent material in a ways that might not occur to the inmates.

However, whether one follows the social science approach of providing explanations, or Wolcott (1990) and Woods' (1996) humanist approach in just conceptualising situations, or even the postmodern largely reflexive strategy, there is a general agreement that description lies at the heart of the qualitative aspect of ethnography (Brewer 2000). Description is the basis of qualitative research products such as explanations, evaluations, and theorisations (Hammersley, 1992). However, this sub discipline of ethnography known as descriptive anthropology, a social science of people (Vidich, 1996, p. 705), is no ordinary description that anybody could provide. The rich details of several layers of reality, classifications, categories, typologies, conceptual refinement and representation amounts to what Geertz (1973) calls 'thick description'.

Accurate description (Strauss and Corbin, 1990) entails a necessary selection of data through categorisation (due to the amount collected) and requires great skill in weaving descriptions, conversations, fieldnotes and own interpretations into a rich believable descriptive narrative.

This is further supported by those (e.g., Wolcott, 1995) who argue that description should be kept separate from interpretation so the researcher starts by not knowing anything and seeks understanding through description and analysis. This is the 'thick description' (Geertz, 1973) which is the verisimilitude we provide, unbounded by plausibility and credibility of validation. In contrast, others see 'thick description' as thick interpretations (Vidich and Lyman, 1996).

This chapter uses and explains Lofland's (1971) characterisation which was applied to social settings and the collection of data separated into what he called six units.

His qualitative activity of analysis—characterisation—is based on such questions as: What kinds of things are going on here? What are the forms of these phenomena? What variations do we find in these phenomena? 'That is, qualitative analysis is addressed to the task of delineating forms, kinds and types of social phenomena; of documenting in loving detail the things that exist' (p. 15). Six units of observation to analyse social phenomena or situations are listed from the microscopic to the more macro similar to progressive focusing (Strauss and Corbin, 1990).

- Acts: Action in a situation that is temporarily brief, consuming only a few seconds, minutes or hours.
- Activities: Action in a setting of more major duration—days, weeks, months, constituting significant elements of person's involvement.
- Meanings: The verbal production of participants that define and direct action.
- Participation: Person's holistic involvement in, or adaptation to, a situation or setting under study.
- Relationships: Interrelationships among several persons considered simultaneously.
- Settings: The entire setting under study conceived as the lens of analysis.

Social phenomenon can now be seen to translate into at least six more specific categories. Instead of asking 'What are the characteristics of a social phenomenon, the form it assumes, the variations it displays?' Lofland (1971) now asks, 'What are the characteristics of acts, activities, meanings, participation, relationships, and settings, the forms they assume, the variations they display?' (p. 15).

However, Lofland, in this 1971 methodology appears to eschew the interpretative element of the researcher's role, as he sees the data collected as facts. It is therefore necessary to take these arguments into account when using his useful lenses. It is also useful to make it clear that this observational process is more inclined towards the data generation than the broader aspect of fieldwork, the former more technical and the latter the embedding and immersing of the researcher in the research site over time (Wolcott, 1996). However, the data collected in an ethnography should be that collected in deep familiarity with the social setting gained by personal participation (Lofland, 1995).

This chapter will explore how these units were used in a recent research project focusing on creative learning in primary schools. The focus of the paper is the observational fieldnotes collected during data collection as determined by Lofland's units which we prefer to call lenses. We will be clearly acknowledging the involvement of the researcher in choosing sites to record, for interpreting the data through the frames of creative teaching and learning. We will also add to the Lofland methodology to acknowledge the power of the language and the writing we employ to influence the data outcomes of characterisation. This was another area that Lofland eschews, the influence of the writer/researcher's tone and style of writing on the characterisation of settings.

The anthropological research tradition in the UK—from which ethnography derives—begins with description as does the USA interactive analysis approach but the latter uses pre-ordained categories whereas the anthropological/ ethnographic tradition allows new categories so potentially fertile descriptive language is possible. It can identify common phenomena from small samples showing the character of classrooms (Delamont and Hamilton, 1976)

Fieldwork that does not get written is partial and incomplete and description is the starting point with early writing of memos and further descriptions seen as ferreting out bias. Descriptive writing should use panache and style to lighten up contexts and according to some written for the self first (Wolcott, 1995).

Rounded, instead of flat characters, are created in these descriptions and as they help to transcend the shallow understanding of outsiders in a complex and authentic version of social reality. The language used in the descriptions is central to the problematic and construction of reality (Atkinson, 1990) and comprehensiveness and comprehensibility (Hammersley, 1993) compete as the describer seeks to provide both pictures and understanding invading science through narrative ethnography, writing the poetry of engagement (Rose, 1990). An ethnography is a piece of writing and the result can be seen as the blurring of art and science e.g., Geertz, Douglas, Levi-Strauss and Turner (Viditch and Lyman, 1996).

From a postmodern perspective descriptions evoke the sound and hearing simultaneously as well as the harmony but there are no pictures of reality for whatever is there is only an imitation of the continuing symbols of signifiers and signified. An ethnography according to this tradition has no path from perspective to concepts for it begins and ends in concepts challenging Wolcott's (1995) notion of an absence of interpretation on entering the field. Ethnography is not a record of experience but a means of experience, i.e.: the experience becomes the experience of writing the ethnography (Tyler, 1986).

However, descriptive accounts may be more persuasive for primary readers, i.e., those being studied and peers rather than policy makers. Case studies do not readily lend themselves to data collapse and they are never finished only left. Lofland's (1971) comprehensive model for analysing social settings encourages the researcher to record events, understandings, agency and adaptations, interactions and finally, and perhaps most important, an analysis of the 'entire setting', which encourages a holistic analysis of the previous lenses and at the same time counters a selective approach. The middle three lenses—meanings, participations and relationships—again force the researcher to carry out some higher level of analysis for something has to be said about them based on the detailed collection of acts and activities. A reader can then be confident that if higher order analysis or tentative theories are produced they are based on detailed observations, of qualitative analysis of the social setting and an overall analytical description of the whole setting. Using this model for research indicates clearly to the reader that any interest in assigning causes and consequences will be obliged to include a quantitative approach.

Characterising creative learning.

The English part of a ten partner European Socrates project entitled 'Creative Learning and Student Perspectives (CLASP)' (Jeffrey 2006a) investigated creative learning in three primary schools between 2004-5. Two of the schools were selected because they supported creative teaching and learning and the third involved a dance programme for Year 6 (aged 10-11) to help improve overall confidence and self esteem, leading to hopes of higher achievement levels. The fieldwork was carried out by the author over two years with visits to the schools taking place over a year. There were some conversations with relevant adults but the main recorded conversations were with learners from ages 5-11 and the fieldwork covered all age classes, some outdoor activities led by local creative partnership artists and other invited external projects were observed (Jeffrey, 2008). The main objective of the fieldwork was to try and gain and analyse learner's perspectives and to characterise creative learning.

The Lofland (1971) six lenses of observation were used as frame for the participant observation and our fieldnotes provided some examples of analysis derived from this research through these frames. To illustrate his practices Lofland used research material from a variety of well known ethnographies whereas this paper will only focus on our research. The main objective is to show how these lenses or frames constitute a comprehensive form of characterising research sites and how they can also assist in avoiding any misuse of qualitative data.

Acts

As indicated above 'acts' are temporarily brief actions involving solitary, collective (the class together), co-participative (drawing on others activities to enhance or distinguish one's own or a group's efforts), or collaborative engagements (working together) (Jeffrey, 2006b). In order to characterise these acts in this research we recorded narratives and we tried to evoke a feeling for the act. A fieldnote narrative describes action over short periods of time and gives a flavour of the development of the action, in this case, a workshop on the Tudors,

> Joe finds something relevant to Greenwich—close to the school—and Mickey says 'nice find'. Their worksheet suggests that each person in the group should have a role and a subject. Joe reads out more from his search on 'the Palace at Greenwich and the Royal Maritime Museum. The old palace, of Tudor times, no longer exists' and Leighthan reads a book. Mickey says 'I'm going to give you a new job Joe. Find a web site with loads of text and select what we want and then download it to *Microsoft Word* and Duran will print it'. Nathan draws, Duran and Joe use the computer tablets to seek facts, and Mickey supervises, 'I'm still looking for more, is that okay Mickey' says Joe. Mickey co-ordinates, organises, facilitates and stimulates. (Yr. 5)

Mixing the facts of what's happening and the dialogue in a narrative description supplies some of the character of creative learning to be encapsulated in higher level categories later.

Recording the nature of the engagement of individuals or groups provides initial analysis of 'what's going on' and at the same time gives the researcher the opportunity to take their observation data a stage further in this dance act..

> The children are learning how to work in a circle, going in and out and circling round in different directions. Their faces are serious as they have to concentrate on the beat and the direction of turning when the circle goes round in the opposite direction. They are learning about unity in the

universe. As they practise their birth and sound sequence they watch the leader with a serious intent, the flash jump, the smooth roll, the scrunch roll, the flame leap. Their eyes follow their arms looking into space with slow stretched turns. Nadine smiles as she explodes and follows this with a spiky roll and a swirl. She purses her smiling lips and swirls so fast she loses her balance and laughs at herself. (Yr. 6)

These qualitative engagements could not be captured without a qualitative approach of the recording of the acts, for example, 'pursing her smiling lips'.

An adjunct of this qualitative data collection is using the opportunities of one's writing skills to evoke (Tyler, 1986) the nature of the act through literary devices (Atkinson, 1990) such as listing actions to reproduce the sense of dynamism in the setting as in this account of a drama lesson of the story of Faust with a Year 5 group led by a National Theatre director.

The children are divided into three groups and they have to pick a scene from their story and show it as a tableau to represent the whole story. As they talk in the groups about the composition of the story their hands shooting in the air, they jump excitedly. They point, call to one another, take a position or pose, cajole, suggest, wave their arms, spring, threaten in role, purloin a chair, enjoin their bodies, wrap themselves around each other and squeal. They mimic screams, push people into position, watch, wait, listen, frown, persuade, experiment in groups, compose in different groups, argue, insist, shunt, volunteer, propose, and look perplexed.

There is always more happening in Acts than maybe at first apparent and recording the detail of settings, through narratives, engagements and evocations (Tyler, 1986), writing the poetry of engagement (Rose, 1990) provides a rich source of data for further analysis for language constructs the reality (Woods, 1996), albeit a subtle reality (Hammersley, 1992). Ethnography is not just any piece of writing (Viditch and Lyman, 1996). There is also no denying that the unstructured data is structured by our selection of fieldnotes and conversations (Lancy, 2001) but any bias can be seen as early level theorising (Wolcott, 1995). However, it differs from novelists and journalism in that there is an external and internal validity (Woods, 1986), a verisimilitude of 'thick description' (Geertz, 1973), a subtle reality (Hammersley, 1992) validated by plausibility and credibility.

Activities

These are actions of a longer duration constituting significant elements of a person's involvement but again it is the qualitative nature we must describe using our interest in other's perspectives and our literacy skills, all part of the researcher as research instrument (Woods, 1996). Our broad theory of creative teaching and learning is characterised by relevance, control, ownership and innovation (so the research could be seen as adding to the theory of creative learning) and we were looking to characterise these in this research. The first three could be applied to many other qualitative research sites, particularly ethnographic, as they provide some dimensions for the recording of agency or its limitations. Our recordings focused on how these developed over time and therefore fitted neatly Lofland's (1971) assertion that it is important to try to ascertain the significance over time of people's involvement and gives the ethnographic researcher an extra interest in carrying out research over time. In this case the dance project showed the temporal nature of control.

> They remember much of the dance from a previous week and perhaps the cause of their focus is the enjoyment of anticipation and becoming more competent as they take control. Martin, the dance teacher, walks round the hall to another spot and the children's eyes follow and they take a new position facing him occasionally swinging an arm or two. They march towards an imaginary ladder and begin to climb it, anticipating the next movement. They are slightly ahead of the instructions from Martin as they recall the next movement in the composition. There is not a word spoken. (Yr. 6)

Again all narrative, engagement and evocation are used to show involvement over time and out of this passage a possible characteristic of control is constructed, that of 'anticipation'. Although we began the research with a theory of creative learning we are not asserting it in these fieldnotes or promoting a position but characterising it for further development.

Ownership follows control as Amy (Year 2) demonstrates as she describes her adventure playground made out of scrap material.

> I made the slide. You go up there, through the hole and down the slide. This is a lamp post made from pipe cleaners and we both did the sand

> pit together. We put in a bucket. There are some flowers and a bench made out of matchsticks and I have put a very steep slide on it. I got some matchsticks on paper and made a roundabout. I did some knots to keep the material on the slide tower on. This is a monkey bar slide. You can climb on the second swing across and let go into the sand pit. We used the matchsticks stuck into the ground to make little areas to play in. I liked doing the swirly, whirly bits of the slide because it was quite fiddly and I like doing fiddly things. You have to hold them and play with it a lot. When you pull the whirly slide the little girl on the high bridge wobbles. She's on high bar above the ground balancing on the bridge. We've put steps up to the slide. I've learnt how to more things and to really make things and to make things wobble without touching them. I learnt how to take things and make them into something they really are not.

Being innovative is particular to our research project but again the style of data collection is imbued with the process of initial analysis as the opportunity to be innovative is accompanied with feelings of joy—a category we used later.

As their creative learning develops over time in Lofland's (1991) Activities so does their commitment to an ever increasing complexity of work.

> In the scissors exercise they open and close on their own with many different ideas, a bent back, hands in the air, knees bent the same, some horizontal, some in a circle, closing their feet by turning them, some on their toes, composing and watching, watching and composing. Some pairs focus on each other oblivious of the rest as one girl moves a partner into position to match the music but another pair of girls survey the room and discuss the composition by a pair of boys. The girls talk about their movements together and the boys demonstrate and someone else claps them. There is a lot to do and a lot remember in these lessons and the children have to engage their intellect, the bodies and their creativity. The pairs demonstrate the composition and two girls keep the pace and the rhythm of the maracas that Martin is playing. They fall to a scissors shape together with a turn, a role and a jump. Another pair face each other and march towards each other in a confrontational dance representing a scissor battle.

Here is another feature of creative learning—commitment—that search for the diversity of organising themes (Hammersley and Atkinson, 1995) that will be useful when we come to further analysis.

The recording of data connected to the Activities such as long term timetables in this case are also useful in assisting the analysis and observation of engagements. In this case we noticed full details of the terms timetable on a classroom wall which gave us a sense of the compartmentalisation of learning and led us to investigate how learner's felt about continual lesson switching.

> The fortnight early literacy plans are pinned on the wall together with the learning objectives. The general weekly timetable for the second half of the autumn term is there, as is the autumn term timetable for all the separate subjects. There are weekly numeracy plans also pinned to the wall. Literacy and numeracy takes all morning and other sports and library activities together with music, science, art, religious education, history and personal social subjects are also time tabled. Reading times take place at the beginning of each afternoon and there is a story time. The autumn timetable contains science; keeping warm and circuits and conductors; ICT (Information and Communication Technology)–writing for different audiences and Internet searches; design and technology–money containers , tests before fabrics and using technology for decoration; history–the Second World War; geography–similarities and differences, maps and plans; art–still life, RE (Religious Education)–Hindus; music–sound escapes; and PHSE (Personal Health and Social Education)–emotional development and circle time. Clearly teaches do not have to worry about what to teach each week, just how to fit it in.

This linear approach is in opposition to a circular approach in which investigations are revisited regularly (Woods and Jeffrey, 1996; Watkins and Mortimore, 1999) and we were able to look out for times when teachers abandoned this timetable. This contrasting situation provided us with an opportunity to investigate the teacher's tensions concerned with managing a tight timetable and subverting it, thus challenging the theory that teachers are merely technical operatives and providing evidence of agency. In empirical terms this is done through time spent in institutions recording change and subversions and using them to triangulate recorded conversations which may not reflect reality.

Meanings

This is possibly Lofland's (1971) most difficult frame or lens of qualitative observational research for he recognises the broad extent of encompassing culture, norms, values, understandings, social reality, definitions of the situation, typifications, ideology, beliefs, world view, perspective and stereotypes. He also recognises that all the other lenses contribute to the meanings attached to those being observed and researched. He describes life encompassing, middle range, situated meanings and norms as meanings. His focus for this lens are the words that are spoken to define and direct action, i.e., the discourses they bring to their acts and activities and the meanings these utterances represent. There is much more interpretation by the researcher in this lens than in the previous more factual collection of data but thick interpretations are essentially thick descriptions (Vidich, 1996, p. 705). Nevertheless, the terms people use, in their utterances are key terms reflecting their values and norms and the contradictions between them, their explorations of typifications, understandings and realities and their situated use of ideologies, beliefs and world views.

In this creative learning research we took a more literal approach to this lens by focusing more on the use of language than on its symbolic meaning but still found it useful for our research and we believe this lens or frame is still a legitimate one in spite of straying from Lofland's (1971) approach. (Our most recent research on performativity in primary schools focuses more on symbolic utterances or discourses (Troman, 2007). We recorded tonal indicators, verbal utterances, shared dialogues, role switching, involved engagements, dynamic interchanges, conflicts and evaluations.

> Alice does some verbal comprehension work asking them when, where, what do you know about certain characters, poverty, ages, hunger, what do you feel about them, what does the writer make you feel about them. She encourages them to talk to somebody they are sitting next to about the story and how they feel about the characters. 'I feel sorry for them because that they are orphans'. She asks them 'how does the writer make you feel about two of the characters. 'I think the two ladies are cruel' [Georgina]. Alice asks for some key words. She gets—disgusting, mad, disgraceful, meaning, cruel, selfish, disrespectful, ashamed. She accepts them all. She asked them how they feel about the characters and accepts all the responses even if they are not appropriate 'I think they are mad'.

Characterising social settings as the basis for qualitative research in ethnography 151

> She asks them about Scrascult 'he is helpful because he is getting them a job and giving them money' [Georgina]. She then asked them what they think of the character. They think he is suspicious, joyful [this was accepted without comment], untrustworthy, that he was blackmailing them [Alice suggested that he might be tricking them rather than blackmailing them], that he might want children to work for him, that he is a merchant, that he might not give them enough food, that he won't pay them enough. She then asks them how the story might continue. 'he might make them follow him and then he would pretend he can't find work and make them work for him and tell a lie and not pay them. He will starve them and not give them anything to eat. He will eat in front of them when they are in a cage' [Georgina].

It is not just words that are helpful in producing description for analysis of the tone of the engagement. Recording shared dialogues can also reveal different ways of being with peers, as in this case of a Year 5 learner.

> The group who are designing the seats in the playground use a tablet PC and the *Paint* software. Sophie asked Rodney 'what would you like behind the seat. What colours would you like?' He said he would like 'big bushes behind the seats'. Sophie said 'I don't mind going last and putting your ideas and Bethany's in first'. She continues to construct the design while asking Rodney and Bethany what they want. She asks him if he would like apple trees, how big he would like them to be and whether they wanted it to cover the whole space. If you want grey you can have it. There you are Rodney draw a squirrel where you want', and she gives him the tablet.

The words indicate one of Sophie's values, that of contributing to the organisation of collaboration and shows it to be a feature of creative learning. Comprehensiveness and comprehensibility compete productively (Hammersley and Atkinson, 1995). Dialogues also give an insight into the extent to which members are becoming involved in the social context.

Participation

Lofland's (1971) lenses move from micro to macro and the fourth frame explores the holistic involvement in, or adaptation to the situation or setting under study.

As Lofland's lenses draw back from the minute detail of acts, activities and meanings we begin to see the qualitative nature of members' engagement. The CLASP project identified the following indicators of involvement, colourful descriptions, playful and skilled engagements, immersion and a final taking of ownership as key features of this participation lens. The first—contextual description—is exemplified by a Year 6 group's full descriptions of the construction of tangram (a square cut into seven pieces all with different geometric properties) pictures.

> This is a numeracy week where the whole school is focusing on shape and pattern. Caroline's class (Yr. 6) are making Tangram pictures. Jake makes a duck, then an Elvis picture, then a duck's head and a funnel followed by a chimney. 'I'm seeing what I can make. I don't decide beforehand but I've decided on the dinosaur. It's interesting and it's the best of all I have done. It's the most creative. I've made a pocket for my tangram pieces from paper'.
>
> Cloe tries to make a 'spooky' picture because the background picture is black. 'Does it look like a ghost? It's floating. It has a tail like some ghosts and these are the arms like wings helping them to fly. I'm going to do a spider. It's hanging from there. I decided to make it because you find them in spooky places.
>
> Stephen says, 'I'll make anything that nobody else has made. I go a bit crazy drawing a scientist holding a test tube and getting his face blown up. I have made a sign that goes on a 'baby changing door'. It struck me straight away. It's my first choice and it looked real. It looks like a baby holder'.

Their personal involvement is exemplified in the way they bring their interests and experiences to the activity and also indicates the way in which they are personalising their engagement. Their experience of creative learning obviously involved the imagination but this is broken up into both playful and skilled use of imagination, another example of early analysis (or index coding) as opposed to open coding later (Brewer, 2000)—countering neglectful misuse. Exemplifying the former were two nine year old learners who were working in the IT suite on a project on representation.

Characterising social settings as the basis for qualitative research in ethnography 153

> The Yr. 4 children had taken pictures of themselves on a digital camera and put it onto a *Dazzle* file. They then worked on reconstructing their friend's picture, 'making her weird and making her crazy and putting weird clothes on her. I put a beard on her and big cracked yellow ears and purple hair with blue spots and I put a crown on her big hair do. She thinks it's disgusting. She'll say "Tara, you're going crazy" as I put on a funny blue nose and weird black eyes'. Hannah is amusingly outraged, 'Tara made it crazy. It's funny. If I did look like that I would freak out.' Tara responds 'I like being horrible. It's really fun making people weird. It's funny when you print it out. You say "What have I done to Hannah. Look at her. Look you're weird" Hannah says, 'I think you have made me absolutely disgusting. I hate it. Tara shows no regret, 'I made it disgusting. I made the scriggly bogies go on her silky dress. The eyes are in different places. That's why there are three. It's turning into a monster and her hands are creaky and freaking'.

These two close friends were enjoying this form of imaginative playing with their relationship through the creative IT programme and their holistic engagement is plain to see. However, the learners' use of their imagination is also skilfully employed.

> Andrea, the dance teacher, then asks the class to compose a sequence for a group of four in the centre of the hall. They suggest: 'go fast and high, show a turn, circle arms and legs, work in line clicking fingers, canon along the line'. The children clap the efforts. They suggest 'three go high and three low, push each over like dominoes in a canon, do a low-high split and then reverse it, all fall over, separate from one another, get into a row and finish sitting, make a letter p'. Last week the children composed a set of movements suggested by Andrea—high, low, turn, etc.—modelling. After the class last week Nimra suggested to Andrea that they come up with ideas for each other so she included it in this week's programme.

Their gradual expertise was developing, resulting in their imaginative use, again, giving an indication of their holistic involvement but at the same time intervening to change the direction of pedagogic control. Descriptive engagement, and playful and expert use of imagination were indicators of immersion in the acts and activities as this example of Year 5 learners engaged in a dramatic conflict concerning the dilemma for Faust.

> They are split into two lines facing one another across the dance studio. One group represent God and the other group Mephistopheles. They are challenging one another for the soul of Faust. Each group say the lines in turn and as they do it they create the appropriate actions and emphasis. They also construct a physical reaction while the other group are speaking. One boy in the Mephistopheles group turns and taps his feet and looks bored and puts his hand to his mouth in a yawn while he listens to God. There is an angry shout from Joe who is part of the group playing God and he has his hands on his hips and is pointing 'Lead him on the downward course, but be ashamed when you fail'. He stands sidewards and says it with the vehemence and his compatriots wave their arms. Those playing Mephistopheles answer in dramatic gestures when God is speaking and in response the opposition group grow much louder and aggressive. One boy puts his hood over his head and pouts aggressively.

Immersion in the case of creative learning leads to the taking of ownership over their products as in these examples of the construction of futuristic classrooms by a Year 5 group.

> Freia and Mickey input loads of novelty things like launchers that launch bad teachers into the sky. There is also a teacher cage for bad teachers who are two bossy and old-fashioned and who think the cane should be used. However Geoff, their teacher, is allowed in the classroom but he is not allowed to teach although he still gets his salary. His job is to search the Internet for teaching ways to help the children with their games. The children can play any game but they have learn something from seventy-five percent of them and the games have to be fun. 'Bad teachers breath is toxic so we have an airlock so that bad teachers cannot breathe on us. The classroom has a teacher cage, learner's workstations, a huge and lemon and chocolate cake and a celebration bowl that you jump into with giant sweets similar to a play ball park, a teacher airlock and a swimming pool.

Participation data collection has identified creative learning features of involvement through the merging of personal involvement, the use of playful and expert imagination, and shown how this leads to immersion and the taking of ownership, supporting the generation of categories early on in the research. (Lancy 2001)

Relationships

These are particularly pertinent aspects of qualitative data collection as they indicate the nature of power relations as well the social ones. It must be obvious that Lofland (1971) was not advocating a linear approach to his six lenses for all of them may be seen in any specific situation but they span the lenses we use and at the same time ensure that we consider the micro to the macro.

It is not surprising that the area of creative learning involved collaborations but the nature of the enfolded relations was also there to see.

> Carly's Yr. 3 class are constructing a soup for sale in a Design and Technology project. 'We planned the advert and had a chance to get it ready. We didn't have to do it all in one day'. 'You know what you're to do in the future but you can change it when you are unhappy with it. We had a rough idea without having to start all over again.' 'I liked working together with all of us doing different things.' 'I liked watching the other crew and laughing.' 'We agreed things by changing it as we discussed it.' 'If you belong to a team you feel you are being listened to. It's good to have others caring about your ideas.' 'We have learnt how to co-operate and how to use tools and how to be creative with vegetable leftovers and to make pictures.'

Collegiality, being listened to, having others care about you are all features of these relationships and possible features for later broader analysis for example, developing a social role as appreciators of creativity itself and of each others' ideas, commitments and products, a product of creative learning (Jeffrey, 2007). These early codes are heuristic tools that add to the topography of the research landscape, its features and its details (Seidel, 1998). Relations are often dynamic in that they develop rapidly, revolve, create tensions and reconciliations. In our case they were mainly enjoyable but nevertheless dynamic.

> In groups of four in a circle they begin to build their fists on top of one another. They discuss who is to go first and then enjoy the sensation of the explosion after the construction as they throw their fists into the air, smiling and laughing and allowing their bodies to fly away. They then make a ladder of their heads placing them on top of each other ear to ear all facing the same direction. They laugh as the hall becomes a fall of crisis, falls, giggles, screams, shouts and chattering. (Yr. 6)

The collaborations related to creative learning we observed were warm ones and yet as they developed they became a complex interweaving of relationships.

> The children sit in groups colouring in the designs, discussing the appropriate colours and trying out some of the maths attached to the games they are planning for the playground for the younger children in the school with a Creative Partnership artist. They are working on the fine detail of the game, 'they will have to roll the dice once, and remember the number, and roll it again'. They practice the figures on scraps of paper asking each other's permission, 'shall I put a number in here', measuring accurately the position of signs, evaluating each indecision before continuing. 'If it's too full you won't to be out to see the numbers from below', shooing away those who disturb them or interfere, 'go away, we know what we've doing'; sometimes arguing over a central aspect; and measuring themselves to decide on the appropriate height for the game, colour coding numbers, science and texts; borrowing, sharing and problem solving; 'we could put the numbers in a container,' 'it would be too difficult to make it like that,' 'no it won't,' 'how will you open the doors'; offering opinions and cracking relevant jokes.

That is not to say that conflicts didn't exist for they did and they added to the nature of the dynamic relations.

> Martin shouts at one girl for walking aimlessly. He didn't ask what she was doing, 'It was an endless walk with absolutely no effort whatsoever'. He complains that they are still not focusing hard enough and he is disappointed with the amount of effort being made by the children. 'Some

of you can't be bothered. Here is a chance to see what you can do. I am disappointed'. There is not much circulation of ideas in this session.

The description of these relations has provided a rich seam of features and characteristics for the analysis of the nature of relations involved in creative learning. Wolcott (1995) argues that analysis seems to be winning over interpretation creating a lack of authenticity and he sees the artistic challenge as preserving, conveying and the celebration of complexity, messing up science. Reality gives analysis an undeniability to be matched by plausibility with which to assess the interpretive effort. It is the analytical imagination of the researcher based on detailed description that is needed to counter any misuse and the last of Lofland's lenses is where this has the most force.

Settings

Ethnography involves the collection of research data that is relatively unsystematic and open ended, a holistic frame that accepts complex scenes and begins with a broad perspective that reduces breadth of enquiry to give more attention to emerging issues. (Delamont and Hamilton, 1976). Lofland (1971 saw this lens as his most macro perspective seeing the entire setting under study as a lens of analysis, in our case a creative learning setting. This is the lens that allows the researcher to gather together much of the detail from the other lenses for a broader reflection or analysis. However, there is also a more complex use of this lens which is to make the leap from any of the lenses the researcher is considering to the broader picture, where questions are asked and puzzlement becomes a major feature. Understanding settings requires a broader holistic approach and the ethnographic search for meaning as a complete as possible body of data, thick description. This is where the researcher is freer to pose questions to oneself, of the settings, to try out some broader analytical characteristics, to critique the settings, to bring in more open reflections to bring in relevant literature references and lenses, to play with the whole research setting, the site of activity of participants, the environment they inhabit, the cultures that proliferate and the relationships that exist.

Critical reflection by the researcher is an essential part of the characterisation process.

> Martin, the dance teacher, insists on a climate of commitment. He doesn't want any lounging, chatting or loss of focus, fidgeting or fiddling. How far

is this essential for creative dance? The chatterers and the loungers and the fidgets still complete the tasks and construct the compositions. There doesn't seem to me to be a loss of commitment if they behave in this way. It might be argued that they can't help it anyway. How far does this put them off modern dance? More important how far have does it constrain or restrict their creativity? Probably not very much but it may have an effect on what could be seen as their informal creative learning, learning situations in which they are innovative because the atmosphere and the climate is supportive and warm. But does it make any difference?

Contrasting situations can be used for enhancing the qualitative analysis of the enquiry as well as triangulating the data collection as this critique of a secondary teacher's approach in a visit by a Year 6 class shows.

This type of pedagogy seems to be so different to that in the primary school. Every little detail is included and no doubt the teacher has relayed this narrative many times. Nothing is left to chance or to creativity or and none of it is investigative. She didn't let the children do two things differently and then discuss the most effective or hygienic approach. How creative is it if children have little control over the exercise, to design one quarter of a piece of dough but do no investigation? Is creative learning different to being creative, i.e., should creative learning include an investigation, and opportunity for the learner to make decisions about effectiveness through reflection and experimentation? Is a major part of the concept of possibility thinking weighing up possibilities and comparing them, i.e., is suggesting a possibility just that or does possibility thinking include reflection, comparison and evaluation? What kind of learning is going on in the secondary teacher's classroom and how far is it determined by the circumstances and the context?

This is a form of comparative analysis to bring out the nature of the main focus, creative teaching and learning. In another situation with Year 4 we identified a preference by teachers for the development of self esteem, rather than collective investigations and the fieldnotes included a critical observation.

Teachers give affirmation as a matter of course. I wonder if an inclusive co- participative approach would be more critical and focus more on the quality of learning rather than just affirming the child. The affirmation of suggestions and proposals from children, which are either not relevant or contributions that a misplaced or where the child has misunderstood, does not seem very creative or have much to do with creative teaching and learning. It has more to do with creating a climate of involvement and building confidence in children but not directly to do with learning.

Contradictions are another form of analysis that can be applied to the whole setting acting as an analytical tool.

Ben had brought in his book on the brain and the teacher noted that we don't use a lot of our brain. One child offered the statistic that it was about half but it was ignored. This is a classic example of a non-participative action/contribution. Another child suggests that they can help one another if they get confused and the teacher says yes 'but not doing other people's work'. This is another example of discouraging the participants adopting a collaborative approach.

We must be aware of our biases emerging—as exemplified in the last sentence—but broader reflections are part of this data collection and analysis of the setting.

More open reflections contribute to this characterisation of settings but at the same time the researcher used this opportunity to raise questions for the research.

The staff room at Suburbia school playtime is jolly and warm as teachers tease each other, tell amusing stories from their weekend, discuss what they have given up for Lent and crack a joke with a small child as he comes to tell them that the bell is going for the end of break. It is a relaxed atmosphere with the head joining in the jokes as she passes. During the lunch hour three or four staff organise some of next term's activities. This role doesn't appear to have been designated to them by the head.

It doesn't seem to matter what position they have in the school as to whether they contribute or not. This is one of those schools that develops and changes dynamically. Creative teaching has a human aspect to it. It involves the emotions, care and interest in others and it generates appreciation. It is an appreciative business, just as involvement in the arts is a matter of qualitative appreciation. However, one wonders if there are over any clashes of values or of value positions. How do they resolve them? How is every creative suggestion, proposal accepted and incorporated?

More detailed reflective analysis is often possible in the quieter times of fieldwork as well as afterwards (Brewer, 2000) when 'nothing appears to be of interest' and contributes to the analytical induction.

Can we talk about less constrained/bounded contexts and more constrained/bounded ones. I should have asked the learner how that felt and looked for examples of how copying and working collectively is approached more positively, for example, have you made any changes? Which aspect is your idea? How did copying this or working collectively assist your creativity? Creativity does have roots and connections. It is what individuals and groups do with them. All different approaches— need analysing and categorising.

Obviously other theories are drawn into the reflections but as a tool to unpack reality, to stumble across wholes and holes (Seidel, 1999).

So, any curriculum subject may have been experienced by learners in a different context. Subjects are often integrated into other subjects because the pedagogy draws on different subjects, for example, design draws on maths and literacy, literacy development draws on aspects of shape and pattern. There is more integration than separation of curriculum subjects. How is Bernstein (Bernstein, 1971) and Coombes (Jeffrey and Woods, 2003) going to be helpful here?

We used this lens to make the links between Acts and Activities and broader research issues. The involvement of the researcher's reactions to Acts and Activities are an integral part of the researcher's characterisation of the site. The problem for ethnographers is not that they are in danger of becoming part of the situation but that they fail to do so (Walker, 1986).

Althea takes an art lesson with Yr. 4. She refers to an artist they have looked at in the past and she gives them each a large flower which they have to draw. As the children look at it they discuss what they know about flowers. 'That's the pollen. I remember when it fell over me, it stains the clothes,' 'if you put it on yourself these will come after you for that is what they want.' 'It makes a scent, that is what they really want' 'My mum's friend owns a gallery and we threw flowers in a pond. I have seen giant daises in my neighbour's garden.' 'Creativity stands for art and cooking.' 'Flowers, trees and bushes can be used by people to be creative.' 'Creativity is creating more things, poems and stories.' Nadia says to Emmanuel 'Why don't you rub the pastel with your finger. I prefer that look because the shade of the colour comes out.' He says thank you gratefully. 'Creativity is my hobby.' However all this information is irrelevant to this particular lesson and is put aside or ignored or not encouraged. Does this fracture school and learner knowledge, constrain or restrict creativity or creative learning? Should we be doing both appreciating the aesthetic quality of flowers and the role they play in the biological, social and environmental aspects of our lives?

These fieldnote observations go alongside the other lenses and at the same time they encapsulate the other lenses in a recursive manner as questions, critiques, puzzles and musings go back and forwards acting as the warp and weft of the fabric as it is created by the detailed collection of data in the other lenses. Qualitative software such as *Ethnograph* are also based on a cyclical approach of noting, collecting and thinking, an iterative progressive, recursive and holographic approach (Seidel, 1998).

The adherence to a set of frames like these shows how the inductive analysis is a further construction of the description the research is providing through data collection. Analysis, as we hope we have shown, goes on a the same time as the data collection, progressive focusing and escalation of insights (Hammersley, 1993) within the bounded lenses that Lofland has identified to assist our fieldwork. The lenses allow some early analysis to take place, a form of subtle analysis (Wolcott, 1990) in which the descriptive material is mainly written before analysis but is interpreted *in situ*. This is similar to Hammersley's (1993) preliminary stage in which the researcher highlights, adds comments, identifies important points, contradictions and inconsistencies, common themes, references to literature and introduces comparisons with other data.

Conclusion

Arising from the operation of these six lenses and observation and analysis the CLASP project constructed a creative learning identity, its characteristics being meaningful engagement, meaningful experience and a meaningful role (Jeffrey, 2008). Meaningful engagement was characterised as consisting of joy (corporeal freedom, dynamism and collective delight) and authentic labour (resoluteness, assured engagement and peak perfection). Meaningful experience was characterised as playing with identity, celebrating achievement and inhabiting a sense of place and meaningful role by acting as active participants as co-participators, collectivists, collaborators and learnicians who were skilled acted as creative learning analysts and evaluators.

This analysis does not constitute a general theory but attempts to characterise in more detail the features of creative learning found in these specific sites and are an invitation for other researchers to test them in new situations or to add to the characterisation or to add more features (Woods, 1987). The characterisations are additions to the qualitative nature of creative learning.

Ethnography, alone in all the methodologies requires site immersion in order to gather the empirical data upon which any analysis and any theory building depends. Recorded conversations alone away from the site of focus or without any immersed data on the acts, activities, meanings, participations, relationships and settings do not constitute ethnography. This does not mean that ethnographic studies have to be done over many years for there are different categories of time that can be employed (Jeffrey and Troman, 2004). Lofland's (1971) lenses constitute six different essential aspects of the character of a site or situation that can greatly assist any temporal ethnographic process. It is obvious that at least the first five lenses may well be employed at once or alternatively in very quick succession but the more the researcher is aware of these different lenses the richer will be the quality of their data and thicker their descriptions or thick interpretations (Vidich and Lyman, 1996). Although the researcher is the research instrument they need some technology upon which to base their work and these lenses provide some very effective tools.

References

Atkinson, P. (1990) *The Ethnographic Imagination: textual constructions of reality*, London: Routledge.

Bernstein (1971) On the Classification and Framing of Educational Knowledge, in Young, M. F. D. (ed.) *Knowledge and Control: New Directions for the Sociology of Education*. London: Collier Macmillan.

Brewer, J. (2000) *Ethnography*, Buckingham: Open University Press.

Delamont, S. and D. Hamilton (1976) Classroom research: A critique and a new approach, in Stubbs, M. and Delamont, S. (eds.) *Explorations in classroom observation*, Chichester: John Wiley and Sons.

Geertz, C. (1973) *The interpretation of cultures: selected essays by Clifford Geertz*, New York: Basic Books.

Hammersley, M. (1992) Some reflections on ethnography and validity, *Qualitative Studies in Education* 5(3): 193-203.

Hammersley, M. (1993) Using Qualitative Methods, in Bogue, D. A. and D. J. (ed.) *Readings in Population Research Methodology*, Chicago: Social Development Centre.

Hammersley, M. and P. Atkinson (1995) *Ethnography : principles in practice*, London, New York: Routledge.

Jeffrey, B.(2006a) (ed.) *Creative learning practices: European perspectives*, London: the Tufnell Press.

Jeffrey, B. (2006b) Creative teaching and learning: Towards a common discourse and practice, *Cambridge Journal of Education*, 36(3): 399-414.

Jeffrey, B. (2007) Creative Learning in Europe: Making use of global discourses, in Craft, A., Burnard, P. and Cremin, T. (eds.) *Creative Learning 3-11 and how we document it*, Stoke-on-Trent: Trentham.

Jeffrey, B. (forthcoming) Meaningful creative learning: The development of primary learner identities *Education* 3(13).

Jeffrey, B. and G. Troman (2004) Time for ethnography *British Journal of Educational Research*, 30(4): 535-548.

Jeffrey, B. and P. Woods (2003) *The Creative School: A framework for success, quality and effectiveness*, London: RoutledgeFalmer.

Lancy, D., F (2001) *Studying children and schools: Qualitative research traditions*, Prospect Heights, Illinois: Waveland Press.

Lofland, J. (1971) *Analysing social settings*, Belmont CA: Wadsworth.

Rose, D. (1990) *Living the Ethnographic Life*, London: Sage.

Seidel, J. (1998) *Qualitative Data Analysis*, London: Sage.

Troman, G., Jeffrey, B., and Raggl, A. (2007) Creativity and performativity policies in primary school cultures, *Journal of Education Policy*, 22(5): 549-572

Strauss, A. and J. Corbin (1990) *Basics of Qualitative Research*, London: Sage.

Tyler, S. (1986) Post-modern ethnography: from document of the occult to occult document, in Clifford, J. and Marcus, G (eds.) *Writing Culture*, Berkeley, CA: University of California Press.

Vidich.A and Lyman. M (1996) Qualitative Methods: History of Sociology, in Norman, K. D. and Yvonne, S. L. (eds.) *The Landscape of Qualitative Research: Theories and Issues*, London: Sage.

Walker, R. (1986) The conduct of educational case studies: ethics, theory and procedures, in Hammersley, M. (ed.) *Controversies in Classroom Research*, Milton Keynes: Open University Press.

Watkins, C. and Mortimore, P. (1999) Pedagogy: What do we know?' In Mortimore, P. (ed.) *Understanding Pedagogy and its impact on Learning*, London: Paul Chapman

Wolcott, H. (1995) *The art of fieldwork*, London: Sage.

Wolcott, H. (1990) *Writing up qualitative research*: Newbury Park, CA: Sage.

Woods, P. (1986) *Inside Schools: Ethnography in Educational Research*, London: Routledge.

Woods, P. (1987) Ethnography at the crossroads: a reply to Hammersley, *British Educational Research Journal*, 13(3): 297-307.

Woods, P. (1996) *Researching the art of teaching: ethnography for educational use*, London: Routledge.

Woods, P. and B. Jeffrey (1996) *Teachable Moments: The Art Of Creative Teaching in Primary Schools*, Buckingham: Open University Press.

Chapter 8.

Ethnography and representation: About representations for criticism and change through ethnography

Dennis Beach

The present chapter is about the dialectics of representation in critical ethnography and what Barthes says about where meanings begin and end with the issue of codes (also Bernstein, 1971, 1990). It concerns how signs can only convey meaning when there is access to codes that allow us to translate concepts back into language. These codes are outcomes of social and cultural conventions that help form the shared maps of meaning making that make words and things function as signs within and across discursive fields. There is an analogy in the chapter on the basis of this fundamental recognition. This analogy is between ethnographic representation and the art or craft of drawing and it lies in the coded nature of a drawing, which, according to Barthes, can be seen at three levels. First; a drawing requires a set of rule governed transpositions; secondly, it requires a division (coded) between the significant and the insignificant to be made. A drawing does not reproduce everything. It rather demonstrates certain aspects that are seen in certain ways by the drawer and then recognised in these or other ways by the reader. Finally, like all coded practices, drawing requires an apprenticeship of some kind by which the drawer learns 'the tricks of the trade' (Beach and Larsson, 2006).

'Drawing' is thus, as ethnography also is, very often a process of inscription that involves periodically turning away from the external objects of the representation that are usually assumed to be its focus, toward *what* it is that *has been recognised* as important or interesting. It is *an interpretative act*. What is 'drawn' is never be (nor can it be) what was simply there in an objective sense, or even what was simply seen. 'Drawing' (and thus by the analogy also ethnography) involves *perception* not just seeing and as perceptual it is shaped by implicit or explicit theories or ideas that privilege certain meaning formations. The diffusion of information through drawing (and by likeness ethnography) thus does not mask its constructed meanings as given (natural, real) as photography may. A drawing, and by inference the representation of ethnography in a metaphorical likeness to drawing, is clearly ideological, skilfully crafted and therefore also trans-formational.

The question of ethnographic representation

The question of ethnographic representation has been debated throughout the history of ethnography. Malinowski spoke about it in his seminal work, *the Argonauts of the Western Pacific*. Clifford Geertz wrote a book entirely about the representational practices of leading anthropologists (Geertz, 1988) and is himself widely quoted in relation to his seminal piece (in Geetz, 1973) on thick description. Paul Atkinson (1990) paraphrased the importance of representations in his book *The Ethnographic Imagination*. Howard Becker used to run an informal seminar on representation for his graduate students and wrote a book dealing with some of the problems of writing as representation (*Writing for Social Scientists*, University of Chicago Press, 1986) has been focused on in chapters and part chapters of just about every ethnographic methods book written (Wolcott, 2001; Elliott, 2005).

Nevertheless, the question of the quality and possibilities of representation is still today an unclear, and at times contradictory and enigmatic issue. What is admissible and what roles can and do different techniques (photography, drama, theatre, dance, film or just plain writing) play? Moreover, how should we conceptually position representation? It is, on the one hand, work and part of the production system of contemporary research. In this sense it is governed by researcher self-discipline and the performance demands of competition based on publication lists that link publication both to work security and to salaries. On the other it is also a way of formulating an understanding of important issues and a tool for critical scrutiny with a real-use-value even beyond academia (Beach and Larsson, 2006).

How to organise an ethnographic representation is thus obviously a difficult task to give advice on, with the exception of the need to accept it as a transformational craft-practice and art-form that is caught between the two moral edifices of the use-value and productive-value of labour. Debord (1977) speaks of the spectacle of representation as a form which chooses its own technical content that is inseparable from general cleavages within society as a product of the division of social labour and as a possible organ and aspect of class domination. There are different audiences to relate to in terms of background knowledge and these are often motivated by and interested in different aspects of an ethnographic account.

So how do we cope with these edifices and also at the same time capture and illuminate things for people with different motivations and interests; including different class interests? Usually not very well according to critical accounts! Richardson (2000) for instance finds representations qualitative research (including ethnography) on the whole very boring and she points to a relationship between artistic qualities, depth of interest and the possibilities of/for producing really moving interpretations (Beach and Larsson, 2006; Beach, 2006). For her there is an internal relation between interpretations and these qualities (Lather, 1991; Willis, 2000), even though the success of ethnographic texts among researchers is commonly based on them being judged as providing clear and convincing accounts that are also demonstrated as having scientific validity (Atkinson, 1990; Hammersley, 1992).

Ethnography and/as representation

There is no singly accepted clear definition of what ethnography is in social and educational research, beyond it being seen and expressed as a family of methods involving direct and sustained social contact with social agents in their everyday encounters with social life (Beach et al., 2004) and a process that involves richly writing up and/or otherwise representing the lives and activities participant observed in ways that respect, record and show key aspects of the irreducibility of human experience in its own terms (Willis, 2000; Beach, 2005). To quote Willis and Trondman (2000), ethnography is in this sense not a closed system of thought and only really has one disciplining base line, which is a belief in Nussbaum's notion of 'reason' as having a 'special dignity' as a worldly knowledge of practice for the conduct of everyday life as it grapples with the play of everyday forces and helps us to understand analytically the culture in which an ethnographer's richly described 'experiences' have been located and formed within a flow of contemporary history that is made and remade inside lived experiences that are socially sprung and dialectically produced and responded to (Beach, 1997; Willis and Trondman, 2000). The history is, to paraphrase Paul Willis (2000), an expression of life as art. And ethnographic representation is the art or craft (i.e. the coded/coding practice) of representing life as art. It is therefore always to a degree going to be both irreducible and enigmatic as both product and practice.

However, at the same time as it is irreducible and enigmatic, ethnographic representation is also an established and distinctive *method* and *product* that has been systematically described and reflexively examined within a variety of disciplines, most prominently cultural and social anthropology (Burgess, 1984; Beach, 2005; Geertz, 1988; Clifford and Marcus, 1986). As Willis and Trondman (2000) make clear, in this vein a series of theoretical challenges have been mounted against what is sometimes, if wrongly, taken as, on the one hand, the inherently uncritical humanism of ethnographic representations and, on the other hand, their impenitent empiricism. These two extremes are deconstructed to suspend tendencies toward forms of discursive *naïveté* that cause ethnographers to ignore the importance of the ways representations are produced. This is sometimes called an essential reflexivity.

This kind of consideration of the relations of production of ethnographic representations can of course be simply termed as being (part of) a reflexive understanding of the practices and products of a theoretically informed writing craft (Beach, 2006). But there is a risk of loosing the strengths and continuities of the ethnographic tradition in this turn. Because whilst it recognises that our written discourses cannot be treated as if their contents can be equated with lived outcomes (Willis and Trondman, 2000), in order to sustain a critical contribution from ethnography to the positive development of social theorising that allows voice to those who live their conditions of existence in the situations described and analysed, ethnographic representations must also utilise at least some of the critiqued strengths of modernist ethnography, at the same time as it puts them under suspicion (Lather, 1991). This is a key element of critical ethnography and its forms of representation.

Some key distinguishing characteristics for critical ethnographic representation

There are a number of characteristics I would like to claim for critical ethnographic representations in education. These are listed and also briefly discussed below.

1. The first point recognises the role of critical theory as a pre-cursor, medium and outcome of ethnographic representation that helps us understand the social phenomena developed in ethnographic research as dialectical products. However, this theory is not theory as a (rationalist) scholastic reason or an 'abstracted' (naïve realist) empiricism. It is a 'theoretical informed-ness' involving the use of what Glaser and Strauss have termed 'sensitising concepts' as a means of developing patterns from the texture of everyday life that are also possible to subject to further examination (Geertz, 1973; Beach, 1995, 1997, 2005). This cultural and historical view of theory which operates even though

ethnography, in order to be scientific, has to have aspects of generalisability and must bear upon some main organising feature or principle of change which it then also graphically describes and or critiques, is part of a broader project of communication about contemporary education in contemporary society and its discourses. It is a kind of theory is constantly brought into question, tested and modified by data production and analyses that incorporate both openness and predictability (Beach, 1997, 2005).

2. Theoretically informed critical ethnographic representation is thus not primarily about 'applying' a specific theory to descriptions of an outside given set of activities or situations in the production of a research result. It is about using theory to expand the resources of knowledge and understanding about subject positions, genuine agency and the consequences of the actions subjects as agents take. Associated with this aim is the representational venture of producing and communicating knowledge about different human 'life forms' and their social settings, and an intention to comparatively test different possible or imagined worlds against and within the grain of these lives (Willis and Trondman, 2000).

3. Ethnographic representations are in this sense about how life forms can be re-conceptualised in ways that bring 'registered experience' into a productive relationship to 'critical theory' to establish analytical products with a potential to change the ways lives are understood and then lived (Beach, 1997). The role of theory in the representation is thus very specific. It is to carve out relevant sensitising dimensions of thought that remain sufficiently open and are plastic enough to be able to recognise and respond appropriately to empirical questions without automatically generating given answers about how social actors must of necessity experience and shape their conditions of existence (Willis and Trondman, 2000). The theory must allow a dialogue between 'scientific knowledge' produced by specialist institutions and the practical common sense and self-reflexivity of common culture. And it is this that must be communicated in and by the ethnographic representation (Troman et al., 2006) through the theoretical and practical scope of ethnography's representational *techniques* (dance, drama, illustrations, photographs, texts) that can attend to the detail of the mundane practices of everyday life. It has to do with a struggle for openness and predictability in developing knowledge that is both theoretically informed and yet not fully pre-figured in a theoretical position that is given in advance (Willis and Trondman, 2000; Willis, 2000; Dovemark, 2004; Beach, 2005). It concerns accommodations between the

predictions and contradictions of critical theories and lived, documented experiences that can reshape, re-articulate and rewrite existing knowledge. As Willis and Trondman (2000) claim, social phenomena are shot through with indeterminacy, so a very important role is to express something about the always existing and irreducible modes of human life that are more than just blank reflections of pre-existing and straightforwardly reproduced economic and social conditions.

4. Representing *broader culture* as context is important. However, as also for (Willis and Trondman, 2000), the concept of 'culture' represents a broader notion of the mull in which people make their own roots, routes and 'lived' meanings in life. This involves, in Willis and Trondman's terms, noting the importance of the contemporary disarticulations between 'social being' and 'social consciousness' that raise the salience of 'culture' as an 'independent' and all pervasive category, interpenetrating, continuous with, and running parallel to established social forms. Often cultural contexts (such as institutions like the school and the family) are undergoing profound processes of change, often between contradistinctive elements: currently re-structuring and de- or re-traditionalisation are mentioned regularly. This aspect of the representation is about adopting a critical focus in the extended senses meant by the Frankfurt School. That is, in the senses of recording, questioning and rethinking the lived social relations of the cultural forms described, in our case in education, from the point of view of how they embody, mediate and enact the operations and results of specific, identified, described and accounted for forms of educational/cultural power (Debord, 1977; Bourdieu and Passeron, 1977). It is about tracing the lines of evidence of individual and group responses to power as well as how the interests and views of the powerful are often finally secured within educational processes and practices (Carspecken, 1996; Beach and Dovemark, 2007).

5. Ethnographic representation *is a form of symbolic production* that works through the consciousness and self-understanding of the ethnographer with a partial 'autonomy' that should never, to paraphrase Debord (1977), become a simple mirror of surrounding economic conditions of existence. However, at the same time, an ethnographic representation also has to be understood in relation to the conditions of existence within which we humans (including both ethnographers and 'their subjects') act and work. Symbolic creativity and meaning making are not entirely free floating social practices (Beach, 1997). So the autonomy has to be understood and accounted for in a very precise

Ethnography and representation

non-reductive way as existing inside specifically culturally produced social constraints.

6. Autonomy, both in cultural life and in the element of culture that is the representation (the spectacle), thus exists here only in the Althusserian sense of unpredictability (over-determination and un-decidability) in the ways in which humans (including ethnographers) handle problems in their specific social locations and *is not* about how the workings of the human psyche are able to stand outside and suspend the effects of powerful social and cultural restraints and ideologies on their everyday practices. For this reason critical ethnographic representations are about showing the relations of indeterminacy as the autonomy of culture within larger processes of social reproduction and it is this quality that is the elegance of the best critical ethnographic work (Willis, 1977, 2000). It is about encoding recognised issues regarding the social, cultural, individual and interactive negotiations of the relations of indeterminacy that are embedded within socio-cultural and socio-economic conditions to help us explore, analyse and theorise about these issues.

7. These notions of ethnographic representation emphasise the importance of encoding everyday cultural practices so they may be understood, theorised and talked about in relation to the social, individual, economic, political, juridical, ideological and institutional 'levels' of education. No educational relation or process can be understood outside of the mediations of culture and one should for this reason always ask 'what do the analytically observed and described features mean (as consequence and outcome too) for those affected' (Willis and Trondman, 2000). The focus here is on the materials put to use in the ethnographic representation and the ways these 'catch' the details of the historical and social context participant-observed. Critical ethnographic representations do not try to suspend the conditions of existence, as these are constantly present and in some way always in force. The representation is about figure-background features and their ability to both anchor and relay critical meaning. A critical ethnographic representation 'draws out' lived experience to explore critical questions about how it comes to be that the subjective beliefs, practices and actions of social agents act against their own interests (see Willis, 1977, critical ethnography as a classical example) within the taken-for-granted meanings and everyday practices of education institutions (Beach, 1997; Dovemark, 2004). It is about representing the way power is formed over subjectivity through dominant discourses, social

representations, (cultural) literacy and social-cultural-historical practices and traditions and keeping track of the complex, contradictory and sometimes unintended consequences of the politics, interventions, institutional practices, writing and other productions within the 'public spheres' of society on the emergent human practices of human individuals and groups as they try to make sense of the at times profound structural and cultural change which bear on their possibilities for ordinary meaning-making in educational life (Willis, 2000; Carspecken, 1991; Beach, 1997; Gustafsson, 2003; Dovemark, 2004; Beach and Dovemark, 2007).

8. The interest here is for recording and presenting the grist of everyday life in ordinary cultural practices (Willis, 2000) in ways that can help produce more than just an 'Ah ha' effect. Such an effect is essential but the intention is to generate moments where new understandings and possibilities are opened up in the space between experience and discourse in a manner that enables people to deconstruct and reshape their taken for granted world-view. 'Ah ha' effects fuse old experiences with new ones, thus opening up readers' minds towards new horizons (Willis and Trondman, 2000). This is by all means essential but in the representations of critical ethnography engagement with the 'real' world is intended to bring 'surprise' to theoretical formulations and theoretical resources are meant to bring 'surprise' to how empirical data may be understood and can be made use of (Beach, 1997, 2005; Beach and Dovemark, 2007). This is a pivotal moment. It is about, to paraphrase Willis and Trondman (2000), producing a 'dialectic of surprise' through a continuous process of shifting back and forth between 'inductive' and 'deductive' readings of culture from data into other analytical representations as a basis for a new (hybrid) concept or idea. The notion of hybrid is important. It has to do with the potential for awakening qualitatively different thoughts than those expressed in data and theory as separate entities emerges in a representation as a zone of transitional and transgressive meaning making that shifts the boundaries of thought about cultures and their practices and changes the meaning of these practices in a surprising way.

The above points make explicit how theoretically informed critical ethnographic representations build upon a dialectic between ethnographic data and thinking about this data in evocative, imaginative and transformational ways, in order to provide important new questions for (new) life projects and important new answers to existing life questions as a catalyst for a re-examination of the (hegemonically) accepted parameters of common culture (Lather, 1986). This is an intention which is very much in line with the aims of critical ethnography more generally (see also Carspecken, 1996; Carspecken and Walford, 2002). It is about showing and reversing the historical, ideological and contemporary effects of upper-class perspectives and position dominances on other actors as agents (Beach, 2005) so they may, in the senses of Althusser (1969), break free from the corpus of the vast majority of subjects who are constantly subdued by the dominant ideologies of the State.

As in Beach (2005), critical ethnographic representations should thus be looking to provide a real examination of the social and structural conditions which both give rise to and 'normalise' the rules, actions and beliefs that are at play in the specific contexts of our researched settings, as well as the relations of structure that privilege a particular social order by helping promote its favoured forms of behaviour, distinction and belief as natural (Debord, 1977). This moves us beyond both post-structuralist deconstructions and Marxist ideology criticism, as the aim is to represent not just what the dialectics of human agency and 'hidden' forces are and what hides them to confound progressive reform (Beach, 1995, 1997), but also how they work in a specific local community so they may be opposed and changed in the development of really practical knowledge and a critical subjectivity (Heron and Reason, 1997, Beach, 2003). This is possibly the main aim of critical ethnographic representation in demonstrating the confounding structuration processes and the inter-play of institutional relations that obstruct self-fulfilment and educational development through the enactment of particular ideological forms in material practices so new and more 'progressive' action can be built (Lather, 1986; Beach, 2003).

Presentation and organisation of ethnographic representations

The critical ethnographic representation is a reflexive, purposive, meaning making and catalytic text according to the reasoning above. Tony Ghaye (2006) has recently written a short piece about the characteristics he looks for in such accounts, in the Editorial of a recent issue of the international journal *Refelctive Practice*. Two principle characteristics are raised. They concern, as here, research writing as a *craft*. They are the characteristics of *presentation* and *organisation* respectively.

By presentation is meant things like spelling, grammar, paraphrasing, the use of suitable sub-headings to provide an overall structure for the representation, consistency in the use of sub-headings and concepts and the selection of relevant terminology for the subject matter and the audience (including any identified journal a piece may be intended for). However, even issues such as punctuation, length of sentences and complexity of sentence structure are focused on. Bad presentation leads to confusion and sensations that the writer is not bothered about the impression their paper creates. Organisation concerns different ways of presenting work. Organisation has to do with the framing of representations in terms of sequencing rules, pacing and spacing. Atkinson (1990) spoke of chronological, thematic and natural history based accounts as common ways of varying the organisation of ethnographic representations.

However, in addition to considering the two general and common principles of organisation and presentation, Ghaye also went into detail regarding criteria for judging research representations. These criteria were developed from Ghaye's reading of a book by Gelb called *How to Think like Leonardo da Vinci*. They are relevant not only to theoretically informed critical ethnography of education, but to all three 'metaphors' of ethnographic work supplied by Fine (1994: 17). These are *the ventriloquist*, who transmits information in an effort toward neutrality, *the positionality of voices*, where the subjects themselves are the focus and their voices carry indigenous meanings and experiences in opposition to dominant discourses and practices, and *the activism stance*, in which the ethnographer takes a clear position in intervening on hegemonic practices. Slightly edited, the da Vincian principles taken up by Ghaye (2006, p. 2) are as follows (also Beach and Larsson, 2006):

- *Curiositá*: This concerns whether the representation shows a curiosity about the subject and awakens a feeling that the author wants to show more about their chosen topic than was previously known.
- *Dimostrazione*: This is about the relevance of evidence and the use made of other works and others' experiences. Have these been taken into consideration and are they also accounted for? Also, how far does the representation make it clear that new ideas have been put under pressure and questioned against existing orders of knowledge?
- *Sensazione*: This is about the forms in which the representation engages with the reader or viewer. What different ways of telling the story are present and how are they used? Are the ways creative? What techniques of representation are present and how skilfully are they combined to both anchor and relay meaning? In Ghaye's terms how skilled are we in the art of *visualisation*.
- *Sfumato*: This characteristic is about how the representation succeeds in embracing ambiguity, paradox or uncertainty. It is linked to a further characteristic: *Arte/Scienza*, which as Ghaye writes, is about how the

representation deals with the fuzzy worlds that ethnography becomes engaged with (Lather, 1991, 2001). Is 'an holistic view' taken and made evident (Ghaye, 2006, p. 3) with respect to the part whole relationship in the production of what Larsson (2004, 2006) calls a balanced gestalt that weaves in empirical materials in a surprising and satisfying way?

- *Corporalita*: This is about the position of the self. Is the self visible or invisible, present or absent, concrete or abstractly represented?
- *Connessione*: This is the principle of inter-connectedness (Lather, 1991) that ties things together and shows a recognition and appreciation of the principles and processes of reflection and representation with regard to the object of the representation itself (Atkinson, 1990; Beach, 2005, 2006).

The ethnographic representation and/as art genres

The above section connects ethnographic representation with rules of art (see also Atkinson, 1990; Willis, 2000). This was also attempted in a previous work, where artistic genres were compared to ethnographic writing to provide some food for thought regarding the framing of ethnography as a representation. The genres of realism, impressionism, pop-art and expressionism were considered in some detail (Beach, 2006). In the present chapter three of the genres (realism, impressionism and expressionism) are revisited. The presentation begins by considering the framing characteristics of ethnographic and artistic realism.

In realist representational forms the artists (and by extension the ethnographer's) intention was to try to represent distinctions in their work along the line of the photography metaphor to show distinctions that are acted towards as if they were *inherent in the world rather than created* by our gaze upon or confrontation and interaction with it. Landscape artists who accomplish meticulous detail and 'natural' toning in their paintings through the use of diligent brush-strokes and hues of brown and green are a good example (Beach, 2006), and their work can be used to symbolically represent the techniques and intentions of ethnographic realists, who try to reflect the characteristics of an objective world through neutral languages. This is sometimes called a *reflectionist* position on representation (Beach, 2006). Ethnographic realists try to represent the world objectively and in detail, and their intention is to show or as exactly as possible describe a distinct, real existence of objects in space and time, that are fully independent of the ethnographer's engagements with them. That is, they claim to tap into properties which are genuinely present in a particular location or group, which they then also describe with an as neutral and objective a language as possible.

In Mulkay's (1989) terms realist approximations in scientific writing are almost inevitable, because as he put it, human language cannot escape an essentialising character as a tool for controlling and refashioning the world. Speech and writing always create the appearance of an independent world beyond our speech and we have no option but to act as if the illusion created is the real world in which we and others have our being (Mulkay, 1989: 35-36). However, writer-critics of realism (such as Lather, 1991; Richardson, 2000 and Clough, 2000) see such realist narratives as power-texts that inevitably tend toward totalistic claims and treacherous translations that are falsely represented as neutral and objective facts that are beyond contention.

Ethnographic realism dominated the Golden Ages of ethnographic writing according to Denzin and Lincoln (2000), Viditch and Lyman (2000), and Van Maanen (1988), but has became increasingly difficult to uphold, after the literary turn in the social sciences. It has now given way to the impressionistic and the confessional tales of the field, both of which represent a revolt against realist traditions, although quite different ones (Troman et al., 2006). When attempting to convey elements in the lived world, writing impressionistically allows the impressions of the world on the author's senses or, as in art, vision or view, to freely form the focus of what is represented. In contrast to realism, impressionism tries to lift out the different possible textures of meaning that can be composed from an experience rather than claiming to show absolute and objective truths. This puts emphasis on the *literary skills* and *narrative ingenuity* of the researcher as author.

Impressionism has, according to Ash (1988), its most important roots in the impressionist painting that developed in France during the late nineteenth and early twentieth centuries, through the work of artists who shared related approaches and techniques for representing their *experiences of visual reality* in terms of its transient effects of light and colour (i.e., its visual impressions). The impressionists used a mixture of vivid and contrastive colour combinations to emphasise the play of light and shade on the senses, which was of course made possible by the new technologies and pigments from the bourgeoning textile industry. But impressionism also came about in part through an internal revolution. The impressionists shared a common dissatisfaction with the conventional treatments of academic painting and sought a new aesthetic standard in which attention was shifted *from a realist reflection* of the world *to the artist's manipulation* of colour, tone and texture. Rather than trying to capture an illusive multi-dimensional space and fix it two dimensionally, as in realism, the objective of impressionist representations is according to Ash (1988) to be a vehicle of *artful composition* that embodies a relief from traditional approaches to subject matter (Beach, 2006). This is carried over also into impressionist writing, where the *literary or poetic effect* is primary, as is noted also by van Maanen (1988) in his discussions of impressionist tales of the field.

The intention behind a creative representation is not always only an aesthetic or poetic one. There may be a politics involved as well (Clough, 2000). This likens more *expressionist art* as a tradition of representation. There is a strongly critical perspective in expressionist art, which is premised on the idea that modern societies have turned into closed totalitarian systems that are heavily determined by stinting and dehabilitating (post-)colonialist world views and their forms of science and communication (Beach, 2005), through which individual autonomy and full subject possibilities for all human-kind have been eliminated (see also Marx concept of Alienation and Marcuse's notion of one dimensional man). Expressionist art aims to get the intense emotional experiences invoked through participation in such circumstances into a communicative media in a way that *gives voice* to the subjective emotions that these experiences arouse. There is an intention to call forth a critical subjectivity. This intention is shared in critical education ethnography (Beach, 2005).

The strongly critical dimensions within expressionist art were according to Beach (2006) clearest amongst the group of German artists called Die Brücke (including Heckel, Schmidt-Rottluff, and Bleyl) who were all in revolt against the *superficial naturalism of a decadent academic impressionism and realism*, and who used primitive, highly personal and spontaneous forms of representation to develop harshness, boldness, and intensity in an emotionally charged manner that could express frustration, anxiety, disgust and discontent about contemporary situations and the contradictions of modern life (Beach, 2006). Traditional bourgeois values (such as charity and consensus institutions) were satirised whilst values that are more concerned with political and social reform and which express the hope for a coming revolution were admired.

The representational intentions of critical education ethnography are very easy to link to the expressionism of Heckel, Schmidt-Rottluff, and Bleyl. For instance, like expressionist painting, the representations of critical education ethnography have developed as *a reaction against materialism, complacent bourgeois prosperity, rapid mechanisation and urbanisation*, all of which are common themes in the critical ethnographic writing of the main schools in the tradition, such as the Birmingham School (see also Kuper, 1987), and like expressionist play-writers and novelists, critical ethnographers such as Carspecken (1991) and Willis (1977) try to forge dramatic representations from forms of social protest to try to convey a concern for the contradictory truths embedded in contemporary social situations. Finally, there is also a historical corollary. Expressionism became a dominant artistic movement in Germany just after World War I, close in time to the growth of the Frankfurt School of critical social theory (Held, 1980) that inspires critical education ethnography in several ways, and like the Frankfurt School many expressionist painters and dramatists were hounded by the National Socialists and the movement was outlawed by Hitler in the 1930s.

The educational research of the Birmingham school almost deliberately developed their work in a similar way to expressionist writers', through the use of symbolic types (the bikers, the lads, the earoles, the sisterhood, the black sisters, Asian warriors etc.) rather than of fully developed individualised characters to attend to the general drama of everyday life (see e.g., Willis, 2000; Mac An Ghail, 1988). Common tropes in CCCS (Centre for Critical Cultural Studies) work include the spiritual malaise of youth and its revolt against an older generation and those who 'obey' it by conforming to its conventions, rules and regulations, the derision of middle-class values and a valorisation of opposition, resistance or revolt.

As mentioned earlier, Paul Willis (2000) speaks of the concept of 'life-as-art' in the context of his work in the CCCS tradition, as a way of showing the cultural viewpoint and hidden knowledge of exploited classes and the way entrapping decisions are often taken in life in a sense of liberty, but nevertheless contribute to the perpetuation of oppression, marginalisation or exploitation. However, his point is that things can be different if sufficiently and sensitively critically re-presented and re-theorised as part of a project that is concerned not only with description or general theoretical elaboration but also with organic intellectualism. The purpose of representations in critical education ethnography is to contribute to such a project. It doesn't matter which expressive forms, technologies or media are utilised (text, dance, theatre, other). It is how they are used that matters, inside which alliances, to which ends and with what kind of surprise in whose interests.

Endnote

In this chapter representation is regarded as a way by which meaning is constructed through language and other symbolic systems such as photography and art as both an object and a process or even strategy of signification that uses symbolic or semiotic techniques. In ethnography this most usually becomes the production of meaning through a language that symbolises or references objects, people and events in visual and literal culture and is concerned with the capacities of producing and conveying meaning across broad discursive formations and populations. This takes place, the chapter suggests, thus, on the basis of a dialectics of visualisation and literacy within institutions of communication. These historical inscriptions of ideology enable particular articulations of meaning to occur rather than others (Hall, 1997, p. 310). This is not just a question of simple object-subject relations. It is one of interpellation in the sense of Althusser. It concerns the workings of a system of ideological relays in poly-semiotic and poly-vocal situations (Bernstein, 2000). As Stuart Hall has written, the image and its meaning is not externally fixed but relative to and implicated in the positions and schemas of interpretation that are brought to bear.

This means nothing more than that all discourses have different possible positions of interpretation (from which they 'make sense') and the subjects must always bring their own subjective desires and capacities and take up positions of identification in relation to their meaning. This 'little system' of interpretation is composed of two inter-dependent but relatively autonomous moments according to Stuart Hall (1997: 310) and the present chapter has been concerned with nothing more than this system and how to make it work in critical interests in ethnographic research. This was the point of origin of the chapter, which has been about ethnographic representation as an image-text that likens more the skilled-craft of drawing than it does the analogical technique of photography. Critical ethnography is not recording. Its representations are never simple records of events. As also Clifford and Marcus (1986) point out ethnographic representations make culture they do not simply discover or reflect it. And ethnographic representation is thus a humanistic and creative, open ended activity reflecting processes of production, reproduction, identity and tradition.

However, the chapter also says something about the subjects as 'targets' of representation. This is not an audience as such, in the original senses of that term, as these subject are not the simple recipients of completed representations, they are rather made by and make these representations themselves; at least to some degree. Representations are never self-sufficient entities and they are always capable of bearing more than one interpretation for any one subject. As also Barthes suggested in *Image, Music, Text* from 1964, the power of the representation to convey meaning is thus virtual not real. Meanings are realised through representations in culturally inscribed practices of seeing/hearing and interpretation inside ideologically formed social and material arenas and architectures of knowledge within which subjects and their capacities are formed. The reader-hearer-seer of the representation has to make the images of the representation signify something through a changeable internal relation to the things figuratively inscribed.

References

Althusser, L. (1969) *For Marx*, Harmondsworth: Penguin.
Ash, R. (1988) *The Impressionists and their Art*, London: MacDonald.
Atkinson, P. (1990) *The Ethnographic Imagination: Textual Construction of Reality*, London: Routledge.
Barthes, R. (1964/1977) *Image Music Text*, New York: Hill and Wang.
Beach, D. (1995) *Making sense of the problem of change: an ethnographic study of a teacher education refor*, (Göteborg Studies in Educational Sciences 100), Göteborg: Acta Universitatis Gothoburgensis.
Beach, D. (1997) *Symbolic control and power relay: Learning in higher professional education*, (Göteborg Studies in Educational Sciences 119), Göteborg: Acta Universitatis Gothoburgensis.
Beach, D. (2003) A problem of validity in education research, *Qualitative Inquiry*, 9(6): 859-874.
Beach, D. (2005) From fieldwork to theory and representation in ethnography, in Troman, G., Jeffrey, B. and Walford, G (eds.) *Methodological issues and Practices in Ethnography. Studies in Educational Ethnography* Vol 11, Oxford: Elsivier.
Beach, D. (2006) Artistic representation and research writing, in Troman, G. Jeffrey, B. and Beach, D. (eds.) *Researching Education Policy: Ethnographic Experiences*. London: the Tufnell Press.
Beach, D and Dovemark, M. (2007) *Education and the Commodity Problem: Ethnographic Investigations of Creativity and Performativity in Swedish Schools*, London: the Tufnell Press.
Beach, D., Gobbo, F., Jeffrey, B., Smyth, G., and Troman, G. (2004) Guest editors' introduction, *European Educational Researcher Journal*, 3(3):534–538.
Beach, D. and Larsson, S. (2006) *Research Writing as Work and Artful Practice*, paper presented at the 2006 Oxford Conference in *Ethnography in Education*, September 4-5, St Hilda's College, Oxford, UK.
Becker, H. (1986) *Writing for Social Scientists*, Berkley: University of Chicago Press.
Bernstein, B. (1971) *Class, Codes and Control Vol. 1: Theoretical Studies Toward a Sociology of Language*, London: Routledge and Kegan Paul.

Bernstein, B. (1990) *Class, Codes and Control Vol. 4: The Structuring of Pedagogic Discourse*, London: Routledge.
Bourdieu, P. and Passeron, J-C. (1977) *Reproduction in Education, Society and Culture*, London: Sage.
Burgess, R. (1984) *In the field: An introduction to field research*, London: Allen and Urwin.
Carspecken, P. F. (1991) *Community Schooling and the Nature of Power: The Battle for Croxteth Comprehensive*, London: Routledge.
Carspecken, P. F. (1996) *Critical Ethnography in educational research: A theoretical and practical guide*, London: Routledge.
Carspecken, P. and Walford, G. (2002) (eds.) *Critical Ethnography and Education*, Amsterdam, London and New York: Elsevier.
Clifford, J. and Marcus, G. E. (1986) *Writing Culture: The Poetics and Politics of Ethnography*, Berkeley: University of California Press.
Clough, P. (2000) Comments on criteria for experimental writing, *Qualitative Inquiry*, 6(2): 278–291.
Debord, G. (1977) *Society of the Specatacle*, Michigan: Black and Red.
Denzin, N. and Lincoln, Y. (2000) Introduction: Entering the field of qualitative research, in Denzin, N. and Lincoln, Y (eds.) *Handbook of Qualitative Research*, New York: Sage.
Dovemark, M. (2004) *Ansvar-flexibilitet-valfrihet. En etnografisk studie om en skola i förändring* (Gothenburg Studies in Educational Sciences 223), Göteborg: ACTA.
Elliott, J. (2005) *Using Narrative in Social Research: Qualitative and Quantitative Approaches*, New York: Sage.
Fine, M. (1994) Reworking the hyphens, in Denzin, N. and Lincoln, Y. (eds.) *Handbook of Qualitative Research*, Newbury Park: Sage.
Geertz, C. (1973) *The Interpretation of Cultures*, New York: Basic Books.
Geertz, C. (1988) *Works and Lives: The Anthropologist as Author*, Cambridge: Polity Press.
Ghaye, A. L. (2006) Editor's introduction, *Reflective Practice*, 7(1): 1-7.
Gustavsson, J. (2003) *Integration som text, diskursiv och social praktik: En policyetnografisk fallstudie av mötet mellan skolan och förskoleklassen.* (Göteborg Studies in Educational Science, 190). Göteborg, Acta Universitatis Gothenburgensis.
Hall, S. (1997) *Representation: culture, representation and signifying practices*, London: Sage.
Hammersley, M. (1992) *Reading Ethnographic Research: A Critical Guide*, London: Longmann.
Held, D. (1980) *Introduction to Critical Theory*, Berkeley and Los Angeles, CA: University of California Press.
Heron, J. and Reason, P. (1997) A participatory inquiry paradigm, *Qualitative Inquiry*, 3(3): 259-273.
Kuper, A. (1978/1987) *Anthropologists and Anthropology: The British School 1922–1972*, London: Routledge.
Larsson, S. (2004) The Joy and Despair of Writing, *Nordisk Pedagogik*, 24(2): 97–112.
Larsson, S. (2006) Ethnography in Action. How ethnography was established in Swedish educational research, *Ethnography and Education*, 1(2): 177–195.
Lather, P. (1991) *Getting Smart: Feminist Research and Pedagogy with/In the Post-modern*, New York: Routledge.

Lather, P. (1986) Research as praxis, *Harvard Educational Review*, 56(3): 257-77.
Lather, P. (1991) *Getting Smart: Feminist Research and Pedagogy with/in the Post-modern*, New York: Routledge.
Mac An Ghail, M. (1988) *Young, Gifted and Black*, Milton Keynes: Open University Press.
Malinowski, B. (1964) *The Argonauts of the Western Pacific*, London: Routledge.
Marcuse, H. (1964) *One-Dimensional Man*, Boston, MA: Beacon Press.
Mulkay, M. (1989) Textual fragments on science, social science and literature, in Mulkay, M. (1991) *Sociology of Science: A sociological pilgrimage*, Milton Keynes: Open University Press.
Richardson, L. (2000) Writing. A Method of Inquiry, in Denzin, N.,K. and Lincoln, Y., S. (eds.) *Handbook of Qualitative Research*, Thousand Oaks: Sage.
Troman, G., Jeffrey, B. and Beach, D. (2006) *Researching Education Policy: Ethnographic Experiences*, London: the Tufnell Press.
Van Maanen, J. (1988) *Tales of the Field: On Writing Ethnography*, Chicago: University of Chicago Press.
Viditch, A. J. and Lyman, S. M. (2000) Qualitative methods and their history in sociology and anthropology, in: Denzin, N. and Lincoln, Y (eds.) *Handbook of Qualitative Research*, London and New York: Sage.
Willis, P. (1999) Labour power, culture and the cultural commodity, in Castells, M., Flecha, R., Freire, P., Giroux, H., Macedo, D. and Willis, P. (eds) *Critical Education in the New information Age*, Oxford: Rowman and Littlefield.
Willis, P. (1977) *Learning to Labour: How Working Class Kids Get Working Class Jobs*, Farnborough: Saxon House.
Willis, P. (2000) *The Ethnographic Imagination*, Cambridge: Polity Press.
Willis, P. and Trondman, M. (2000) Manifesto for ethnography, *Ethnography*, 1(1): 5-16.
Wolcott, H. (2001) *Writing Up Qualitative Research, s* New York: Sage.

Notes on Contributors

W. Douglas Baker, Associate Professor, Eastern Michigan University, Department of Language and Literature. His research interests include local disciplinary knowledge in classrooms and how it is constructed through discourse and action, collaborative aspects of reading and writing, and research methodology. A former secondary school English language arts teacher, Doug teaches writing and methods courses and graduate classes on literacy, writing assessment and research methodology. He is a co-director of the Eastern Michigan Writing Project and co-editor of *Language Arts Journal of Michigan*, and Treasurer of the Special Interest Group on Language and Social Processes of the American Educational Research Association. He has published articles on video analysis and disciplinary knowledge construction and writing processes and practices.

Dennis Beach, Professor of Education at the University College of Borås, Sweden and Visiting Professor at the University of Roehampton, London, England and Kalamar University College, Sweden. He is an experienced ethnographer of education and the author of several books in the field. His current main research interests are in the politics of education change and the globalisation of neo-liberal education policy. He is research leader on three major national research projects and a participant in international research in these areas.

Sara Delamont is Reader in Sociology at Cardiff University. She was elected to the Academy of Learned Societies for the Social Sciences in 2000, and was the 1st Woman President of the British Educational Research Association in 1984. Her areas of research include the sociology of education - especially classroom interaction, school ethnography, higher education and gender; the sociology of the professions including science; qualitative methods; and habitus and embodiment, as exemplified through *Capoeira*. Sara is one of the two Founding Editors of *Qualitative Research*, and Joint Editor of *Teaching and Teacher Education*. Her recent publications include: *Successful Research Careers* (with P. Atkinson) (2004, Open University Press), *Narrative Methods* (edited with P. Atkinson) *Four Volumes* (2006, Sage), *Supervising the Doctorate* (with P. Atkinson and O. Parry) (2004, Open University Press), *Key Themes in Qualitative Research* (with P. Atkinson and A. Coffey), (2003, Alta Mira Press), *Feminist Sociology* (2003, Sage), *Feminism and the Classroom Teacher: Research, Praxis Pedagogy* (with A Coffey) (2000, Falmer), and *Handbook of Ethnography* (edited with Atkinson, Coffey, Lofland and Lofland) (2001, paperback edition, 2007, Sage).

Martin Forsey, Lecturer, Anthropology, University of Western Australia. He teaches introductory Anthropology, as well as Australian culture and society and the Anthropology of organisational enterprises. Martin's research interests include the organisational culture of schools, school choice and educational reform and he has written about ethnographic method, neo-liberal reform of schooling and organisational change. His monograph, *Challenging the System? A Dramatic Tale of Neo-liberal Reform in an Australian Government High School*, was recently published by Information Age Publishing.

Judith Green, Professor of Education, University of California, Santa Barbara and Director of the Center for Literacy and Inquiry in Networking Communities (LINC). Her research focuses on the social construction of knowledge and equity of access to academic knowledge in classrooms with linguistically and culturally diverse students. She has published research in *Review of Research in Education* (10 and 23), *Discourse Processes, Linguistics and Education, Applied Linguistics and Pedagogies*. She is co-Editor of the *Review of Research in Education* (30, 2006; 32, 2008) and of *Complementary Methods for Research in Education* (Green, Camilli & Elmore, 2006, LEA) for the American Education Research Association (AERA) and of *Multidisciplinary Perspectives on Literacy Research* (Beach, Green, Kamil & Shanahan, 2005, Hampton Press) for the National Conference for Research on Language and Literacy. She has also published research syntheses in handbooks for AERA, National Council of Teachers of English (NCTE) and the International Reading Association (IRA). She is a Fellow of NCRLL and the American Anthropology Association (AAA).

Bob Jeffrey taught in primary schools for over 20 years and joined the Open University in 1992 as a researcher, working with Peter Woods and Geoff Troman, specialising in primary teacher's work and teacher and pupil creativity from a sociological perspective. These two strands have been held together by an interest in exploring the agency of the individual under conditions of tension and constraint and in particular the effects on their creativity.

Having recently completed a nine nation European research project into creative learning and Co-Directing an ESRC seminar series on Creativity in Education with Anna Craft, his current research is leading, with Geoff Troman, an ESRC two-year study of the effects of creativity and performativity policies in primary schools and another on primary teacher identity. He is co-founder and deputy editor of the *Ethnography and Education* journal, and commissioning editor of a series of the same title with the Tufnell Press. He was co-founder of the European Ethnography Research Network at ECER, the Open Creativity Centre at the Open University with Anna Craft, and the Creativity SIG at BERA. Recent publications include: Jeffrey, B. and Woods, P. (2003) *The Creative School*, London, Falmer Press, and Troman, G., Beach, D. and Jeffrey, B. (2006) *Researching Education Policy: Ethnographic Experiences*, London, the Tufnell Press.

Audra Skukauskait, Associate Professor, University of Texas, Brownsville, Department of Curriculum and Instruction. Her research interests include discourse and ethnographic research in education, open-ended interviewing methodology, and impact of reforms on teachers. Recently she has published a chapter 'Examining peripheries of substantive democracy in Lithuania from the point of view of teachers: Intended and unintended outcomes of the financial reform in education' in *Reimagining Civic Education* (2007). She is a co-author of the chapter 'Epistemological Issues in the analysis of video records: Interactional ethnography as a logic of inquiry' in *Video Research in the Learning Sciences* (2007). She was an assistant editor for the *Handbook of Complementary Methods for Research in Education* (2006) and a co-editor of special issues of the *Journal of Classroom Interaction and Pedagogies* 3(2). Currently she serves on the editorial boards of *Educational Researcher* and *Family Journal*. She has worked with teachers and school administrators in a professional development program sponsored by the American Professional Partnership for Lithuanian Education (APPLE) and the Lithuanian Ministry of Education.

Mats Trondman, Professor of Cultural Sociology, Department for Social Sciences at Växjö University, Sweden, where he has been working for more than twenty years. He was the founding editor of the Sage journal *Ethnography* together with Paul Willis, with whom he also wrote the *Manifesto for Ethnography* in 2000. Over the years he has covered a large number of theoretical empirical research topics such as: musical taste and lifestyle; social and cultural mobility; counter cultures; the transformation of the Swedish Welfare Society during the 1990s; sports; the Arts; social and cultural policy; and education and schooling. His main focus now is youth culture research and social and cultural theory. He has published eight books in Swedish. The most well-known is on class travelling, that is, working class kids becoming academics. He has also published more than hundred articles and reports, as well as being an occasional writer for the Arts pages in the Swedish press.

His most recent publications have been on Emile Durkheim's Science of Education and articles on Multiculturalism. The most recent in English is an article, Disowning Knowledge. He is currently working on two projects - one is about youth cultures and postindustrial and multicultural Malmoe. The other is a theoretical project called 'The Road to Cultural Sociology' which is on the sociology of Jeffrey C. Alexander.

Geoffrey Walford is Professor of Education Policy and a Fellow of Green Templeton College at the University of Oxford. He is author of many academic articles and book chapters, and his books include: *Life in Public Schools* (Methuen, 1986), *City Technology College* (Open University Press, 1991, with Henry Miller), *Doing Educational Research* (Routledge, editor, 1991), *Choice and Equity in Education* (Cassell, 1994), *Researching the Powerful in Education* (UCL Press, editor, 1994), *Policy, Politics and Education - sponsored grant-maintained schools and religious diversity* (Ashgate, 2000), *Doing Qualitative Educational Research* (Continuum, 2001), *Private Schooling: Tradition and diversity* (Continuum, 2005) and *Markets and Equity in Education* (Continuum, 2006). Within the Department of Education at the University of Oxford he teaches on the MSc in Educational Research Methodology course, and supervises masters and doctoral research students. He is Editor of the annual volume, *Studies in Educational Ethnography*, and has been Editor of the *Oxford Review of Education* since January 2004. His research foci are the relationships between central government policy and local processes of implementation, private schools, choice of schools, religiously-based schools and ethnographic research methodology.

Printed in the United States
125413LV00004B/157/P